Mediating Science Learning through Information and Communications Technology

Mediating Science Learning through Information and Communications Technology (ICT) focuses on how contemporary science education has been affected by recent developments in educational technology. More specifically, this book deals with changes in the ways in which science is taught and learnt following developments in ICT, for example, the increased use of multimedia, web-based learning and communication technology.

The book is divided into three parts and contains chapters on the theoretical and practical considerations of using ICT in the teaching and learning of science. Examples are drawn both from higher education, science in schools, and open and distance education. The book discusses approaches to learning and teaching in science accessible over the web, and science learning mediated through disc-based resources. Emphasis is given to formal learning contexts. These approaches include the role of current developments and future prospects for research in this area.

Mediating Science Learning through Information and Communications Technology will be a valuable resource for teachers on Masters courses in science education and academics in science education.

This is a companion reader to *Reconsidering Science Learning*, also published by RoutledgeFalmer.

Richard Holliman and **Eileen Scanlon** are both members of The Open University MSc in Science team.

SEH806 Contemporary Issues in Science Learning

The companion volume in this series is *Reconsidering Science Learning* by Eileen Scanlon, Patricia Murphy, Jeff Thomas and Elizabeth Whitelegg.

Both of the Readers are part of a course, **Contemporary Issues in Science Learning** (SEH806), that is itself part of an MSc in Science Programme at The Open University and also counts towards the MA in Education and the MA in Online and Distance Education.

The Open University MSc in Science

The MSc in Science at The Open University is a relatively new 'distance-taught' programme that has been designed for students who want to explore broad scientific topics at postgraduate level. It provides opportunities to pursue some of science's most pressing issues using the innovative teaching methods pioneered at The Open University.

Structure of the MSc in Science

The MSc in Science is a modular programme that allows students to select modules that best fit with their interests and professional goals. The Programme has two main themes or 'strands': Science Studies and Frontiers in Medical Science.

Modules currently available

> *Science and the Public*
> *Communicating Science*
> *Imaging in Medicine*
> *Molecules in Medicine*
> *Issues in Brain and Behaviour*
> *The Project Module*

It is also possible to count other OU modules towards the MSc in Science and to count MSc in Science modules towards other OU awards such as the MA in Education.

OU supported learning

The MSc in Science Programme, in common with other OU programmes, provides great flexibility. Students study at their own pace and in their own time, anywhere in the European Union. They receive specially prepared study materials and benefit from tutorial support (electronically and at day schools), thus offering them the chance to work with other students.

How to apply

If you would like to register for this Programme, or find out more information, visit our website http://www.open.ac.uk/science/msc. If you would like more general information about available courses, please contact the Course Information and Advice Centre, PO Box 724, The Open University, Walton Hall, Milton Keynes MK7 6ZS, UK (telephone 01908 653231). Details can also be viewed on our web pages: http://www.open.ac.uk/courses

Mediating Science Learning through Information and Communications Technology

Edited by Richard Holliman and Eileen Scanlon

RoutledgeFalmer
Taylor & Francis Group

LONDON AND NEW YORK

The Open
University

First published 2004
by RoutledgeFalmer
11 New Fetter Lane, London EC4P 4EE

Simultaneously published in the USA and Canada by RoutledgeFalmer
29 West 35th Street, New York, NY 10001

RoutledgeFalmer is an imprint of the Taylor & Francis Group

Typeset in Goudy by
Bookcraft Ltd, Stroud, Gloucestershire
Printed and bound in Great Britain by
TJ International Ltd, Padstow, Cornwall

British Library Cataloguing in Publication Data
A catalogue record for this book is available from the British Library

Library of Congress Cataloging in Publication Data
A catalog record has been requested

ISBN 0–415–32832–2 (hbk)

ISBN 0–415–32833–0 (pbk)

Contents

Figures

Tables

Sources

Where a chapter in this book is based on or is a reprint or revision of material previously published elsewhere, details are given below, with grateful acknowledgements to the original publishers.

Chapter 1.3   This is an edited version of a chapter originally published in Wellington, J. (ed.) *Teaching and Learning in Secondary Science,* pp. 195–225, RoutledgeFalmer (2000).

Chapter 2.1   This is an edited version of an article originally published in *Studies in Science Education* 38, pp. 115–42 (2002).

Chapter 2.4   This is an edited version of an article originally published in *Active Learning* 8, pp. 1–6, Institute for Learning and Teaching in Higher Education (1998).

Preface

This collection of readings has been chosen to complement The Open University's course on contemporary issues in science learning, which is part of the MSc in Science. This is the second of two volumes which together provide our students with a set of readings for their use in the course. The other reader deals with a reconsideration of science learning.

These two volumes of readings form a small part of the Master's module on contemporary issues, which is part of a Master's course in Science being produced in the Science Faculty of The Open University by a team from the Faculties of Science and Education and Language Studies, and the Institute of Educational Technology. It is studied by students aiming for the Master's degree in Science , but it also can act as a subsidiary course for other Open University Masters awards in Education and Online and Distance Education.

Study materials provided by the University also include a study commentary, set texts and disk-based resources with a library of additional paper and video material. Students also have access to a wide range of materials and resources over the Internet (including access to selected web resources, an e-desktop and The Open University's library available to students online). Most of the tuition is conducted online, using conferencing software that facilitates one-to-one and one-to-many asynchronous and synchronous conferencing.

Much of the material in this reader is newly commissioned by the editors for use in our course. Other chapters have been adapted and edited from previously published papers in journals and books. As a result, a range of styles has been used by the authors which were appropriate for the original contents and a range of referencing styles is also in use in this volume. Students of our course may notice that these references do not all conform to our course referencing styles.

This is a collection of chapters dealing with science learning and the use of information and communications technology (ICT). It is divided into three parts. The first part acts as an introduction to the book through discussion of how students learn science, mediated by new technology, and through consideration of what value might be added to the learning experience by using ICT. The second part examines the role of design and evaluation of ICT by drawing on theoretical and practical explanations of these issues. The final section examines the potential for extending access to science learning using ICT. It also considers the future prospects for learning using ICT by reviewing trends in educational research and current developments in technology.

The editors would like to thank the other members of the course team for their help in selecting the chapters. We would also like to thank Shelagh Ross and Josie Taylor, for their helpful comments in preparing the newly commissioned chapters, and Cheryl Newport, Carol Johnstone, Gillian Riley and Pat Forster for their invaluable help in the production of this volume. Opinions expressed in the chapters are not necessarily those of the course team or The Open University.

The editors of the volume would also like to thank the authors who produced newly commissioned chapters: Diana Laurillard, UK Department for Education and Skills; Marcia Linn, University of California at Berkeley; Tom Boyle, London Metropolitan University; Martin Oliver, University College London; Martyn Cooper, Open University; and Terry Di Paolo, Chetz Colwell, Victoria Uren and Anne Jelfs, Open University.

Richard Holliman
Eileen Scanlon

Introduction

Richard Holliman and Eileen Scanlon

The past twenty-five years have seen an unprecedented period of growth in the development and use of information and communications technology (ICT) to facilitate science teaching and learning at primary, secondary and tertiary levels. These developments have attempted to utilize the combination of educational and technological input, supported by educational research (into design and evaluation issues, for example) and developments in learning theories. This volume introduces a series of readings that consider these developments from the perspective of educational researchers working in a contemporary UK and international context.

This is not to underplay the role of technological developments, however, as these have also been a key factor in the adoption of ICT. These technological advances, and in particular the ability to converge the computational potential of computers with new communication technologies, have extended the possibilities for using ICT to facilitate science teaching and learning. Boohan notes this development:

> When computers were first introduced into schools, they were known simply as 'computers'. Then the expression 'information technology' was introduced – computers, after all, did more than just computation. Then 'IT' became 'ICT'. 'Information and Communications Technology' is intended to emphasize that computers are powerful tools for communicating information. ICT can be used to support pupils' reading and writing science and the communication of scientific ideas.
>
> (Boohan 2002: 213)

This quotation illustrates the importance of the interrelationships between the three elements. In combination, ICT introduces new prospects for education (for example, ICT has the potential to represent the same information and to structure the learning activity in different ways to suit the learner). ICT also includes the potential to communicate information interactively from student to tutor and from student to student (on a one-to-one, one-to-many, or many-to-many basis). And there are an increasing number of examples that demonstrate that these communications can range from two individuals, to classroom-based discussions, to exchanges in a global context. Collaborative teaching and learning is now a possibility at local, regional, international and global levels. This raises new opportunities but also new challenges for those involved in science learning.

These developments are obviously ongoing, although the uptake of ICT is far from comprehensive (particularly at the tertiary level). They are reflected in the contributions of educational policy makers who remain enthusiastic about the prospects of ICT (for example, see Sitters 2003). An example is the UK government's new policy whereby all schools should have access to the Internet. Once online, students can access the National Grid for Learning (NGfL) and the National Curriculum online. In addition, a wealth of resources is now provided by companies who have expanded into the educational resources market.

These developments have led to new demands on teachers and learners, not least because both are required to be progressively more ICT-literate. Further to this, UK schools are increasingly looking to their science teaching staff and ICT coordinators to explore the use of ICT resources to facilitate science learning and even to develop their own ICT resources (for example, for delivery via school-based intranet sites). This raises important issues for teachers, of course, not least because the introduction of ICT is likely to affect pedagogic strategies. This book also addresses these issues.

However, there are also issues of access to these resources for education, both at the local level (for example, in schools and pupils' homes), and also when we consider students studying in developing nations who may not have access to these resources (for example, see Mbarika *et al.* 2002; Norris *et al.* 2002 for further discussion). The danger is that the information age will focus on specific groups of learners, thus increasing existing structural inequalities. For reasons of length and focus, these are issues that are largely outside the scope of this volume. Notably, however, Linn's chapter does introduce these issues. The volume does consider issues of access in a different context, however, that of extending access to learners with special educational needs (see below).

It is also important to note that the use of ICT raises new challenges for science education and, in particular, for teachers who need to decide whether there is sufficient evidence that using ICT will benefit students. These teachers can draw on a growing body of research evidence that examines the effectiveness of using ICT to facilitate science learning. The conclusions drawn from these analyses range from those who offer qualified support and enthusiasm for the use of ICT such as noting increases in student understanding following the introduction of ICT (see Linn and Hsi 2000), to those who are more sceptical (for example, see Cuban 2001). The overall picture therefore remains contested. What is clear is that, should teachers choose to use ICT in the classroom, they should only do so when they are confident of the benefits to their students. Having made this decision, they also need to develop their pedagogic strategies to ensure that all students get the most from these technologically facilitated approaches. This volume considers issues relevant to these debates.

The book is split into three broad sections that examine theoretical and practical considerations of using ICT to teach and learn science. The chapters in the first part explore current issues in using ICT to teach and learn science. The second part considers the role of design and evaluation issues. The final part documents some of the prospects for extending access using ICT, alongside a chapter that considers possible future developments in the use and study of educational technology.

Part 1   What are the current issues in using ICT to teach and learn science?

The first part consists of three contributions from leading educational researchers. The section acts as an introduction to the book through discussion of how students learn science mediated by new technology, and through consideration of what value might be added to the learning experience by using ICT.

In the first chapter, Marcia Linn provides an overview of the principles that have informed her work on a number of US-based projects developed to facilitate science learning. She begins by considering the goals for science learning in a modern information-rich societal context, noting a key role for developing students' skills in independent learning and emphasizing the role that ICT might play in this process. She goes on to argue that the principles that inform the design of ICT should be based on an understanding of how science is taught and learnt and should promote knowledge integration. In doing so, she briefly reviews the literature in this area and acknowledges the role of evaluation studies in informing the development of a range of projects, including the *Computer as Learning Partner* and the *Knowledge Integration Environment*.

Linn introduces four meta-principles that support knowledge integration. These are: to make science accessible, to make thinking visible, to help students to learn from each other, and to promote autonomous learning. They inform the design of the most recent project with which she has been involved – the *Web-based Inquiry Science Environment*. The chapter concludes by considering the future for learning using ICT and the challenges facing educational researchers.

In the second chapter, Diana Laurillard provides an overview of an analytical framework, which she calls the conversational framework. This framework characterizes complex learning as an iterative conversation. She argues that the introduction of an ICT element to this process introduces a novel level of mediation to this conversation. To ensure that ICT is effective, she points to the need for it to be designed with pedagogic principles firmly at the forefront. She notes that, without this principled design strategy, there is a danger of uncritically accepting the rhetoric that expounds on the possibilities for educational media while failing to realize their full learning potential. Laurillard argues that the conversational framework can inform the development of new ICT materials by specifically considering which elements of the framework are supported by these materials. The model is not limited to this function, however. It can also facilitate systematic examination of the effectiveness of existing ICT materials.

In the final chapter in this section, previously published in a book that examined the teaching and learning of secondary science (Wellington 2000), Jerry Wellington examines the prospects of ICT from a teacher's perspective. In doing so he addresses a series of questions, including why and when is it useful to use ICT to facilitate science learning. He then introduces critical discussion of how a range of applications, including simulations, multimedia, word processing, spreadsheets, data logging, databases and the Internet, could be used in the secondary science classroom. In each case, he describes how these applications could be used to promote science learning, while acknowledging the potential challenges that they raise for secondary school teachers.

Part 2   Designing and evaluating ICT to teach and learn science

The second part examines the role of design and evaluation of ICT by drawing on theoretical and practical explanations of these issues. In the first paper, Leach and Scott consider the design and evaluation of teaching sequences. They offer an alternative perspective to current approaches to such sequences, basing this on social constructivist theories and the concept of learner demand.

In the following chapter, Tom Boyle considers the design of multimedia e-learning for science education. This process, he argues, begins by considering the strategic approach to design. Here, he briefly outlines two examples: instructional systems design and constructivism. Next, he considers two key challenges facing educational designers: abstraction and complexity in science education. He then discusses how design concepts, such as visualization and the use of transitional objects, and scaffolding can address these twin challenges. In the penultimate section of the chapter, Boyle considers the importance of ensuring ICT is accessible to all users. He argues that design for accessibility should mean improved access for everyone because it starts with the premise of 'design for all'. To achieve these ends effectively, accessibility issues have to be introduced at the start of the design process and then reconsidered at each stage of development. Finally, Boyle considers current issues surrounding the development of learning objects, including the importance of standardization.

In the following chapter by Martin Oliver, the debate moves from considering design issues to focusing on the role of evaluation. He begins with a definition of evaluation, leading to a brief history of evaluation research, noting the different theoretical influences on these approaches. The chapter then switches to more practical issues by providing an introductory guide to educational evaluation. This involves a series of stages ranging from consideration of the audience for the evaluation to choice of data collection methods and consideration of the type of analysis. Each stage is described and linked to existing examples from the research literature. In conclusion, some of the technical, ethical and philosophical challenges to conducting evaluation research are considered.

The final chapter in this part, written by Martin Oliver and Grainne Conole, continues the examination of evaluation issues. It considers evaluation in a practical context by introducing a tool kit for those with little or no previous experience of evaluation work. In keeping with the practical nature of a tool kit, the chapter adopts a step-by-step guide to conducting an evaluation, examining the key issues associated with each step. This is followed by a descriptive example and concluding section.

Part 3   Extending access to science learning

The final part examines the potential for extending access to science learning using ICT. It also considers the future prospects for learning using ICT by reviewing trends in educational research and current developments in technology.

In the first chapter, Martyn Cooper documents current issues in the provision of accessible learning using technology in the light of the recent UK legislation in this area. He argues that ICT can provide an extremely useful pedagogic resource to extend access to learning. In doing so, he documents some of the existing assistive technologies that support learning for students with a range of special requirements. Ensuring that all learners can make the most effective use of ICT, however, requires that these materials are designed for accessibility. This requires careful consideration of how end-users will access them, alongside clear advice and guidance on what a course requires of a student.

Cooper argues that design for accessibility should be considered at all stages in the development process and that this should be facilitated by ongoing formative evaluation. To this end, he introduces several principles of accessibility, linking these to issues of design. These are key to developing successful ICT that is flexible and adaptive to a wide range of end-users. Finally, by introducing the issues of registration and assessment, Cooper notes the importance of flexibility, both in the institutional provision of information and registration facilities and also in pedagogic strategies. By ensuring flexibility in these two key areas, support for learning for students with special educational needs (SEN) will be greatly enhanced.

The following chapter, written by a team from The Open University, takes the principles outlined in Cooper's chapter and illustrates how they can be put into practice, in this instance to facilitate access to real-world practical work from remote locations. The chapter reports on studies conducted for the *Practical Experimentation by Access to Remote Learning* (PEARL) project, a European Union-funded endeavour involving four participating universities from across Europe. The PEARL team sought to address the practicalities of providing remote access to real-world experiments for a number of reasons. Not least of these was to provide opportunities for access that would be difficult to achieve in other ways, for example by extending the boundaries to science learning, that would otherwise have been prohibitive on the grounds of access, cost or time to travel.

The chapter focuses on work conducted at The Open University to provide access to chemistry and physics experiments that normally form part of a residential school. In doing so, it documents the design principles, technological challenges and evaluation work that informed the development of these materials.

In the final chapter, Eileen Scanlon explores some of the prospects for future research and development of ICT to facilitate science learning. She reviews a wide range of approaches to using and researching educational technology, including current approaches to the use of simulation and modelling and to computer-mediated communication. The chapter concludes by considering future trends, introducing discussion of portability, reuse and virtual reality.

References

Boohan, R. (2002) 'ICT and communication', in S. Amos and R. Boohan (eds) *Aspects of Teaching in Secondary School – Perspectives on Practice*, London: RoutledgeFalmer.

Cuban, L. (2001) *Oversold and Underused: Computers in the Classroom*, London: Harvard University Press.

Linn, M. C. and Hsi, S. (2000) *Computers, Teachers, Peers: Science Learning Partners*, Mahwah, NJ: Lawrence Erlbaum Associates.

Mbarika, V., Jensen, M. and Meso, P. (2002) 'International perspectives: cyberspace across sub-Saharan Africa', *Communications of the Association for Computing Machinery* 45(12): 17–21.

Norris, C., Soloway, E. and Sullivan, T. (2002) 'Examining 25 years of technology in US education', *Communications of the Association for Computing Machinery* 45(8): 15–18.

Sitters, R. (2003) 'Ministerial déjà vu', *Guardian*: educ@guardian 11 March: 2–3.

Wellington, J. (ed.) (2000) *Teaching and Learning in Secondary Science*, London and New York: Routledge.

Part 1

What are the current issues in using ICT to teach and learn science?

1.1 Using ICT to teach and learn science

Marcia C. Linn

Learning technologies have spurred researchers and curriculum designers to create and test instructional materials to meet the needs of today's students (DISessa 2000; Krajcik *et al.* 1994; Linn and Hsi 2000). Designers use these technologies to create learning environments that combine curriculum, instruction, logistic support and communication. Learning environments enable teachers to carry out complex projects by turning the logistical and managerial aspects of project work over to technology. They connect resources, such as molecular models, geographic information systems (GIS) and Internet sites, with pedagogical advantages, such as collaboration among experts, teachers and students. Learning environments can amplify the effectiveness of teachers, freeing them to use their talents to customize instruction, guide individuals and tutor small groups. Initiatives such as the *Web-based Inquiry Science Environment* (WISE) (Linn *et al.* 2003), the *Cognitive Tutor* (Koedinger and Anderson 1998), *BGuILE* (Reiser *et al.* 2001), *Model-It* (Krajcik *et al.* 1994), *Thinker Tools* (White and Frederiksen 1998) and *World Watcher* (Edelson 1999), address complex science topics, engage students in scientific inquiry, take advantage of the technologies used by experts, support research on learning and prepare students to carry out their own projects in the future.

Ideally, science instruction will ensure that students learn complex science in the context of inquiry and have an experience of mastering new topics or technologies relevant to their personal needs or goals. Inquiry refers to the ability to plan, carry out and interpret novel investigations. Inquiry knowledge is central to new science standards in most countries (Third International Mathematics and Science Study (TIMSS) 1999). In spite of the prominence given to inquiry in all of these standards, few science classes teach for it (Becker 1999).

Information and communications technology (ICT) generally comprises resources found on the Internet and supports for discourse about these and other resources. ICT is a part of the range of technology used by scientists and citizens for learning, research, leisure and efficiency. For the purposes of this paper, technology refers to the broad range of advances that impact the field of science, including ICT, automated data collection, genetic engineering, data mining, molecular modelling and integrated circuit design. Learning technologies refer to any uses of these technologies designed to promote understanding of science or technology. These include varied input devices such as personal digital assistants (PDAs) and data loggers; the full range of digital technologies including computer-assisted design, visualization, modelling, search, data mining and GIS; varied digital resources such as photos, films and video clips; as well as versions of complex applications used by experts for cloning, nanotechnology or space exploration. These distinctions between ICT, technology and learning technologies have blurred over time and now refer more to the activities that they support than to distinct applications. Advances such as cloning entwine computation, mechanical systems, lasers and micro-technology as well as Internet resources and electronic discourse. This chapter follows the convention of using ICT to refer to Internet resources and communication supports, learning technologies to refer to learning environments and technology to refer to the full range of engineering advances used in scientific research.

It discusses current opportunities with ICT for science learning and teaching. Fundamentally, ICT supports and fosters learning when informed by deep understanding of mechanisms governing learning and teaching. The introduction briefly identifies central issues in ICT, including equity, expertise and learning mechanisms. The main section discusses promising uses of learning technologies. The final section identifies trends, opportunities and criteria for using ICT in science learning.

Equity and ICT

Well-designed learning environments can enhance science learning and prepare students for tomorrow's dilemmas, but they require access to computers and the Internet. More and more schools add computer laboratories or mobile laboratories and connect to the Internet but neglect professional development, software and technical support. Schools complain that the costs of technical support, upgrades and software interfere with making ICT effective. Students with access to ICT at home often have special advantages. Even programming courses often provide only 10 to 15 hours of access to technology during a semester. Younger students and those from wealthier families have more access to computers than do older and less wealthy students (American Association of University Women (AAUW) 2000). Inequitable access to learning technologies could thwart efforts to prepare students for satisfying lives and remunerative careers. At the same time as innovators create new learning opportunities with ICT, they also need to ensure that these materials reach all students.

Scientific advance and student learning

Rapid advances in technologies of all sorts have changed the landscape of science dramatically and necessitated new goals for science courses. Lasers, chromosome mapping, genetic engineering, nanotechnology, supercomputers, space telescopes and other technologies have led to new fields of science, raised new ethical issues, enabled new medical treatments and revealed new challenges. Citizens today need a firm foundation in science and technology as well as the ability to learn new topics just-in-time for the next course, job or personal dilemma. Citizens face numerous challenges directly connected to advances in science and technology. Health decisions often involve interpreting new treatments, researching alternatives and making sense of persuasive messages. Environmental stewardship raises complex questions about energy conservation, endangered species and global warming. Scientific advances in cloning, genetically modified crops and data mining raise ethical concerns. Contemporary scientific controversies play out in the news media. Many people learn about complex scientific phenomena and products from the Internet. As a result, citizens need more critical abilities and better techniques for evaluating complex information than have been offered historically by courses. To prepare students for these complex tasks, science courses need to be regular updated as well as having an increased emphasis on independent investigation of scientific questions. New learning technologies, including information technologies like computation, communication technologies like networks and resources including Internet pages and modelling environments, align well with changing goals for science courses.

Mechanisms governing learning and teaching

Successful uses of ICT take advantage of growing understanding of the mechanisms governing learning and teaching. The research base, coming from psychology, educational psychology and science education, tells a consistent story about how students make sense of science (see Anderson and Schunn 2000; Bransford *et al.* 1999; DISessa 2000; Linn *et al.* 2003; Linn and Hsi 2000; Scardamalia and Bereiter 1992). These authors generally agree that students appear to develop new ideas in multiple contexts – developing a repertoire of ideas about a given phenomenon rather than a single perspective.

Results from science education research tell us that this repertoire may include compelling but non-normative ideas about complex topics, such as thermodynamics (DISessa 2000). Most people believe, for example, that aluminium foil is a better insulator than wool for a cold drink because 'metals feel cold and wool sweaters warm things up' (Linn and Hsi 2000). This belief draws on useful observations that metals feel cool to the touch at room temperature and that sweaters feel warm on cold days. However, it ignores other observations, such as how metals feel on a hot day. Many believe that Styrofoam™ is a good insulator, that materials which keep things cold may not keep them hot, that thermos flasks 'know' when to keep things hot or cold and that metals conduct electricity (Linn and Hsi 2000). As these examples illustrate, learners come to science with a repertoire of disconnected ideas and the learning task involves both adding new, more normative ideas and sorting out the repertoire.

Effective instruction involves motivating students to consider new ideas, sort out their existing ideas and develop the capability of making sense of new information throughout their lives. Designing opportunities that help students sort out and prioritize their ideas therefore requires some knowledge of the ideas that students typically hold. Most curriculum materials simply transmit the normative view of science topics (for example, the molecular kinetic view of thermodynamics), but do not enable students to make connections to their existing ideas. This results in the addition of new (perhaps normative) ideas to the student's repertoire, but with few connections to previously held ideas. These new disconnected ideas are easily forgotten, as many students report when asked what they learned in science (Bransford *et al.* 1999).

Research results offer mechanisms that describe how people learn, understand, recall and reuse information. For example, cognitive psychology studies demonstrate that, when learners have to generate connections among elements in a list or ideas in a paragraph, they learn more than when they study the material for the same length of time without generating connections (Bransford *et al.* 1999). Psychological research also demonstrates that all explanations are not the same – explanations succeed when they connect to the specific dilemmas faced by learners. Such general findings leave many questions about science learning unanswered. For example, in helping students generate their own connections, which ones should we encourage, how often should they generate connections, and what forms of generation are the most successful?

Instruction that helps students connect ideas requires both the addition of ideas that reveal the connections among existing views and the provision of opportunities to compare, contrast, explore, reconsider and reflect on views of a science topic. To facilitate this, curriculum designers can construct 'pivotal cases' that prompt students to reorganize their ideas in order to explain challenging phenomena. This results in a more coherent understanding that supports recall of normative ideas one, two or four years later (Linn and Hsi 2000). For example, a pivotal case for the heat and temperature example discussed earlier in this chapter could contrast how wood and metal feel on cold days and how they feel on hot days. To encourage students to integrate this information, instruction needs to support the process of generating connections between this case and other ideas. Combining this case and others like it with prompts to generate connections may lead many students to distinguish their tactile experiences – how hot or cold an object feels – from evidence provided using a thermometer. Thus, this pivotal case could also serve as a firm foundation for later courses that introduce molecular kinetic theory.

Learning environments to support teaching and learning

Learning environments such as the *Web-based Inquiry Science Environment* (WISE) reflect the research base in science learning and instruction and support designers who wish to take advantage of this research (Figure 1.1.1). For example, WISE designers can introduce new ideas with an evidence page and use a wealth of methods to support the integration of ideas including argument construction tools such as *SenseMaker*, reflection notes, causal modelling tools and data representation techniques (Linn and Slotta 2000).

Research using learning environments also advances research in science education, because investigators can easily create alternative versions of projects and test their impacts on learning. For example, science educators have designed alternative versions of instruction to show that generating predictions before conducting an experiment results in more inquiry learning than just designing and conducting the experiment (Linn and Hsi 2000). Researchers using the *Cognitive Tutor* (Figure 1.1.2) have shown that representations of problem solutions that enable students to work

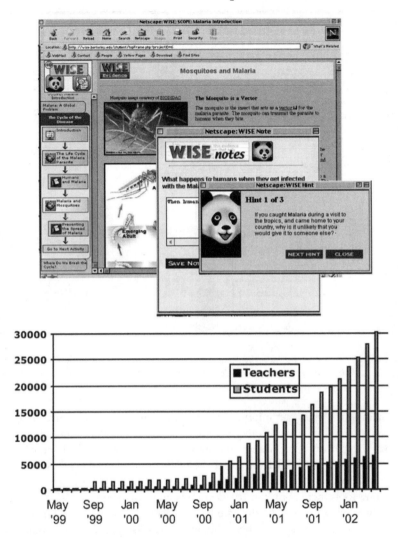

Figure 1.1.1 The *Web-based Inquiry Science Environment* (WISE) guides students with an inquiry map as shown on the left side of the screen, encourages students to reflect by providing a note function and enables instructors to investigate various forms of hints as shown in the hint facility. The bottom of the figure shows recent usage figures for WISE. WISE is used by teachers in the USA, England, Germany, the Netherlands, Norway and other countries.

both forward and backward result in more efficient and effective learning than traditional representations that encourage top-down problem solving (Koedinger and Anderson 1998). Likewise, science educators demonstrate that students develop more robust ideas about water quality when they construct models using *Model-It* (Figure 1.1.3) rather than keeping a laboratory notebook (Krajcik *et al.* 1994).

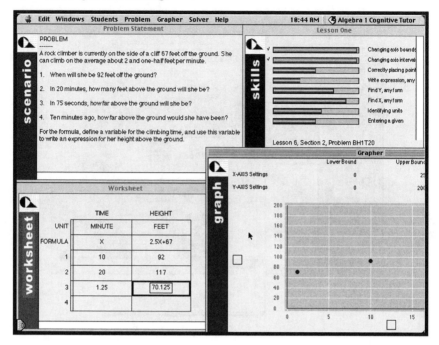

Figure 1.1.2 The *Cognitive Tutor Learning Environment.* Students are guided by a scenario and can keep track of skill development, show their work and get feedback and use resources such as graphing software.

Findings like these can inform those designing new curriculum materials. For example, the WISE learning environment incorporates similar findings in curriculum design patterns that connect the array of tools available in the learning environment. Starting with the basic pattern of 'elicit ideas, add ideas and use a variety of methods to integrate the ideas', designers have created more specific patterns for modelling tools, argument construction tools and discussion tools. One pattern emphasizes pivotal cases. In this, students explain why metals feel colder than wood, they make predictions about the rate of heat flow in these materials, they test their predictions using a dynamic simulation where heat flows at different rates within different materials and they construct an argument using the *SenseMaker* software (Linn and Hsi 2000; Linn and Slotta 2000). These patterns are captured in an inquiry map (see Figure 1.1.1) to guide students. Designers can use these patterns to create instruction that reflects the research base, resulting in varied projects that build on the same pattern. These patterns suggest a new form for the transfer of instruction. Basically, students who perform multiple projects where they use the same pattern in new contexts have the potential of learning how to use the pattern in their own independent investigations.

This research programme emphasizes the challenges of inquiry for both students and teachers. Students need to make sense of their existing and new ideas as well as learn how to identify and research new questions independently. The WISE

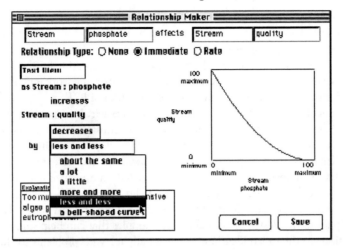

Figure 1.1.3   Screen layout from the *Model-It* software. *Model-It* enables students to measure indicators of the quality of water in a local stream, river or lake, specify a model of water quality and enter their findings into the model. *Model-It* then computes the quality of water in the location. At this point, students can modify their model and change the values of the indicators to investigate ways to improve the quality of the water.

inquiry map guides students to engage in this sense-making; the WISE evidence pages introduce pivotal cases; and the WISE embedded assessments provide teachers with evidence about how well the curriculum is working. The WISE authoring environment serves as a database of curriculum design patterns as well as pivotal cases that have succeeded in specific settings. The WISE learning environment therefore gives new designers a head start in creating powerful instruction.

Scaffolded knowledge integration framework

Both designers and users of technology need criteria to guide their activities. To help designers take advantage of research using learning environments, researchers have synthesized the findings from numerous investigations conducted in science classrooms. The *Computer as Learning Partner* project designed a 12-week thermodynamics curriculum based on real-time data collection and conducted eight iterations of the materials. Each time, the research team used findings from classroom trials to improve the materials. These revisions resulted in a 400 per cent increase in student understanding of the distinction between heat and temperature (Linn and Hsi 2000).

The research team combined the results of these studies and related research to devise a framework that informed the design of the WISE learning environment, can guide future designers and can help users of technology to devise criteria to guide their decisions. This framework, called scaffolded knowledge integration, describes practices that promote knowledge integration. Research and development of technologies to promote science learning can be organized under four meta-principles that capture the main cognitive advantages of technology. These principles are beginning to guide designers of learning environments and also synthesize promising designs that have begun to emerge. They form the basis for a database of design principles that Kali *et al.* (2002) are creating for the Center for Innovative Learning Technologies. In this chapter, the framework is used to create criteria for those selecting from among promising uses of ICT.

First, effective innovations can *make science accessible*. Inquiry science instruction needs an appropriate level of analysis for the scientific content so that students can restructure, rethink, compare, critique and develop more cohesive ideas. For thermodynamics, the *Computer as Learning Partner* project researched models at various levels of abstraction and ultimately settled on a heat-flow model, rather than a molecular kinetic model, because it did a better job of connecting to students' knowledge about heat and temperature (Linn and Hsi 2000). This principle applies to the design of pivotal cases, examples that can help students make connections to their own ideas and to personally relevant problems so they have the opportunity to revisit their ideas regularly. The *Jasper Project* demonstrated the advantage of this principle by designing problems that connect to student experience (Cognition and Technology Group at Vanderbilt 1997).

Second, innovations can *make thinking visible*. Technologies can illustrate the ideas behind assertions and help students understand the process of linking and connecting ideas. When students observe others sorting out more or less promising notions they can learn about appropriate criteria for distinguishing among ideas. Inquiry instruction can make scientific ideas and arguments visible in a number of ways. For example, if implemented carefully, models and simulations can help students understand complex scientific ideas. As an illustration of this potential, the *Model-It* software enables students to build and test water quality models (Krajcik *et al.* 1994). Ideas can be made visible when teachers offer compelling explanations, as well as when students write answers to complex science concepts. By embedding opportunities to make thinking visible in the curriculum, students encounter models of scientific phenomena and explanations that clarify the ideas behind them, as well as having opportunities to make their own thinking visible in embedded assessments and in other tools.

Third, innovative technologies can *help students learn from each other*. Instruction featuring inquiry should include opportunities for students to collaborate, discuss ideas and debate consequential science issues, such as the causes of the declining population of amphibians in North America. These discussions enable students to make their own thinking more visible and also provide explanations that more readily connect to their ideas, both because they might be in vocabulary that students understand and because accounts of scientific phenomena responding directly to student comments are often easier for them to connect to their own thinking (Brown and Campione 1994).

Fourth, innovations can *promote autonomous learning*. To become lifelong learners, students need investigatory skills that they can use throughout their lives. To develop these skills, inquiry projects can help them reflect on their progress and learn to critique their own ideas and those of others. For example, the *BGuILE* learning environment helps students to understand the population dynamics for Galapagos finches (Reiser *et al.* 2001). As noted above, the curriculum design patterns implemented in WISE can reinforce inquiry practices by illustrating similar approaches for quite distinct science topics.

Applying the scaffolded knowledge integration framework

Teaching for knowledge integration can incorporate many genres of technology. These elements often fail to improve learning on their own, but add value when combined with curriculum design patterns in a learning environment.

Web pages

A huge assortment of web pages have been developed to transmit scientific information. These pages vary in their quality, effectiveness, validity and content. Designers seek web pages that make the science accessible to the audience. Often, web pages address particular audiences and are difficult for younger, or older, or less experienced, or more experienced individuals to use effectively. To convert these resources into supports for knowledge integration requires consideration of how students will use the information. The pattern requires eliciting student ideas, introducing resources to contribute to understanding, supporting the search for additional resources, encouraging argument construction, conducting a classroom debate and revising the argument.

Web pages can introduce pivotal cases. In one classroom, students were researching light propagation and a group of students located a web page about night goggles. This turned out to be a pivotal case that helped them distinguish between visual acuity and the physics of light. This activity not only makes the science of light accessible to students but also implements a curriculum design pattern that promotes autonomy.

Web pages can also make thinking visible, as was the case for the night goggles page, which provided an animation of night vision when using the goggles. Making thinking visible adds value to web pages that make science accessible. To this end, pages can include visualizations, models, illustrations and animations.

However, even very powerful web pages, such as that on night goggles, could fail to support knowledge integration if used for the wrong curriculum design pattern. Too often, web pages become an electronic textbook with little motivation for forming cohesive arguments. Designers may need to perform classroom research to find out whether a potential pivotal case or animation promotes knowledge integration. Rather than expecting each teacher to find appropriate web pages, designers should create projects in learning environments and make it easy for teachers to customize the instruction by adding, modifying or substituting pages. The WISE research programme achieves this by engaging partnerships of teachers, natural scientists, pedagogy experts and technologists to create a library of projects and then supporting new schools and teachers who wish to customize the projects.

Probeware and data collection tools

An important technological support for science learning, probeware refers to a variety of sensors that connect to a computer, calculator or handheld PDA (personal digital assistant) and allow students to record data about their environment in real time. Common probe types include temperature, voltage and motion sensors.

These technologies can make thinking about experimentation visible, but can also lead to confusion and frustration. The *Computer as Learning Partner* project took advantage of probeware to create knowledge integration activities around heat and temperature. Initiated when the first Apple II computers arrived in classrooms, this project researched ways to use temperature-sensitive probes and real-time data collection to teach complex concepts such as thermal equilibrium. *Computer as Learning Partner* researchers demonstrated that many uses of probeware left students confused and unable to interpret the data that they had collected. For example, early applications could not support labels on graphs, so many students assumed that the graphs supported their conjectures.

Using the WISE learning environment, researchers combined probeware with animations of the underlying heat flow process and developed curriculum design patterns that involved conducting experiments, writing a principle to synthesize the results, discussing the principles in an online discussion and revising the principles, based on feedback. This revision combined the principle of making thinking visible with the principle of learning from others and engaged students in critiquing results. This curriculum design pattern improved student learning (Linn *et al.* 2003).

Modelling and simulation environments

Modelling and simulation environments are touted as ways to make thinking visible. They make it easy for students to perform 'what if?' experiments or to simulate an experiment that would be dangerous or difficult to perform using real-world materials. For example, researchers have developed powerful ways for students to study emergent phenomena, such as traffic jams, by modelling the behaviour of individual objects using *StarLOGO* (Colella *et al.* 2001). Learners typically manipulate objects in their simulations to see how they react under different conditions. To ensure that these experiences contribute to knowledge integration, designers need to encourage students to synthesize their results. For example, in modelling falling objects, where the underlying rule such as the force of gravity is already defined, students can compare the simulated behaviour of two objects with different masses falling in a vacuum. However, unless they also generate conclusions and compare their ideas with experiments in the classroom, they may not learn the underlying principles. The *Thinker Tools* learning environment combines these activities to improve student understanding (White and Frederiksen 1998).

In many cases, models make thinking about the phenomena visible but do not require that students make their thinking about the model visible. Research suggests that models where students can vary the conditions and test their ideas help them explore complex relationships. For example, they might model a simple predator–prey relationship by defining the rate at which the predator species successfully hunts its prey and the rate at which both species reproduce. Running a model on the computer simulates how the relative populations of the two species fluctuate over time. Researchers using the *BGuILE* software have devised curriculum design patterns that enable students to explore a complex ecosystem and gather evidence to support their arguments (Reiser *et al.* 2001).

Kit-based inquiry activities and disk-based resources

A large number of technology-enhanced programs are available as disk-based resources (for example, provided on CD-ROM or DVD-ROM), or kit-based activities at all grade levels. These activities are self-contained, in the sense that they come with the materials needed and can be used without any supplemental software or curriculum. Some disk-based resources provide a vetted set of web pages and videos, like an online encyclopedia. Materials can be self-paced and even self-guided.

These materials often claim to make thinking visible, but they also implement a broad range of pedagogical approaches including transmission of knowledge that does not lead to knowledge integration. Some emphasize hands-on activities, others are more suited to memorization and still others provide descriptive accounts of complex phenomena similar to videos. To evaluate these resources, users need to study how students use them to integrate their ideas. These materials may require that teachers guide the students in knowledge building.

Furthermore, disk-based materials differ from learning environments in that they typically have no capability for students to record their own information or for teachers to customize their use. They cannot respond directly to the comments and experiences of students. Rather, these technologies provide a means for students to seek resources that might make thinking about a topic visible. Often, disk-based activities were created before more interactive formats were available, and today they would be more successful if they were implemented in a learning environment.

Synchronized collaborative courses

Researchers have created synchronized collaborative courses to enable students to learn from each other. These courses are opportunities for students in different geographical locations to participate in the same activities and interact with one another. In the *Kids as Global Scientists* programme (Songer 1996), as part of a weather unit, students from different parts of the country or the world might make weather measurements and then compare notes on weather patterns in their respective locations. These curriculum units can require a commitment of anywhere from a few days to a few weeks or to the full semester. These programmes work best when several classrooms use the curriculum at the same time and share their findings with each other. They draw on communication technologies to coordinate activity and discussion among the school sites. In some of these programmes, students at a school are required to serve as the resident experts in a particular kind of data and they must communicate with students at other sites to help compare their local environments.

Today, many learning environments, including WISE, *BioKids and World Watcher,* allow classes to engage in synchronized activities such as comparing the geological features of diverse environments. These courses support students as they learn from others, taking advantage of the distributed understanding available in a community. In most studies, students do make progress in integrating their understanding around their area of specialization but they may, or may not, make progress in learning about topics from others. These materials lend themselves to local customization in that teachers can direct their students to local resources and involve local experts.

Comprehensive curricula

Comprehensive curricula include programmes that provide all the written materials, technology and supplies needed to support students' activities and to involve them in a complete, full-length science course. For example, *Constructing Physics Understanding* incorporates visualization and modelling tools to illustrate all of the physics content included in the curriculum. These courses intend to make science accessible, make thinking visible, help students learn from others and promote autonomy. Evaluating their impact may require them to be studied in classrooms, as these courses are often difficult to customize. They could also turn more of the logistics of the course over to the technology and take some advantage of learning environment features.

Distance learning models

Many advocate distance learning using ICT to extend instruction to geographical areas where courses are not available or are difficult to access. Current distance learning design systems such as *Blackboard* and *Web CT* focus on logistics and grading more than on cognitive supports. For example, the *Virtual High School* uses *Blackboard* in an innovative format. The programme invites schools to participate in a consortium where individual teachers offer courses that can be taken by students at other schools. Students can take courses not offered at their own school. The *Virtual High School* model therefore requires collaboration among schools. Each school identifies one teacher to offer an online course for up to twenty participants from other schools. In exchange, up to twenty students from the participating schools can enroll in other courses that are offered through the *Virtual High School.*

The *Virtual High School* enables students to take courses in a wide range of subject areas not covered at their own schools and it offers teachers the opportunity to teach new subjects and gain experience teaching in a new medium. The *Virtual High School* course offerings vary with regard to their use of technology to promote knowledge integration. Courses might be primarily textbook driven with online discussions, or they could take advantage of a complex learning environment.

Summary

In summary, the varied uses of technology require careful evaluation to determine their effectiveness in promoting science learning. Technology is neither a panacea nor an obstacle to learning. Rather, for any technology-enhanced course, users need to evaluate its potential for knowledge integration. The scaffolded knowledge integration framework can help those evaluating new approaches by providing criteria. As these examples show, web resources can fail to make science accessible if they are not carefully designed. In addition, resources can make science confusing rather than visible. If these design issues are taken into consideration, science materials can help students learn from others. Finally, encouraging a life-long practice of inquiry takes more than a few science projects, but learning environments offer a good way to increase inquiry experiences in science classes. As these examples illustrate, the field as a whole can learn from the work of other researchers by focusing on testing and documenting the impact of curriculum design patterns on student outcomes.

Conclusions and next steps

ICT enables new resources for learning, new modes of instruction and new forms of science education research. Students today draw on web resources, databases, models and simulations not available in the past. Many students learn from digital materials rather than from texts or hands-on experimentation. In addition, technology enables new forms of educational research because innovators can build alternative treatments into learning environments and contrast alternative forms of instruction more easily.

Although technology permeates more and more of the scientific workplace, many worry about the role of ICT in education. Much of this concern stems from the numerous failures of early technology innovations. For example, programming courses, implemented because BASIC was the only software on early personal computers, failed to teach the scientific thinking skills some had anticipated. Many early applications in technology were poor imitations of effective materials, such as books or filmstrips.

There have also been successful developments. For example, communication technologies have changed the way people interact: individuals now exchange messages and participate in chat opportunities in different ways from when they relied solely on the postal service and the telephone. Online commerce has also changed how many people shop. These opportunities may have the unintended consequence of reducing face-to-face communication. Many worry that these technologies could reduce social capital, but others point out that electronic communication has created global communities who jointly address topics including rainforest preservation, treatment for rare diseases and collections of Ming china. We are still at an early stage in the effort to shape and comprehend the role of technology in society. We need to study, monitor and critique the use of technology to achieve societal goals.

New research paradigms

Learning environments and other customizable uses of ICT provide opportunities to build on mistakes. Many failed efforts to use technology exist, but these should not condemn the process of investigation and improvement. Fortunately, technology changes rapidly, making it easy to replace poor solutions with better ones. Sometimes new technologies enable solutions that were prevented by earlier ones but often new technologies offer an opportunity for developers to try the next version of their applications and correct flaws in the earlier versions.

We now have very promising materials and can envision far more effective uses for technology, as research continues. Learning environments and technology innovations are more and more tailored to the needs of specific audiences and courses. For example, general programming languages have been replaced by specific simulations and modelling environments that can lead to dramatic gains in student learning (for example, see Linn and Hsi 2000; Bransford *et al.* 1999). Learning environments also support far more customization than was possible with early uses of technology. Today, teachers can customize their instruction to local lakes, current weather conditions, new science standards or new technologies.

Criteria for evaluating technology-enhanced science courses have the potential to improve learning outcomes, teacher satisfaction and research impacts. As curriculum design teams, teacher customization projects and school adoption committees experiment with criteria for evaluating innovations, they will become more savvy about what works in their settings. These groups will also contribute to the criteria and make them more effective. In this chapter, four meta-principles are proposed to evaluate technology enhancements. This chapter also suggests the value of reusable curriculum design patterns and the advantages of designing pivotal cases to advance understanding in each complex science topic. This effort is supported by the creation of a database of design principles and features by the Center for Innovative Learning Technologies, enabling software designers to build on the findings and results of their peers (Kali *et al.* 2002).

New goals for science courses

Both students and teachers need new technology capabilities to help them prepare for current employment opportunities, to design solutions to personally relevant problems and to take advantage of numerous opportunities. Understanding technological advances, as well as recognizing the nature of technology and the inevitable unintended consequences of advances, underlies success in modern society. Designing instruction for just-in-time learning means offering students the capability of guiding, designing and monitoring their own understanding. This ability to autonomously make sense of new material serves everyone well and becomes more and more crucial as both technology and science advance.

To achieve this goal, our science courses need to address science literacy along with language literacy and technology literacy. As the examples in this chapter demonstrate, students need to read in order to learn to become scientifically literate. Science literacy includes the ability to critique accounts of contemporary controversies, such as the debate about genetically modified food. Students also need to develop technology literacy to become scientifically literate today.

Recent reports that call for all individuals to gain technology literacy also define the nature of this dimension (American Association of University Women (AAUW) 2000; National Research Council (NRC) 1996; Snyder *et al.* 1999). Individuals analysing the role of technology in science call for programs that provide students with capabilities, skills and concepts related to technology. By capabilities, these writers refer to areas such as planning, de-bugging, communication and analysis of projects that take advantage of technology. These reports call for opportunities for all students to achieve these capabilities by carrying out sustained projects, such as those supported by learning environments. Many reports also call for students to learn contemporary skills, such as word processing, search and spreadsheet usage. Typically, reports emphasize that these skills be embedded in larger projects and learned on an as-needed basis. Finally, most reports call for students to understand concepts relevant to the use of technology and education such as the nature of a stored program, the characteristics of a network and the nature of intellectual property.

Teaching for science, technology and language literacy means including projects where students conduct investigations, often with extensive guidance, so they can develop the capability of guiding their own learning. Fortunately, advances in technology have made this goal for science learning more accessible.

Research on science learning and instruction

Technology has helped advance our understanding of science learning. Records of student activities in online discussions, reflection notes and constructions of models or concept maps give a clearer picture of the process by which they make sense of scientific material. Online technologies with embedded assessments provide teachers with more detailed and useful information about the effectiveness of curriculum materials than has been available historically. We are only beginning to find ways to take advantage of this information.

Retrospective analysis of the impacts of technology on education underscores the complexity of factors influencing teaching and learning. Over the past 20 years, we have seen numerous new technologies, often offered as a panacea for education, along with frequent claims that technology is causing the downfall of effective classroom instruction. In fact, rapid advances in technology offer an unprecedented opportunity for exploration of educational effectiveness, but no straightforward answers to educational questions.

Any attempt to analyse the role of technology in science education must occur against the backdrop of the overall trends in technology. Three important trends influence thinking about technology's role in science education, both historically and for the future.

First, technological applications have become more and more targeted to specific audiences over time. Initially, for example, businesses relied on generic spreadsheets; today, spreadsheets form the backbone for tax preparation programs, personal banking programs, budget planning programming programs, project control systems, business accounting and inventory control. Rather than a single application, specialized applications for each of these important audiences have been developed, tested and refined. As a result, users of spreadsheets spend less time attempting to solve personal problems and more time taking advantage of the power of the software.

Another example concerns computer-aided design. Initial software programs were relatively poor versions of mechanical drawing. These were replaced by more powerful but generic tools, such as *AutoCAD*. Now computer-aided manufacturing tools help engineers not only design but actually produce automobiles or aeroplanes. In addition, software allows electrical engineers to design and produce integrated circuits. There are also specialist applications for the design of houses, office buildings and theatre sets. Furthermore, related programs allow designers to test their chip designs for thermal properties, determine whether their building plans meet local code restrictions, test the logic of integrated circuits and examine manufactured goods for longevity, wear points, etc.

This trend is now emerging in science education where learning environments support the design of multiple projects, each tailored to a specific topic. In addition, researchers are tailoring environments that succeed in pre-college classes so that they work in higher education.

A second major trend in technology concerns the development of customizable applications. Initially, generic word processors, spreadsheets, search tools and budgeting programs provided little opportunity for customization. Today, users design their own styles for the word processors, establish parameters for their budget needs and enter their personal search preferences into their Internet browser. Furthermore, users create their own web pages and have the opportunity to tailor Internet portals to their personal requirements.

Customization is crucial to education, where curriculum standards, student background and teacher experiences vary from one area to another. Customization also enables teachers and districts to adjust learning materials to their particular body of water, geological formations, weather patterns or other scientific phenomena.

A third major trend concerns community collaboration to create powerful applications. Certainly, Linux offers one of the best examples. The Linux community has jointly created an open-source operating system and applications of high quality which are available to all users. Today, educational research groups seek ways to incorporate varied resources into learning environments.

These trends toward the tailoring of applications to specific courses, age groups and users, providing communities with customizable applications and developing community efforts to create powerful learning environments, greatly enhance the appeal and power of digital technologies for science education.

They also raise important research questions concerning the basis for future use of technology. New technologies, by virtue of their customizability, support powerful research activities. Teachers, schools and research teams can customize instruction and analyse the impact for student learning. Many technological tools provide considerable control over learning activity, enabling researchers to create distinct learning experiences for students, while at the same time allowing teachers to behave similarly in the classroom while the students utilize different curriculum alternatives. We need to find ways to synthesize these experiences so we can learn more from each other.

Acknowledgements

This material is based upon research supported by National Science Foundation grants SF96-138, MDR 91-55744 and MDR 94-53861. Any opinions, findings, conclusions or recommendations expressed in this publication are those of the authors and may not reflect the views of the National Science Foundation.

The author would like to thank members of the *Web-based Inquiry Science Environment* project, members of the *Computer as Learning Partner* project, members of the Science Controversies on Line Partnerships in Education Partnership, as well as all the teachers, administrators and students who have participated in our studies.

References

American Association of University Women (AAUW) (2000) *Tech-savvy: Educating Girls in the New Computer Age*, Washington, DC: AAUW.

Anderson, J. R. and Schunn, C. D. (2000) 'Implications of the ACT-R learning theory: no magic bullets', in R. Glaser (ed.) *Advances in Instructional Psychology* (Vol. 5), Mahwah, NJ: Lawrence Erlbaum Associates.

Becker, H. J. (1999) *Internet Use by Teachers: Conditions of Professional Use and Teacher-directed Student Use*, Center for Research on Information Technology and Organizations, Irvine: University of California and the University of Minnesota.

Bransford, J. D., Brown, A. L. and Cocking, R. R. (eds) (1999) *How People Learn: Brain, Mind, Experience, and School*, Washington, DC: National Research Council.

Brown, A. L. and Campione, J. C. (1994) 'Guided discovery in a community of learners', in K. McGilly (ed.) *Classroom Lessons: Integrating Cognitive Theory and Classroom Practice*, Cambridge, MA: MIT Press/Bradford Books.

Cognition and Technology Group at Vanderbilt (1997) *The Jasper Project: Lessons in Curriculum, Instruction, Assessment, and Professional Development*, Mahwah, NJ: Lawrence Erlbaum Associates.

Colella, V. S., Klopfer, E. and Resnick, M. (2001) *Adventures in Modeling*, New York: Teachers' College Press.

DISessa, A. A. (2000) *Changing Minds: Computers, Learning and Literacy*, Cambridge, MA: MIT Press.

Edelson, D. C. (1999) 'Addressing the challenges of inquiry-based learning through technology and curriculum design', *Journal of the Learning Sciences* 8(3/4): 391–450.

Kali, Y., Bos, N., Linn M., Underwood, J. and Hewitt J. (2002) 'Design principles for educational software', Proceedings of the Computer Support for Collaborative Learning (CSCL) conference: *Foundations for a CSCL Community*, Boulder, CO.

Koedinger, K. R. and Anderson, J. R. (1998) 'Illustrating principled design: the early evolution of a cognitive tutor for algebra symbolization', *Interactive Learning Environments* 5: 161–80.

Krajcik, J. S., Blumenfeld, P. C., Marx, R. W. and Soloway, E. (1994) 'A collaborative model for helping middle grade science teachers learn project-based instruction', *Elementary School Journal* 94(5): 483–97.

Linn, M. C., Davis, E. A. and Bell, P. (2003) *Internet Environments for Science Education*, Mahwah, NJ: Lawrence Erlbaum Associates.

—— and Hsi, S. (2000) *Computers, Teachers, Peers: Science Learning Partners*, Mahwah, NJ: Lawrence Erlbaum Associates.

—— and Slotta, J. D. (2000) 'WISE science', *Educational Leadership* 58(2): 29–32.

National Research Council (NRC) (1996) *National Science Education Standards*, Washington, DC: National Research Council.

Reiser, B. J., Tabak, I., Sandoval, W. A., Smith, B. K., Steinmuller, F. and Leone, A. J. (2001) 'BGuILE: strategic and conceptual scaffolds for scientific inquiry in biology classrooms', in S. M. Carver and D. Klahr (eds), *Cognition and Instruction: Twenty-five Years of Progress*, Mahwah, NJ: Lawrence Erlbaum Associates.

Scardamalia, M. and Bereiter, C. (1992) 'A knowledge building architecture for computer supported learning', In E. de Corte, M. C. Linn, H. Mandl and l. Verschaffel (eds) *Computer-based Learning Environments and Problem Solving*, Berlin: Springer-Verlag.

Snyder, L., Aho, A. V., Linn, M. C., Packer, A. H., Tucker, A. B., Ullman, J. D. and van Dam, A. (1999) *Be FIT! Being Fluent with Information Technology*, Washington, DC: National Academy Press.

Songer, N. B. (1996) 'Exploring learning opportunities in coordinated network-enhanced classrooms: a case of kids as global scientists', *Journal of the Learning Sciences* 5: 297–327.

Third International Mathematics and Science Study (TIMSS) (1999) *Facing the Consequences: Using TIMSS for a Closer Look at United States Mathematics and Science Education*, Dordrecht and London: Kluwer Academic.

White, B. Y. and Frederiksen, J. R. (1998) 'Inquiry, modeling, and metacognition: making science accessible to all students', *Cognition and Instruction* 16(1): 3–188.

1.2 Rethinking the teaching of science

Diana Laurillard

What can the new media offer to science teaching?

The development of educational media is driven by an odd mix of engines: technological pull, commercial empire-building, financial drag, logistical imperatives and pedagogical pleas. Between them, they generate a strange assortment of equipment and systems from which the educational technologist must fashion something academically respectable. None of the new technology media was developed as a response to a pedagogical imperative, and it shows. They do not easily lend themselves to a pedagogical classification or an analysis of their usefulness for different kinds of learning objective.

We need principles for generating a teaching strategy, which is where a classification of educational media should begin. It means starting from the learning objectives: approaching the technology with a clear sense of what we want to achieve for learners and challenging the technology to provide it. The alternative is to begin with the technology. It is tempting to do so, because it is the more tractable of the two approaches – it is exciting to think through all the capabilities of the technology and imagine the huge benefits they yield for learning:

> By giving students access to a new world of information, sparking creativity and facilitating rich communication and collaboration across vast distances, computers have long been a powerful tool for education. At the same time, the Internet has brought an unprecedented level of great educational content to a wide audience, encouraging teachers to share curriculums and resources worldwide ... and emerging web services technologies will create further opportunities for collaborative learning.
>
> (Gates 2002)

The rhetoric is undoubtedly exciting – sparking, rich, vast, powerful, unprecedented, worldwide – and yes, the opportunities are there, but where is the real educational substance? If we are seriously interested in transforming the effectiveness of education then we have to get beyond the powerful rhetoric of the excitement of technology and turn instead to the much more intellectually challenging problem of what it takes to learn.

A framework for designing learning activities

We need to think in terms of what a learner needs when they are trying to assimilate new and difficult conceptual ideas. This is not about learning a new piece of information, such as that 'the symbol for chlorine is Cl'. It is rather about learning why, or how? Acquisition of information is not especially difficult and skill in the use of information and communication technology makes it even less of a challenge. Here, we set ourselves the most difficult teaching challenge, that of helping students learn science; of helping them understand difficult concepts or complex systems.

Irrespective of the technology, or the precise content, or the academic level, or the teaching context, what are the basic characteristics of an effective learning encounter in which the learner is trying to reach a deep understanding of a difficult idea? Suppose we think through the optimal learning process:

- Teacher and student need to talk to each other and exchange ideas – the teacher may have the lion's share of the dialogue, explaining the significance of an idea, why it is useful or interesting, how it relates to other ideas and so on. But the learner will want to interrogate the teacher about what precisely is meant by some piece of terminology, or if their idea applies to some other situation, or why it could not be a simpler idea. A *discursive process* of this kind is all too rare, because it is very time-consuming and because learners are not usually invited to interrogate teachers. However, the need for it remains. It helps each side understand the other.

- The teacher will also set a task for the learner, providing the opportunity to experiment and get meaningful feedback in terms of the goal of the task. This *interactive process* could be a laboratory experiment aiming for a particular result, a field trip looking for evidence to explain given phenomena or an attempt to model some system process.

- To make the interactive task work, the learner has to adapt his or her actions in the light of what he or she has learned in the theory, or discursive, part. This process links the theory to the practice. It is the point where the learner tries to put ideas into practice – applying an idea to interpreting a particular event, for example. An *adaptive process* of this kind helps the learner make the link from theory to practice.

- The learners will then need to reflect on what happens as a result of their attempts to achieve the task goal. The feedback should help promote reflection on the interaction, relate the practice back to the theory and adjust any faulty reasoning, so adapting their future actions to be more successful. This *reflective process* is internal to both teacher and student, each of whom reflects on the interaction at the task level in order to re-describe their theoretical conceptions in the discursive process.

These different kinds of process together are sufficiently rich and comprehensive to support the learner through the elaborate intellectual processes to be undertaken.

There is also a kind of engine driving the different stages to motivate the iteration between them. At each stage, there is a reason for the student, as learner, to move to the next one:

- there is an action to carry out, requiring the student to use the theory;
- there is feedback showing how far the student is from the goal, requiring him or her to reflect on the discrepancy, refer back to the theory and adapt his or her actions accordingly;
- and there is a discussion inviting the student to articulate his or her own ideas, reflecting on his or her experience.

These successive ways of engaging with the ideas, the theory, the practice and the re-articulation are the basis of complex learning of the kind that goes beyond mere acquisition of information. Figure 1.2.1 is a schematic representation of the iterative processes contained within a complex learning process. The name 'Conversational Framework' nicely expresses what appears to be going on between teacher and student.

This Conversational Framework for describing the learning process is intended to be applicable to any academic learning situation: to the full range of subject areas and types of topic. It is not normally applicable to learning through experience, nor to 'everyday' learning.

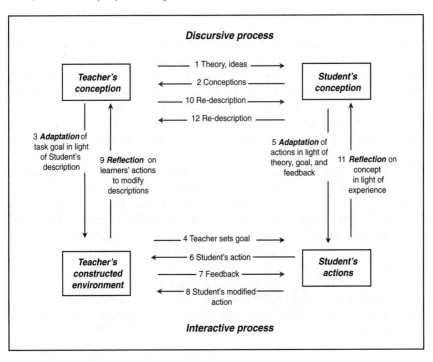

Figure 1.2.1 The Conversational Framework.

The characterization of the teaching–learning process as an iterative 'conversation' is hardly a new idea. Ramsden describes teaching as a sort of conversation:

> ... a teacher faced with a series of classes with a large group of students should plan to do things that encourage deep approaches to learning; these things imply dialogue, structured goals, and activity ... Teaching is a sort of conversation.
>
> (Ramsden 1992: 167–8)

Kolb's 'learning cycle' (Kolb 1984) states that learning occurs through an iterative cycle of experience followed by feedback, which is reflected on and then used to revise action (equivalent to repeating the sequence of activities 6–7–8–11–10–9 in Figure 1.2.1). Pask formalized the idea of learning as a conversation in Conversation Theory (Pask 1976), which included the separation of 'descriptions' and 'model-building behaviours' and the definition of understanding as 'determined by two levels of agreement' (Pask 1976: 22). Many interesting ideas have their counterparts in the culture of Ancient Greece, and this is no exception. The 'Socratic dialogue' is still referred to as epitomizing the tutorial process. A Conversational Framework as a representation of the learning process is at least a plausible idea with a good pedigree, therefore, and serves both to clarify the second-order character of academic learning and to define its essential components.

The Conversational Framework outlined here defines the core structure of an academic dialogue and relates it to content in terms of a topic goal. The dialogue may never actually include the opportunity for students to take actions in practice; it may only refer to former experience or 'thought experiments'; the dialogue may never take place explicitly between teacher and student but as a purely internal dialogue with the student playing both roles. In all these cases, the student has to provide the equivalent – they must imagine the action, or remember a relevant experience to reflect on, or carry out the internal dialogue. This is what makes advanced learning difficult and why it requires some intellectual effort and self-discipline. The full Conversational Framework is rarely present for most learners most of the time. A good teaching strategy will pre-empt what the learner needs and provide those different kinds of support in the way the learning environment is designed. In the context of learning technology, without a teacher present, the educational media themselves must provide what is missing.

The Conversational Framework illustrated in Figure 1.2.1, therefore, is a representation of a principled teaching strategy. There are several different types of learning experience that can be embraced within this framework. Here we focus on some of the most significant.

Attending, apprehending	In the student's conceptual response to the teacher's input at 1 and 10
Investigating, exploring	In the adaptation–action–feedback–reflection loop at 5, 6, 7, 11
Experimenting, practising	In the goal–action–feedback–reflection–adaptation–modification cycle at 4, 6, 7, 11, 5, 8
Discussing, debating	In the discursive process between teacher and students at 1, 2, 10, 12
Articulating, expressing	In the student's discursive activities, fed back to the teacher at 2 and 12

The question addressed here is: to what extent can educational media support these activities in the Conversational Framework and thereby assist the learning process?

Forms of educational media

In the following sections, each type of educational medium is analysed in terms of the Conversational Framework to see how far it offers a principled teaching strategy. Table 1.2.1 shows how the principal learning experiences we are considering link to familiar media or technologies of teaching, both traditional and electronic. The teaching media take distinctive forms, here characterized as 'narrative', 'interactive', 'adaptive', 'communicative' and 'productive'.

The five 'media forms' distinguish between the different ways of using the media, methods and technologies on offer. We can already see that 'e-learning' takes several different forms, just as traditional teaching does. Equally, we can see

Table 1.2.1   Five principal learning experiences with the methods and media forms needed to deliver them

Learning experiences	Media/methods/technologies	Media forms
Attending, apprehending	Talk, print, TV, video, DVD-ROM	Narrative
Investigating, exploring	Library, CD-ROM, DVD-ROM, web-based resources	Interactive
Experimenting, practising	Laboratory, field trip, simulation	Adaptive
Discussing, debating	Seminar, online conference	Communicative
Articulating, expressing	Talk, print, product, animation, model	Productive

that the new technologies have their counterparts in traditional teaching – the five media forms each occur in both traditional and electronic technologies.

As we assess the extent to which the new media offer significant added value to the learning process, we challenge their use – not just accepting them, but forcing the question 'what makes them so much better than the traditional media?'

By analysing illustrative examples of existing learning programs, we can also see which design characteristics enable the medium to fulfil its potential to meet the requirements of the learning experience it has to support. If we want to support exploration with web-based resources, for example, which ways of using them meet the requirements of the Conversational Framework and which do not? This helps us to generate some design principles for developing information and communications technology (ICT).

Narrative media

The traditional educational methods and media, such as lectures, books, films and television programmes, are all narrative in form, and for good reason. Narrative provides a structure that creates global coherence in a text that contains many component parts. In an educational context, print, audio and video all use a variety of structural cues, such as headings, textual signposts, paragraphing, captions, locations and camera movement, to allow learners to maintain a sense of the overall structure of the narrative and hence understand its meaning. Narrative is fundamentally linked to cognition by providing the structure that enables the reader to discern the author's meaning.

However, these media can only offer descriptions of the teacher's conception. The requirements of the Conversational Framework suggest that, if the narrative media are to move beyond the limits of the silent, unquestionable text, then they must engage the learner in reflecting on his or her own experience of the practice and theory he or she is describing. A video cassette is another example of an essentially linear narrative medium. Nothing in the video changes when a student rewinds it, just as nothing in a book changes when you turn a page.

Setting the capabilities of narrative media against the Conversational Framework, we can see, as shown in Figure 1.2.2, that video could support only half of the elements. If the video were demonstrating the characteristics of chemical elements, for example, it could show different elements and their different reactive properties, offering contrastive types (1). The teacher could adapt an exercise for the student (3), but not in the light of the student's own response – the video is designed on the basis of the teacher's previous experience. As a set exercise, the student could be asked to identify which chemicals react violently (4). However, a video cannot give them feedback on their answer. In fact, without the requirement to offer an answer to anyone, they may well not bother to think of one, but just let the video run and tell them what it is.

The same kind of material could be delivered on DVD-ROM. With the video material digitized, it can be accessed much more easily, with a browsable index to each sequence. This makes a DVD-ROM more convenient than video but does

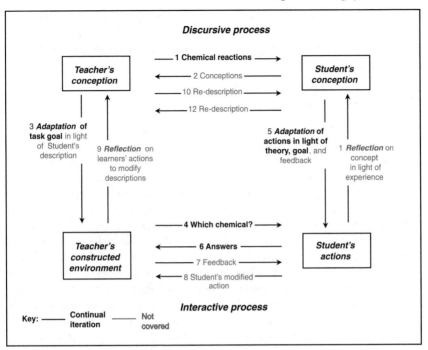

Figure 1.2.2 Interpretation of the Conversational Framework for video material.

not, in itself, change the nature of the learning experience. For that, we need to return to its use as an adaptive medium (see below).

Interactive media

Interactive media are the presentational media that include multimedia as disk-based resources and web-based resources. They share the common property that they are essentially linear media (text, video, audio) delivered in an open, user-controlled environment, either on disk or over a network. Being essentially linear, they offer media resources that remain unchanged by the user, who can navigate and select content at will. The important features of interactive media, from a pedagogical point of view, are the scope of the access and the nature of the user control.

Disk-based resources

The scope of access to disk-based media is clearly small in comparison with the scope of the World Wide Web, but the trade-off, for the learner, is that the more controlled environment of the disk can offer clearer navigation. The teacher designing resources for a disk will select the most important, structure the index, provide relevant contextual information and design the interface to suit the material. Since the disk can also support a programmed environment that offers more support to learners, CDs and DVDs are more likely to be adaptive media (see below), rather than the purely interactive form, which simply provides guided access to a set of resources.

Web-based resources

It is difficult for the teacher to control access to web-based resources – once linked to another website, a learner may choose to link to other material not selected by the teacher. It is a freer environment for exploration but is subject to the navigation and interface designs of others. Of the two types of interactive resource, the Web offers good support to the needs of the lifelong learner who has learned how to learn and has the skills needed to explore and evaluate the multiply connected network of knowledge in their own and related fields. For the student who is a novice in his or her field (which, incidentally, includes the lifelong learner who is exploring a field that is new to them), the scale and scope of this online library requires a kind of 'reading list'. The Web equivalent of the reading list is the 'gateway', a high-quality resource discovery service designed for a target community. Links to other sites are accompanied by searchable descriptions and keywords, which allow users to understand the scope of a website before connecting to it. A gateway of this kind enables a teacher to create a subset of approved websites for students to use as background or as research material that takes them beyond the essential requirements of their course.

By contrast, with a disk, the Web provides an admittedly large, but often bizarrely connected library. Academics are naturally excited by a medium that enables students to explore widely and follow their own research pathways, but students are working under time pressures. Full-time campus students are fitting jobs around their studies and part-time distance learners are fitting studies around their jobs. School students are under pressure to achieve high standards. If they are to use precious learning time efficiently, then the academic must design their use of web-based resources in the light of the whole Conversational Framework. The Web provides an environment that offers hyperlinked access to a range of resources, but gives no further support than that. Figure 1.2.3 shows its limited coverage of the Conversational Framework.

However, a teacher's website could support student learning more efficiently by providing some of the additional activities suggested by the missing elements of the Conversational Framework, such as topics for investigation (Activity 1), suggested task goals (4), a way of collecting and submitting notes on findings (2) and access to expert analyses of those topics (10), with reference to evidence from the linked sites.

The additional support devices in this guided web search reduce the degree of uncertainty for students. They need to be protected from the tyranny of choice offered by the Web. They can easily escape the protection, should they wish to, but it is the teacher's responsibility to make the material learnable. The additional design features suggested by the Conversational Framework transform the Web into a supported learning environment.

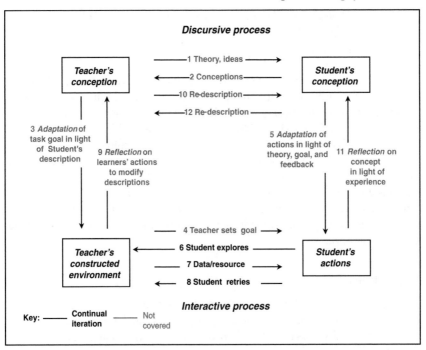

Figure 1.2.3 Interpretation of the Conversational Framework for web-based resources.

The essence of the interactive media is to offer resources for students to explore. Multimedia disks and web-based resources enable students to make their own links between topics and follow their own line of investigation and this is valuable for highly skilled learners. For most learners, however, it is not sufficient to ensure that they are fully supported. Enhanced features, such as suggested tasks, structured note-taking tools or access to expert analyses, contribute much more to ensuring efficient learning.

Adaptive media

For the learning process to be fully supported, students should receive meaningful intrinsic feedback on their actions that relates to the nature of the task goal. The goal–action–feedback cycle constitutes the core of the interactive level of the Conversational Framework. Since 'intrinsic feedback' is such an important feature of the adaptive media, it is worth considering exactly how it differs from 'extrinsic feedback'.

- *Intrinsic feedback* is that which is internal to the action, that cannot be helped once the action occurs – for example, the visual trajectory of a ball kicked towards a goal.

- *Extrinsic feedback* is feedback that is external to the action, which may occur as a commentary on the action – for example, the verdict of the crowd as the ball heads towards the goal, or not.

These definitions reveal their pedagogical significance. The former is inherent in the action and, unlike the latter, requires no third-party judgement on the quality of the action. The student should be able to use the intrinsic feedback to improve his or her performance, so his or her experience is a little like a real-world interaction. That is why adaptive media are so important for teaching science. The informational content of intrinsic feedback is extremely valuable to the learner. It enables them to know how close they are to a good performance and what more they need to do. It is individualized, private, formative feedback, which helps to build the student's understanding of the internal relations between theory and practice. Like the teacher–student dialogue, it is fundamental to the Conversational Framework.

Simulations

A computer-based simulation is a program that embodies some model of an aspect of the world, allows the user to make inputs to the model, runs the model and displays the results. The model could take several forms: a system of equations for describing coexisting plant populations; a set of procedures for guiding a rocket; an operational simulation using experimental performance data of an engineering plant; a set of condition-action rules for operating a nuclear power plant (see Figure 1.2.4, from Moyse 1991).

For all these types of simulations, the program interface allows students to make inputs to the model. These may take the form of selecting parameters to change, choosing parameter values within a range, or choosing when to change parameters. The students' inputs to the model determine its subsequent behaviour, which is then displayed, perhaps as numerical values, or as an animation.

Simulations are useful for representing complex relations. The power plant simulation in Figure 1.2.4 allows the student to explore any combination of parameter values, to test the system to destruction, to find the lowest values at which it still operates or to find the values which give the optimum read-outs for all measures – to explore the system at will.

This kind of access to the teacher's conception within a simulation is a matter of design decision. Simulations are based on a model and in most, the model remains hidden in the depths of the program, inaccessible to inspection by the student. The complexity of its form is usually the main reason for creating a simulation, so that students can become familiar with it by investigating the behaviour it models rather than by inspecting its explicit form. However, having both forms of access – explicitly via the equations or rules and implicitly via the behaviour of the model – gives the student a better chance of relating his or her experience of the world (actions on the model) to descriptions of the world (the formal statement of the model).

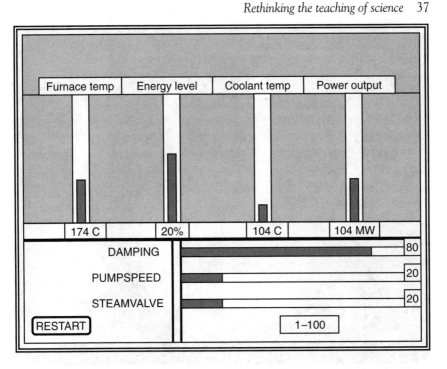

Figure 1.2.4 The screen for the simulated power system. Users click in the horizontal bars to set the related control. Read-outs of the system state are given in the vertical bars.

Source: Moyse (1991: 26)

Virtual environments

Virtual environments are an interesting form of simulation which differ in the nature of the representation of the reality they are simulating. Whereas simulations use a generative mathematical model of the system, virtual environments use a graphical model to display the visual and positional properties of the system, rather than its behaviour. An example would be a virtual field trip, where users can explore a representation of a three-dimensional environment. They may be aiming to understand the positional relationships, which would be important for a geology course, for example, or the visual properties of chemical explosions. A particularly successful virtual environment, the virtual microscope (see Figure 1.2.5) was developed at The Open University initially for students with disabilities. It simulates the views through a microscope of slides displaying different kinds of materials.

The value of such a simulation for students with disabilities is clear: it provides access to key data for those with motor disabilities who cannot visit laboratories, or for students who are partially sighted and find the use of microscopes difficult. Materials designed for students with disabilities invariably add value for other students as well, in this case because the interpretation of microscopic data is

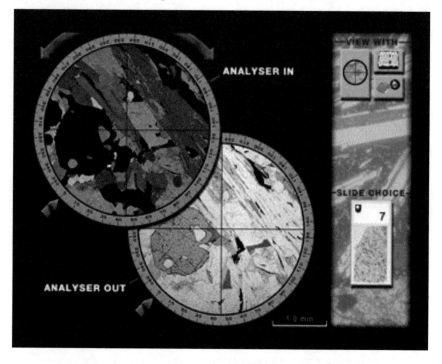

Figure 1.2.5 The virtual microscope, showing the two views through the simulated microscope and the icon for selecting different materials for investigation.

difficult when the view is not being shared. This virtual environment enables tutors
and students to point unambiguously to the same section for discussion and
interpretation.

Do virtual environments cover the Conversational Framework in the same way
as simulations? Interestingly, they are closer to interactive media than to adaptive
media. Like interactive media, they provide new information according to the
user's selection; they are environments for exploration and discovery. They do not
provide intrinsic feedback on actions, as simulations do, because they do not model
the behaviour of a system. A virtual environment that is adaptive to a student's
actions would be one whose positional or visual properties could be manipulated in
relation to some goal.

Tutorial programs

The main difference between simulations and tutorial programs is that the latter
necessarily embody an explicit teaching strategy. For a simulation, there is an
implicit teaching strategy in the choice of model and in the way the interface operates to support the student's exploration. However, there may be no explicit goal.
This constrains the feedback that can be given to a student. In a tutorial, there is an
explicit teaching goal and this fact enables the program to comment on the

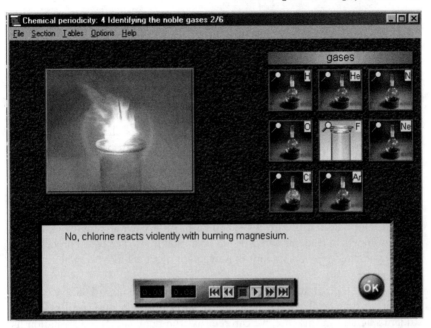

Figure 1.2.6 A tutorial program on chemical periodicity. The student has previously selected reactions with each of the gases, to see which ones yield a violent reaction, and is now being tested on which gases are 'noble' and do not react. On selecting chlorine, the student is give the feedback of a repeat of the demonstration showing how chlorine reacts, together with a brief comment.

student's performance in relation to that goal. This type of adaptivity means that the program uses the student's performance on previous tasks to decide what feedback or subsequent task should be offered. For example, in a tutorial on chemical periodicity (Figure 1.2.6), the goal is to identify the noble gases from their reactive properties. The student can explore the properties of a range of gases and is then tested on what has been learned. In the illustration, the student has misidentified chlorine and the program branches to a re-run of the demonstration showing the violence of its reactive properties.

This embodies a teaching strategy of the form described at the beginning of this section. There is a default sequence built into the program structure, such that the program moves through topics that progress in complexity. Based on the frequency of the student's errors, it may suggest that there is more to be done before moving on to a different topic or taking a test. Thus, adaptivity acts at the level of deciding what task to set and how much practice to offer on each one. The pull-down menus offer free navigation among all the sections of the material, at any stage.

Too many tutorial programs use the multiple choice question format to define the task set for the student, so that the input is easy to analyse. In the case of chemical periodicity, the learning objective is a very simple relation between name and property. The illustration of the property enhances the experience of what it means and may assist memorization. The format is appropriate for such an objective. Objectives that are more complex need the combination of tutorial with simulation to provide intrinsic feedback.

Tutorial simulations

It is quite feasible for a tutorial to offer intrinsic feedback, but only if it has some kind of model of the task it sets. This defines the 'tutorial simulation', being a combination of two complementary media, one offering extrinsic feedback and the other intrinsic. Thus, it is a medium that is different in important ways from either on its own.

The power of the combination is evident in programs such as the geology example in Figure 1.2.7. The task goal is set by the program: to find the shift in the geological formation which gives rise to a given surface feature. It creates an environment in which students can drive an operation in the geological process itself, namely the direction and amount of movement of a rock formation along a fault line.

Because the program provides both the task goal and an interactive environment, it can offer feedback at two levels. The model offers intrinsic feedback on the student's action: in this case, we can see that the right side of the formation has

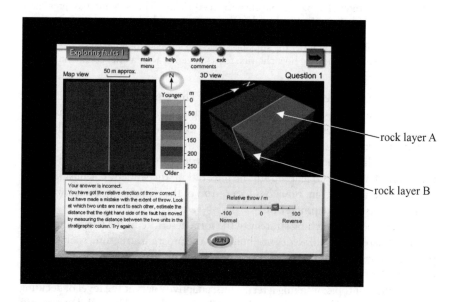

Figure 1.2.7 A tutorial simulation program on geological formations. The student must specify the way the rock formation on the right has to move and erode in order to expose the surface features represented on the left. The direction and amount of the movement are controlled by the slider. The result of the first move is shown on the right, with commentary below left. The target, rock layer B, has not been exposed by the movement specified here. The order of the sedimentary rock layers is shown in the middle.

moved up and the top layer has eroded to expose rock layer A (see Figure 1.2.7). In order to match the surface combination on the left of the screen, it should have moved up more and eroded two layers to expose rock layer B (see Figure 1.2.7). Furthermore, because the program knows what the goal is, it can give extrinsic feedback on the action that emulates the intrinsic: the student has correctly defined the direction of the relative throw, but not the correct amount. This helps to ensure that the student has correctly interpreted the intrinsic feedback.

As research has shown, students of geology experience great difficulty in visualizing the processes involved in these three-dimensional changes over time (McCracken and Laurillard 1994). The intrinsic feedback from the control over the environment provided here helps the visualization. It provides meaningful feedback on actions in such a way that students can see what they need to do in order to correct their input. The extrinsic feedback is possible because the program knows what the goal is and that the student has not reached it. The hint provided in the extrinsic feedback goes beyond that offered by the intrinsic feedback, because it relates the movement to the underlying rock structure.

This simulation model in the program gives students an experiential sense of how the system behaves. With this highly constrained way of experiencing the world of stratigraphs, surface areas and rock formation movements, students begin to see the system as the geologist would wish them to. The tutorial part of the program provides 'canned text' comment on the interaction. This does not make it fully discursive, as there is no provision for the student to articulate his or her own description. The program is capable of offering a re-description of the topic in the light of the student's action, tailored to that event, and is therefore capable of helping the student interpret the intrinsic feedback. Figure 1.2.8 shows the extent to which the program covers the Conversational Framework.

The tutorial simulation is a powerful teaching medium because it provides both adaptation of the environment to the student's actions and reflection on that interaction at the discursive level. In terms of the Conversational Framework, Figure 1.2.8 shows that the tutorial simulation can address almost all of the learning activities, except the iteration around the student's own articulation of the topic.

Communicative media

The communicative media are those that serve the discursive level of the Conversational Framework, having the specific task of bringing people together to discuss. The discussion may be between tutor and student or between students. The medium of communication may be text/graphics, audio or video, or any combination of the three.

A medium that can support discussion immediately addresses the two types of learning activity that we have hardly covered so far: interaction at the level of descriptions and reflection on action, feedback and goals.

Communications media take two forms: synchronous, where participants are together in time, communicating through text, audio or video via a network; and

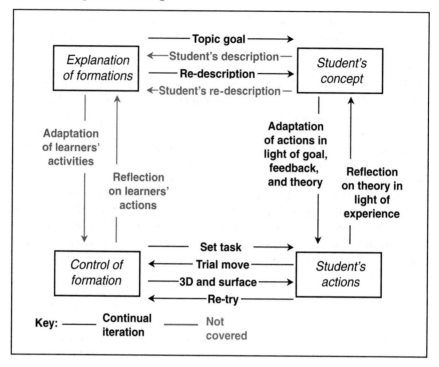

Figure 1.2.8 Interpretation of the Conversational Framework for the geology simulation.

asynchronous, where participants use the system at different times. Tutors and students may be engaged in a one-to-one conversation via e-mail, audio link or desktop video or, more usually, in many-to-many conversations. All these media forms allow an eavesdropping audience of other students to participate vicariously in observing the discussion.

Computer-mediated conferencing

The claims made for the educational value of computer-mediated conferencing (CMC) rest on the assumption that students learn effectively through discussion and collaboration, even at a distance and asynchronously. However, this is not a well-tested assumption as far as the research literature is concerned. It remains a strong belief, given new impetus from the significance of 'communities of practice' (Wenger 1999), but the properties of a medium do not determine the quality of learning that takes place. Collaborative learning is undeniably important and the communicative media are powerful enablers that match what is needed for discussion and collaboration, but to what extent do they succeed in enabling learning?

An obvious pedagogical advantage of asynchronous conferencing over the normal face-to-face tutorial is that students can take time to ponder the various points made and contribute in their own time. Topic negotiation is possible, as in

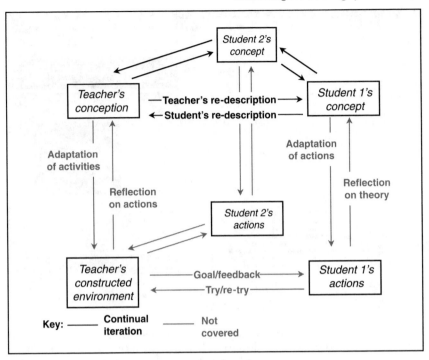

Figure 1.2.9 Interpretation of the Conversational Framework for a computer-mediated conferencing environment. Only two students are shown, but there are potentially many in the same kind of networked relationship.

face-to-face discussion, and a tutor may pursue several lines of discussion with different groups of students in sub-conferences, as the topic develops. Student control is therefore relatively high for this medium.

The fact that conferencing has a one-to-many form, rather than one-to-one, leads to an expectation of the value of eavesdropping by other students. This is largely borne out by what students say about the medium and evaluation studies report many expressions of delight at hearing others express the same worries, confusions or criticisms. As Figure 1.2.9 shows, the Conversational Framework is covered only at the discursive level, but among students, as well as between tutor and student.

A dialogue between a tutor and a student can stand for many such dialogues. In the course of the dialogue, the tutor's viewpoint is also likely to be re-expressed or elaborated, which then benefits all students.

With the appropriate planning and moderating, text-based computer conferencing offers an opportunity for articulation and for reflection on partici-pants' contributions and it helps to build a sense of a scholarly community. The success is largely dependent on a good moderator, of course, and this is likely to be

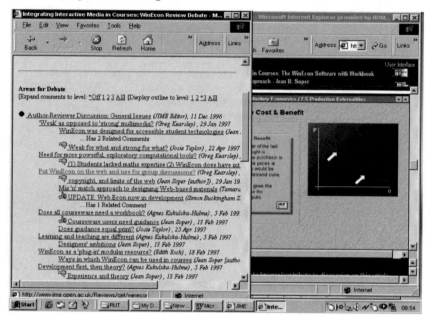

Figure 1.2.10 A digital document discussion environment for a runnable simulation. The top page shows the discussion, linked to the digital document behind it. This example is of a scholarly debate within an electronic journal. The format could equally well be an online class discussion of an interactive simulation.

as time-consuming as any other form of face-to-face tutoring. It is not necessarily the kind of medium where students can be left to work independently.

Digital document discussion environment

Conferencing alone does not support any task-based activity other than the description and re-description of the student's view. The availability of conferencing on the Web, however, makes possible other, augmented forms of communication. A discussion environment can be linked to other 'documents', where the document may be a text, or could be a Java applet running a simulation or animation. Figure 1.2.10 shows an example of a discussion environment linked to a runnable model. If a user wishes to make a comment on some aspect of the model, clicking on the associated comment button gives access to that part of the discussion environment, where a new point can be added or a reply can be given to one raised by someone else.

The digital document discussion environment, known as D³E at The Open University where it was developed, creates an asynchronous network which is a close equivalent of the reading group or seminar. Every member of the group has access to the same material and each can comment on and debate the document –

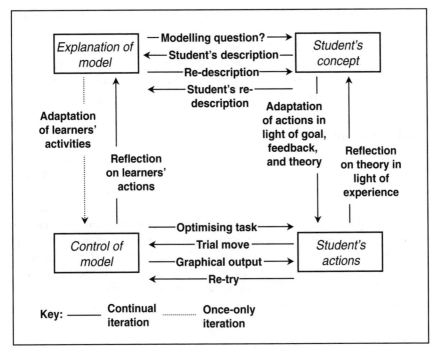

Figure 1.2.11 Interpretation of the Conversational Framework for a digital document discussion environment with a simulation model.

in this case a scientific model – in detail. Being asynchronous, it creates time for reflective responses, free of the cut-and-thrust of face-to-face discussion. The opportunity for detailed commentary on a modelling exercise introduces an inter-active-level task to the discursive-level topic. Students could be set a task to achieve within a simulation environment and link their practice here to a comment or question to the group. The tutor uses students' comments to offer feedback on their interpretation or on the way they have carried out the exercise on the model. It enables comment on their practice, not just on their descriptions of their understanding. In this sense, the environment can emulate intrinsic feed-back and offers an additional dimension of learning activity to the discussion envi-ronment of conferencing alone.

The D³E therefore offers an extremely powerful learning environment. Figure 1.2.11 shows the extent to which it addresses the activities within the Conversa-tional Framework.

In terms of the Conversational Framework, students would be operating the model interactively at the task level and discussing their reflections on the goal–action–feedback cycle at the discursive level. Figure 1.2.11 illustrates that this kind of medium supports almost the full range of the iterative activities. The only non-iterative activity is the adaptation of the model in the light of student needs discerned at the discursive level. In most cases, it would be difficult for the tutor to re-program the model responsively.

Conferencing on the Web should not always be confined to the discursive level. Using a hybrid medium like D³E enables students to be supported through a much more intensive learning process, iterating through communication and interaction in both theory and practice.

Productive media

Paper has always been, and always will be, an important productive medium for learners, still significant in schools but less so in universities, now that production of words is almost entirely electronic. Electronic media have radically extended the range of expression for learners, with some rich and varied tools for building instantiations of ideas. The animation capabilities of PowerPoint, for example, could be a way of enabling a student to express his or her view of how a system works. But what are we actually using as the key enabler for student expression? Microsoft Word. Given what is possible in the electronic world, it might as well be a quill pen. So we have to consider what might be, rather than what is, because there are very few examples in reality that exploit the productive capability of electronic media to allow the student to be the author.

Microworlds

Microworlds made their biggest impact in education in the form of *Logo*, Seymour Papert's programming language for geometry. In his book *Mindstorms*, Papert describes the reasoning behind the development of a Newtonian microworld, and in doing so, expresses exactly the difference between a microworld and a simulation. What makes Papert's microworlds interesting is that they appear to address explicit descriptions of the student's point of view:

> Direct experience with Newtonian motion is a valuable asset for the learning of Newtonian physics. But more is needed to understand it than an intuitive, seat-of-the-pants experience. The student needs the means to conceptualize and 'capture' this world ... The Dynaturtle on the computer screen allows the beginner to play with Newtonian objects ... And programs governing the behaviour of Dynaturtles provide a *formalism in which we capture our otherwise too fleeting thoughts*.
>
> (Papert 1980: 124, my italics)

The formalism provided as an essential feature of a microworld allows the student to express a description of some aspect of the world in a form which can be interpreted by the program itself. The simulation offers no such means of representation. In a microworld, students are building their own runnable systems, whereas in a simulation they are controlling a system that someone else has built.

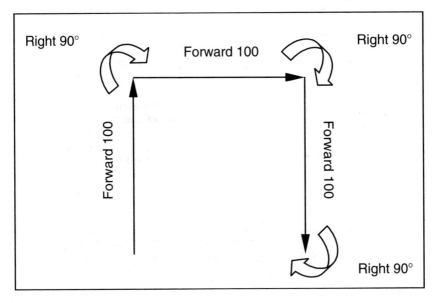

Figure 1.2.12 A microworld for geometry. The program gives visual intrinsic feedback on an incomplete representation of a square as the sequence of commands: 'forward 100; right 90°; forward 100; right 90°; forward 100; right 90°'.

To use Papert's physics microworld, students have to describe their actions in the form of a set of commands, then run them as one would a program, and the result is either the intended behaviour or something unexpected. The feedback operates at the level of the description. In one version of *Logo* geometry, students control the movements of the Dynaturtle. For example, the student types in a set of commands to draw a square (for example, forward 100, right 90°, forward 100, right 90°, forward 100, right 90°), then runs it, and the computer draws three sides of a square (see Figure 1.2.12).

The program provides intrinsic feedback, for example, that the description was incomplete and another command similar to the first should be added by the student. Having perfected the description of a square (by adding another 'forward 100'), the student can adapt and develop that to produce more elaborate outcomes in the microworld. Some create star patterns, others polygons, spirals and so on. Through experimentation of this kind, students will gradually understand the relationship between the behaviour of the system and the form of its representation, to the point where they can control it at will.

Microworlds are productive media, therefore, in the sense that they enable the learner to create and produce a system of their own, designed to achieve a specific end. Simulations are adaptive and the student can only explore and investigate, not create and produce.

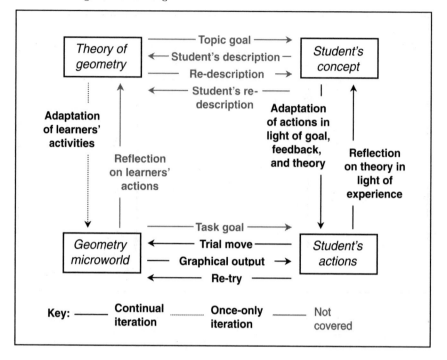

Figure 1.2.13 Interpretation of the Conversational Framework for a microworld on concepts in geometry.

Papert's primary concern is to provide the means for students to enter the Newtonian way of thinking without having to use mathematics as the medium. He wants to give students direct access to the physicist's way of experiencing the world, enabling them to develop an intuitive grasp of the correct Newtonian conceptions. He wants to give them *experiential* knowledge of the world, just as a simulation does, rather than *articulated* knowledge. The intrinsic feedback in a microworld is at the experiential, interactive level, not the theoretical, discursive level, so it covers a much wider range of learning activities than does the narrative medium, as Figure 1.2.13 shows.

The microworld is controllable by the student and therefore supports interaction, adaptation and reflection. Students construct something, see how well it works, use this intrinsic feedback to improve the construction in terms of their immediate goal and, because they can create their own goal, are able to test their own conceptions. But there is no iteration at the theoretical discursive level.

To summarize: simulations and microworlds are similar in the sense that they both operate at the experiential level. They are different because microworlds are also productive, allowing students to go beyond exploration of a given model to the creation of their own model. Does this structural difference have any pedagogical significance in terms of the Conversational Framework? I think it does, and it lies in the fact that a microworld enables the student to define his or her own topic goal in the interaction, therefore giving more encouragement to reflect upon the interaction. A simulation supports a more limited number of possible goals, depending on what parameters are available to the student. It needs to be augmented with a teacher-defined goal, to ensure that the student addresses a goal and does not simply play with the parameters to 'see what happens if …?', and only *sees*, and does not *reflect* on what is seen. Without reflection, the simulation, for all its interactive adaptivity, contributes little to new understanding. The microworld presupposes that the student will define his or her own goal. This may be more motivating than working to a teacher-defined goal, and is also more likely to encourage reflection on how well their interaction is meeting their conceptual, topic-level goal.

Modelling

A modelling program contrasts with a microworld in the sense that the student defines his or her model directly. It is not buried within the design of objects. In a modelling program, the program merely interprets formulae (or rules): it knows nothing about any subject matter, unlike the microworld. A physics microworld can only be used for physics; a modelling program can be used for anything that can be modelled. There is a considerable interface design problem in getting the program to interpret the learner's description of the model and this is the clever part of designing such a tool. Spreadsheets, which offer a template for defining an equation, provide a simple form of productive tool and a useful way of enabling students to articulate their own ideas.

The program may contain its own model, or data, for a particular topic, which it can compare with what has been done by the student. It can then prompt some reflection on the student's outcome in comparison with the goal. It gives feedback on the student's action by running the model and is fully controllable by the student.

The structural form of a modelling system is more iterative than a microworld. The difference is in how the student's conception is expressed: in a microworld as representations of actions in the world; in a modelling system as a representation of the world in which those actions take place. The focus of the students' talk is on how to express the behaviour of a system mathematically. If the aim is not merely to experience the world but also to explain it, then the modelling program comes the closest so far to supporting the learning of academic knowledge. The modelling environment is more generic, allowing students to create their own kind of model. It is the most unconstrained form of productive medium.

Concluding points

Learning technologies can improve the way students learn science because they empower the individual. Whereas the narrative media tell the story of science – the lecture, the video or the multimedia resource explains and illustrates complex and fascinating phenomena – the interactive learning methods enable the student to *do* science. If we utilize the adaptive, interactive and communicative capabilities of the new media, we can enable students to act in some way like scientists – experimenting, analysing, discussing, comparing, interpreting – and this always within a supportive environment that can offer a demonstration or feedback, as necessary. Learning science is difficult for many learners, at all levels. It requires sustained attention to complex ideas, and repeated rehearsal of concepts and intellectual skills. E-learning can support all these. It will not do everything and must be integrated with the inspirational methods offered by the human teacher and the social environment of the class or group, but there is so much it could do to enhance these more traditional methods. If we began with the needs of the learners, we would undoubtedly use a much higher proportion of interactive technology as a major part of our teaching.

References

Gates, B. (2002) *A Vision for Lifelong Learning – Year 2020*, Redmond, WA: Microsoft Research.

Kolb, D. A. (1984) *Experiential Learning: Experience as the Source of Learning and Development*, Englewood Cliffs, NJ: Prentice Hall.

McCracken, J. and Laurillard, D. (1994) 'A study of conceptions in visual representations: a phenomenographic investigation of learning about geological maps', paper presented at the World Conference on Educational Multimedia and Hypermedia, Vancouver, 25–30 June.

Moyse, R. (1991) 'Multiple viewpoints imply knowledge negotiation', *Interactive Learning International* 7: 21–37.

Papert, S. (1980) *Mindstorms: Children, Computers, and Powerful Ideas*, Brighton, UK: Harvester Press.

Pask, G. (1976) 'Conversational techniques in the study and practice of education', *British Journal of Educational Psychology* 46: 12–25.

Ramsden, P. (1992) *Learning to Teach in Higher Education*, London: Routledge.

Wenger, E. (1999) *Communities of Practice: Learning, Meaning, and Identity*, Cambridge: Cambridge University Press.

1.3 Using ICT in teaching and learning science

Jerry Wellington

This chapter is about the use of information and communication technology (ICT) in the teaching and learning of science in the secondary school. We start by looking at the nature of science and science teaching to see where ICT might help. Then we look at what 'computers are good at', to link science as a subject to computers as a learning tool. The chapter then goes on to look at the issues involved in *managing ICT in the school environment*. The specific areas of use of ICT for science are then considered: spreadsheets, databases, data-logging, simulations, multimedia applications and the Internet. Each is examined practically and critically. The key question is the one of *'added value'*, i.e. what value can the use of ICT add to the teaching and learning of science. Teachers need to be able to judge when the use of ICT is effective and *beneficial* and when its use is ineffective or inappropriate.

What can ICT offer to science education?

The use of ICT in science can involve word processing and desktop publishing; database and spreadsheet use; communications; data-logging; simulations and modelling; multimedia of any kind; and control hardware and software. The possibilities are summarized in Table 1.3.1 – the list will grow as ICT itself progresses and becomes available more cheaply to schools.

This chapter considers these various uses. But first, we need to consider why, how and when ICT can be of value in science education.

What's special about science and science teaching?

The emphasis here is to first look at the nature of science and science teaching and learning and to ask what is distinctive about it – then go on to ask what ICT can (and cannot) do for science education (as opposed to starting from the technology, then trying to fit it into science teaching, as many approaches in the past have done).

The first point is that science, and especially school science, is often a very *practical subject*. It involves *doing things*, which is often one of its attractions to learners. It involves observing, measuring, communicating and discussing, trying things out, investigating, handling things, watching and monitoring, recording results ... these

Table 1.3.1 Some potential uses and applications of ICT in science education

Word processing/desktop publishing	*Control*
e.g. in presenting data	e.g. controlling experiments; controlling external devices
Databases and spreadsheets	*Simulations and modelling*
e.g. in pattern searching; hypothesizing; recording and presenting data; accessing and organizing data	e.g. predicting and searching for patterns
Communications	*Data-logging*
e.g. identifying the features of a transmission system; data coding and handling	e.g. using sensors; gathering and recording data
Interactive media (CD, Internet, video-disk, etc.)	*Graphics*
e.g. accessing data; searching	e.g. presenting data

are all things we see happening in the science classroom. ICT can help in virtually all of these activities, as we see shortly.

However, as much as science is a practical discipline, it is equally a *theoretical subject*. It does and always has involved thinking, inferring, having good ideas and hunches, hypothesizing, theorizing, simulating and modelling. Thinking and thought experiments are as important as hands-on activity. ICT can help as much in this aspect of science as it can in the practical aspect.

We also need to see science from two different angles when we talk about learning and teaching it. The two viewpoints involve *process* and *content*. Both are equally important to science education. The content of science – its facts, laws, theories and understanding of them – needs to be taught alongside its processes. ICT can help in learning the *content of science* – information sources such as the Internet and material on CD-ROM can play a part (as can traditional books). ICT can also help in learning the content and facts of science by using it in revision or tutorial mode (as discussed later). Equally, ICT can help in learning the *processes* of science – measuring, recording, processing data, hypothesis and communicating. These skills and processes are vital to science itself, as well as to science education.

Tables 1.3.2 and 1.3.3 sum up some of the areas of activity in science and the specific item of ICT which can enhance them. All these are discussed in more detail later.

Table 1.3.2 Pupils' science activities and the ICT tools which enhance them

Pupils' science activity	What ICT tools will help?
Planning an investigation	Word processing
Researching/learning about a topic	CD-ROM, databases, tutorial programs, Internet
Taking measurements	Data-logging
Making results tables	Data-logging, spreadsheets
Drawing graphs	Data-logging software, spreadsheets, databases
Doing calculations	Spreadsheets, data-logging software
Searching for patterns	Spreadsheets, databases, simulations, modelling programs
Asking 'what if … ?' questions	Simulations, databases, modelling programs
Comparing pupils' results with other people's (reviewing a topic)	CD-ROM, data files, Internet
Presenting information in a report	Word processing, desktop publishing, spreadsheets

Table 1.3.3 Processes in science and appropriate uses of ICT

Process in science	ICT use
Measuring	Data-logging
Hypothesizing (what if … ?), predicting	Simulation, spreadsheets
Recording, processing data	Data-logging, spreadsheets, databases
Thinking	Simulations, modelling programs
Communicating	Word processing, desktop publishing, e-mail, Internet, spreadsheets
Observing	Multimedia, data-logging

So … why use ICT in science education?

We can start to answer this by first listing some of the things that modern ICT systems (hardware and software) are good at. These include:

- collecting and storing large amounts of data
- performing complex calculations rapidly on stored data

- processing large amounts of data and displaying them in a variety of formats
- helping to present and communicate information.

These capabilities all have direct relevance to the process of education and they help us to address the key question of *when to use ICT … and equally importantly, when not to*. One issue concerns the use of computers as labour-saving devices. As listed above, computers can collect data at a rapid rate and perform calculations on them extremely quickly. However, the question arises: should the computer (in an *educational* context), be used to collect, process and display rather than these being done by the learner? For instance, why should data-logging software plot graphs 'automatically', rather than this being done by a pupil using pencil, ruler and graph paper? In other words, when does the use of a *computer* to save labour take away an important educational experience for the learner? A similar issue appears in the use of computers and electronic calculators to perform complex calculations rapidly. This may be desirable in some learning situations, e.g. if the performance of a tedious calculation by human means actually impedes or 'clutters up' a learning process. However, it can also be argued that the ability to perform complex calculations rapidly should be one of the *aims* of education, not something to be replaced by it.

The distinction between what counts as *authentic* (i.e. desirable and purposeful) and *inauthentic* (i.e. unnecessary and irrelevant) labour in the learning process is a central one in considering the use of ICT in education. The notions of 'inauthentic' and 'authentic' labour should be remembered when we look at the added value of ICT in the examples later.

It is also worth noting that computers do exactly what they are instructed to do, very quickly, as many times as they are told to do it. On the one hand, this means that they are not (or at least not yet) capable of making autonomous or independent judgements or personal interpretations. However, it is also the case that they do not become tired, bored, hungry, irritable, angry or impatient and are not liable to error. This may place them at an advantage in some situations as compared with teachers! It has been said that *one* of the reasons why children appear to enjoy learning with computers is precisely because of their impersonal, inhuman 'qualities'.

One final point on the 'abilities' of computers is worth stressing. Computers can, in a sense, speed up, or slow down, reality. As Kahn (1985) puts it 'they operate outside the viscous flow of time in which humans perform tasks'. This is an important point which will be elaborated upon when considering the use of computer *simulations* in education.

Planning for the use of ICT in teaching science

The key question for a school is: how best can ICT be deployed and managed in a school setting? Unfortunately, in schools, as with any organization containing human beings, there are a lot of vested interests, power struggles and micro-politics at work. The science teacher (especially the new one) rarely has the power or status to make whole-school decisions about ICT, what should be bought and where it should be located. We will also see later that the use of ICT is not always compatible or easy to reconcile with the nature and organization of secondary school classrooms.

From a school perspective, teachers need to ask, in their own working setting, which factors in their school promote and enhance ICT use in science? And, conversely, which factors act as a barrier or impediment? For example:

- the logistics of the school
- resources and their location
- the role and attitude of the school ICT coordinator
- school policies and attitudes to ICT
- home background, e.g. home access to ICT.

Science teachers may not always be in a position to decide where resources are situated in a school (unless they become the head or the ICT coordinator!). However, they can judge and consider aspects such as how ICT use in science lessons relates to, and stimulates, use of ICT elsewhere, e.g. follow-up learning in the library, home use. How can they manage its use themselves? When should they go for 'whole-class teaching' (the electronic blackboard)? When should they use small-group activities, involving the whole class in what I call 'battery-hen mode'? – but this would mean booking the computer room; and when should they make it one activity among others? These possibilities are summarized in the crude drawings in Figure 1.3.1.

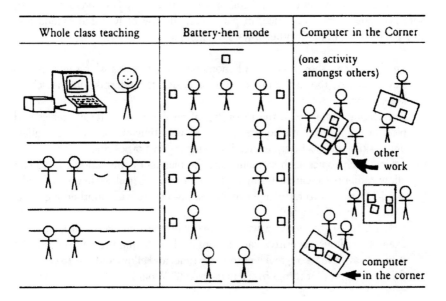

Whole class teaching	Battery-hen mode	Computer in the Corner

Figure 1.3.1 Using computers in the secondary school: three possibilities.

The issue for the science teacher is: *where* is ICT best deployed, e.g. in the science laboratory, the computer room, the library? We can list several modes of use of ICT which are currently in operation, for better or for worse:

- Mode A: as a tool for lecture/demonstration, e.g. using a big screen or projector;
- Mode B: using a single PC with one small group, e.g. as part of a circus in the laboratory;
- Mode C: with half a class using up to five PCs;
- Mode D: with a whole class, using a suite of computers, e.g. in the computer room;
- Mode E: independent use (e.g. at home, in the library or the learning resource centre) prompted and motivated by seeing ICT used in the classroom.

Which of these modes is best for which teaching or learning purposes in science? Table 1.3.4 summarizes the pros and cons of the two polarized approaches.

Classroom applications of ICT in science

Introduction: why bother?

The following benefits or 'added value' can be gained by trying and using ICT in the classroom: motivation, excitement and pleasure; an improvement in pupils' self-esteem and perseverance; and the opportunity for pupils to produce neater, more accurate work. In science, in particular, the use of ICT can extend and enhance learning in many other ways. For example:

- *simulations* can show students phenomena and processes which may be too slow, too fast, too dangerous or too expensive to undertake in the school laboratory;
- *data-logging* can assist in the recording of results, making results tables and plotting graphs so that students can spend more time on some of the 'higher-order' skills such as interpreting, discussing and hypothesizing;
- *databases* on topics such as mammals, the planets or the periodic table can allow students to search through information in a fast, flexible way, to make connections and to try comparing one set of figures with another, e.g. wing span and speed of flight;
- *spreadsheets*, in the same way, can also offer the removal of drudgery, for example, tedious, repetitive calculations such as taking the new length of a spring away from its original length every time, and allow students to get on to the more important things in science – asking 'What if …?' or 'Why don't we try …?'

In the next section, we look at each use of ICT in science, with some illustrations of classroom possibilities. We start with computer simulations.

Table 1.3.4 Computers to the classroom versus classes to the computer room

+ *For*	– *Against*
1 *Classes to the computer room*	
Dedicated room may lead to:	• room may be seen as the province, territory or annexe of certain departments
• tighter security	
• easier maintenance	
• appropriate facilities (e.g. power points; suitable furniture; healthier viewing; distance and positions)	• computing seen as a 'special' activity
	• prior planning, timetabling and scheduling needed (rules out spontaneity)
• ease of supervision (e.g. technical help on hand)	• reduces integration with other aspects of classroom practice or curriculum
• careful monitoring (e.g. of temperature, dust, ventilation, etc.)	
2 *Computers to the classroom*	
• more likely integration into classroom practice and curriculum	Problems of:
• seen as just another 'learning tool'	• security
• not seen as the property of one department more than another	• maintenance and monitoring
	• adequate facilities
• spontaneous, unplanned use made possible	• environmental conditions, e.g. chalk dust, water, chemicals technical support not on hand

Computer simulations in science education

Types of simulation in science education

It is useful to make some fairly crude distinctions between types of simulation which should act as a rough guide:

1 direct copies of existing laboratory activities, e.g. titrations;
2 simulations of industrial processes, e.g. the manufacture of sulphuric acid, bridge building;
3 simulations of processes that are:

- too dangerous
- too slow, e.g. evolution, population growth, an ecosystem of any kind
- too fast, e.g. collisions
- too small, e.g. sub-atomic changes

to be carried out in a school or college environment.

4   simulations involving non-existent entities, e.g. ideal gases, frictionless surfaces, perfectly elastic objects;
5   simulation of models or theories, e.g. kinetic theory, the wave model of light.

Why use computer simulations in science teaching?

The main advantages of using simulations can be summarized as follows:

1   *Cost*: money can be saved in directly copying some laboratory experiments, either by reducing outlay on consumables, e.g. chemicals, test tubes, or by removing the need to buy increasingly costly equipment in the first place.
2   *Time*: using a computer simulation instead of a genuine practical activity may save time, although some teachers are finding that a good computer simulation in which pupils fully explore all the possibilities may take a great deal longer.
3   *Safety*: some activities simply cannot be carried out in a school setting because they are unsafe.
4   *Motivation*: there is a feeling, though with little evidence to support it, that computer simulations motivate pupils in science education more than traditional practical work.
5   *Control*: the use of a simulation allows ease of control of variables, which traditional school practical work does not. This may lead to unguided discovery learning by pupils who are encouraged to explore and hypothesize for themselves.
6   *Management*: last, but certainly not least, computer simulations offer far fewer management problems to teachers than do many traditional activities. Problems of handing out equipment, collecting it back again, and guarding against damage and theft are removed at a stroke. Problems of supervision, timing and clearing up virtually disappear.

Dangers of simulation

So much for the supposed advantages of computer simulations. What of the dangers in using computer simulations in science education? The main ones lie in the hidden messages they convey, classified as follows:

1   *Variables*: simulations give pupils the impression that variables in a physical process can be easily, equally and independently controlled. This message is conveyed by simulations of industrial processes, ecological systems and laboratory experiments. In reality, not all variables in a physical situation can be as easily, equally and as independently controlled as certain simulations suggest.
2   *Unquestioned models, facts and assumptions*: every simulation is based on a certain model of reality. Users are only able to manipulate factors and variables *within* that model. They cannot tamper with the model itself. Moreover, they are neither encouraged nor able to question its validity. The model is hidden from the user. All simulations are based on certain assumptions. These are

often embedded in the model itself. What are these assumptions? Are they ever revealed to the user? All simulations rely on certain facts, or data. Where do these facts come from? What *sources* have been used?

3   *Caricatures of reality*: any model is an idealization of reality, i.e. it ignores certain features in order to concentrate on others. Some idealizations are worse than others. In some cases, a model may be used of a process that is not fully understood. Other models may be deceptive, misleading or downright inaccurate; they provide caricatures of reality, rather than representations of it.

4   *Confusion with reality*: pupils are almost certain to confound the programmer's model of reality with reality itself – such is the current power and potency of the computer, at least until its novelty as a learning aid wears off. Students may then be fooled into thinking that, because they can use and understand a *model* of reality, they can also understand the more complex real phenomena it represents or idealizes. Perhaps more dangerously, the 'microworld' of the computer creates a reality of its own. The world of the micro, the keyboard and the visual display unit (VDU) can assume its own reality in the mind of the user – a reality which is far more alluring and manageable than the complicated and messy world outside. The 'scientific world' presented in computer simulations may become as attractive and addictive as the microworlds of arcade games, as noted by Weizenbaum (1984) and Turkle (1984).

5   *Double idealizations*: all the dangers and hidden messages discussed so far become increasingly important in a simulation which uses a computer model of a scientific model or scientific theory, which itself is an idealization of reality. That is, the idealization involved in modelling is doubly dangerous in simulations which involve a model of a model. A simulation of kinetic theory, for example, is itself based on a model of reality.

Safeguards in using simulations

Given that science teachers will continue to use simulations, what safeguards can be taken to reduce these dangers? First, all teachers and, through them, pupils, must be fully conscious that the models they use in a computer simulation are personal, simplified and perhaps value-laden idealizations of reality. Models are made by man, or woman. Students must be taught to examine and question these models.

Second, the facts, data, assumptions, and even the model itself which are used by the programmer must be made clear and available to the user. This can be done in a teacher's guide or the documentation with the program. All sources of data should be stated and clearly referenced. Any student using a simulation can then be taught to examine and question the facts, assumptions and models underlying it.

Examples of simulation programs

A wide range of simulations is now available for school science, ranging from simulations of chemical collisions, the manufacture of ethanol or the siting of a blast furnace, to the simulation of electric and magnetic fields, electricity use in the home, wave motion, floating and sinking, a 'Newtonian' world of frictionless movement and the construction of bridges. For the life sciences, simulations are available on pond life, the human eye, nerves, the life of the golden eagle and predator–prey relationships.

Multimedia use in science education

What is multimedia?

A simple definition is that 'multimedia' (on either CD-ROM or via the Internet) should involve at least three of the following:

- speech or other sound
- drawings or diagrams
- animated drawings or diagrams
- still photographs or other images
- video clips
- text, i.e. the printed word.

[This mix of media is illustrated by Figures 1.3.2 and 1.3.3. These Open University examples use a mix of media to provide information on the elements of the periodic table. They include a large number of photos of elements and compounds; sounds made by different reactions, e.g. potassium being dropped into water; video clips of such reactions; text and tabulated data; drawings and diagrams which can be seen from different angles, e.g. of models of molecules.]

Value-added … or value (including smell) taken away

A number of CD-ROMs for science now allow quite detailed 'virtual experiments' to be carried out successfully and repeatedly on screen, without using up any of the consumables which science teachers can ill afford to buy (although chemistry teachers lament the loss of smell). The key issue is whether this devalues scientific activity by removing some of the real, hands-on, authentic business of science and placing it in the realm of multimedia.

Should experiments which can be done 'for real' in the laboratory be carried out on the screen? The key issue in deciding on any ICT use is whether it adds value to teaching and learning of science. Table 1.3.5 sums up the aspects of multimedia (from CD-ROM or the Internet) which teachers should examine carefully in deciding when (and when *not*) to use it.

Home–school convergence, or divergence, with multimedia

With the advent of multimedia systems entering homes almost as quickly as schools, we will be forced to consider the links and liaison between the two. This is

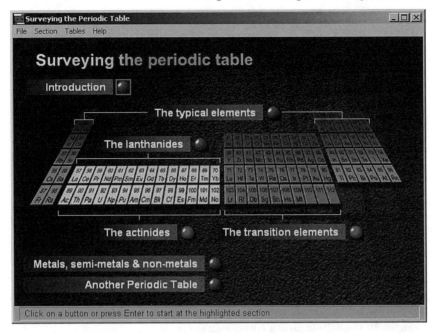

Figure 1.3.2 The Open University program *Surveying the Periodic Table* uses a range of media on a disk which can be used as a tutorial program or 'virtual laboratory'.

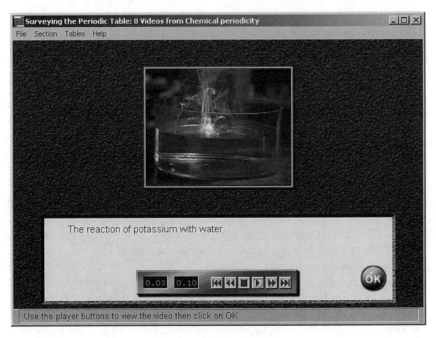

Figure 1.3.3 A still from a *Surveying the Periodic Table* video clip (with sound) of potassium being dropped into water – a 'virtual demonstration'.

Table 1.3.5 Points to consider when looking at multimedia for the classroom

---

What added value can multimedia provide?

What can CDs provide that, for example, a book cannot?

… and therefore why should people use them?

This is an issue which many teachers pose for themselves and to which they rightly expect a satisfactory answer. A crude list of what multimedia can provide which a book cannot shows the technical differences between the two:

1   *Audio*: a CD-ROM can provide speech and sound effects. Does this help or hinder? e.g. poor readers.

2   *Animation*: books can include diagrams but cannot provide the animation which a computer program or multimedia package can. Does animation help explanations?

3   *Video*: many CD-ROMs provide short video clips although their quality is (as yet) commonly quite poor. Do they help learning?

4   *Interactivity/tutorial help*: books are non-interactive in that they cannot provide feedback on a learner's progress – CD-ROMs can also be interactive in other ways although not always (see later).

5   *Substitutes for practical work*: a CD-ROM can provide many possibilities for practical or 'field' work which a book cannot, for example:

- virtual experiments
- simulations
- real-life situations to study
- surrogate walks
- demonstrations.

Teachers need to recognize these attributes and possibilities, and examine each disk to see what 'added value' it provides.

---

given more urgency by the growing number of publishers now producing CD-ROM titles for both the home and school markets – something which has never really happened before in ICT. How will the organizational structures of the school (timetables, bells, teacher-centredness, etc.) manage situations where pupils may know a CD-ROM inside out from using it at home? Will pupils be able to use school disks at home, and teachers use home disks at school? How will teachers be able *to keep control* of children's learning as they do now? Will teachers be flexible enough to exploit home use? How can we hope to create equal opportunities? Will pupils be as excited and motivated by the school disks as they are by those in the home … and so on? The number of questions is limitless – but teachers and schools are certain to face them as the number of multimedia systems at home far exceeds the number in schools.

Word processing (WP) and desktop publishing (DTP)

Why use word processing in science education?

Most pupils and students still write by hand. Write-ups of experiments, evaluations, project work and so on are more likely to be handwritten than typed on a keyboard. Most people would argue that writing with a pen or a pencil is an essential skill and should be preserved. Few would disagree. A small minority would go further and suggest that the use of a keyboard to write words, a computer to process and store them, and a printer to print them will actually hinder or stunt the development of handwriting and even writing generally. I have heard this point of view expressed at meetings, at courses and in discussion. Will the keyboard oust the pen?

In fact, there is little or no evidence to support this understandable fear. In a project where schools and homes were virtually saturated with computers (the Apple Classroom of Tomorrow (ACOT) project) it seemed that pupils' writing was enriched and certainly increased through the use of computers. Pen and pencil were still used. The nature of writing was also changed.

The use of WP can provide the following enrichments and benefits:

1　Pupils are given the opportunity to draft and redraft their own work much more readily. This is well known, and all those who have used a WP system will have experienced it. It seems to affect different users in different ways. Some are much more inclined to actually make a start on a piece of writing (arguably the hardest part of the process), knowing full well that it can be changed or edited easily. Some are actually much more inclined to keep going, just to get their thoughts down onto paper, or the screen, knowing that they can easily be redrafted. This aspect of WP is often said to enhance the writing of so-called 'lower-ability' students – but it affects writers at all levels.

2　Pupils are able to collaborate (work cooperatively) on a piece of writing much more easily with a computer system than with pen and paper. Partnership in writing is encouraged. This occurs for perhaps two main reasons: first, the writing is up there on the screen for all partners to see. This enables them more easily to take an equal share in it. Second, the writing is actually physically done by a shared keyboard, there on the desk or bench. It often does not 'belong' to one person more than another as, say, a pen does.

3　Marking of work done on a WP system can be so much more painless. Again, this applies equally at all levels of education and writing. Writers are far more inclined to seek feedback and critical comment if they know that alteration, addition and editing are relatively simple. This is again said to apply especially to those most likely to make spelling or grammatical mistakes and this is certainly true: the use of WP does remove the need for marks and corrections all over a script. However, it can have an influence on people's writing attitudes and habits at all levels.

4　The final product of a piece of writing can be so much better through the use of WP and DTP, as we will see later. This can produce a positive feedback loop, in turn influencing the earlier stages.

5   Finally, writing done with a WP system can be easily stored and exchanged. On the one hand, this may encourage malpractice with exam coursework (although I know of no cases). On the other, its positive effect is to allow a person or a group to stop writing at a convenient point and take it up again more easily later.

Teachers' use of WP and DTP

A further aspect of interest in the use of WP in schools is that teachers who are otherwise reluctant about using ICT are often willing users of WP and DTP. Their activities tended to focus on the production of teaching materials such as worksheets, assignment sheets and tests, as well as general course and departmental documentation. The seemingly anomalous situation of a teacher owning several boxes of floppy disks while never using a computer in a lesson does not seem to be uncommon. One possible interpretation is that, as WP is an extension of something familiar, namely typing, and the user is firmly in control of events, the technology is therefore relatively non-threatening to the user. It is accepted by ICT sceptics because the pay-off outweighs the threat.

When used by teachers to produce teaching materials and professional documentation, WP can contribute to departmental teamwork (as can e-mail). It is much easier to circulate draft copies to colleagues and accommodate their suggested changes when the document is stored on disk. In this sense, ICT is an aid to management processes in schools and within science departments.

Two key practical issues with WP

Over the brief history of ICT in schools, two key issues related to the use of WP have constantly surfaced and resurfaced:

1   Should pupils be taught *keyboard skills* at an early age, using the ubiquitous QWERTY layout? One of the barriers to the use of WP (and databases) has been pupils' slowness in typing in text. Should keyboard skills be taught to *all* pupils as a matter of course?
     Research shows that these skills are certainly one of the main requirements of employers in connection with ICT (see Wellington 1989, for past research on this question).
2   A second barrier to use, as with many aspects of ICT, is access to a computer system. What will be the effect of increased use of portable/laptop computers on the incidence and use of WP? Should they be introduced into science lessons on a wide scale, especially as pupils increasingly acquire their own laptops and have ICT at home?

Desktop publishing (DTP)

Word processing programs are designed to manage text made up of letters, numbers and other symbols, such as those found on typewriters. The layout of the text can be altered in several useful, but strictly limited ways. Desktop publishing (DTP) programs are more flexible. DTP can accommodate line drawings and sprites (pictures made of groups of pixels: a pixel is a small area of the screen) as well as data from other programs. The DTP user might utilize newspaper format in columns, text flowing round graphics, attractive data display such as a three-dimensional pie chart, text enhancements including a variety of fonts, headings and borders. DTP programs can also operate as simple word processors, which is not as retrograde as it appears because printing can be much quicker in this mode of use.

The presentation of work by pupils can be greatly enhanced with DTP and WP, which raises many issues for assessment, as is discussed later.

Spreadsheets

Introduction

A spreadsheet is a program which deals with information in the form of a table, with rows and columns. The rows are often given numbers and the columns are given letters so that any particular cell or element of the table can be identified, for example, as C5 or J2. Data can be changed or linked to other data by specifying which elements are to be changed and what the nature of the change is to be. An example would be to multiply every number in column D by the corresponding number in column E and put the results in column F. If column D contained data about speeds and column E contained data about time intervals, then column F would represent distances. This facility for data manipulation is a key characteristic of spreadsheet programs. Spreadsheets can also be used for sorting and displaying stored data and for creating and manipulating mathematical models.

Some manipulation processes can be carried out by using either a spreadsheet or a database. Which one is preferable? A rough guide might be that databases tend to offer more powerful search and sort options while spreadsheets tend to be easier to inspect, update and edit.

Uses for spreadsheets in teaching science

A simple form of spreadsheet may be dedicated to accepting only one type of data, for example, the food consumed by every pupil in a class in one day. The data are manipulated in prescribed ways, with the aim of communicating information in a pre-programmed format. Although restricted in use, such programs are accessible to students and they can be a gentle introduction to the use of more versatile spreadsheets.

The more flexible and powerful the spreadsheet, the more the user is required to make decisions about the way the data are stored and manipulated. These decisions may include the user having to classify the data into groups and identifying the relationships between groups of data.

Any activity in science which involves students looking at or building up tables of information might be considered as a candidate for spreadsheet use. Learners can then go on to undertake modelling activities, by asking 'What if?' questions (i.e. the conjectural paradigm). Examples might include: investigating a predator–prey relationship; correlating experimental data, such as current, voltage, resistance and power; looking at food intake over a period of time.

Spreadsheets: pros and cons

The use of spreadsheets can enhance students' learning in science, but what is the balance between pay-off and cost to the teacher? The cost, in its broader sense, involves acquiring and learning to use the software, at least so as to remain one step ahead of the students (or only one step behind!). It also involves building ICT into schemes of work and lesson plans, and booking a computer at the right time, in the right place. Finally, the students must be shown how to use the software. The pay-offs from using spreadsheets must include the potential for improved student learning and motivation, otherwise they would have no place in the classroom. Additional advantages include the following:

- *Flexible learning*: students can work independently and at their own pace.
- *Working co-operatively in groups*.
- *Teacher–pupil relations*: pupils will notice and value the fact that the teacher has bothered to introduce a new and interesting activity.
- *Improved teacher competence in ICT*: teachers may find uses for spreadsheets in their professional work other than with their classes. Two likely areas are departmental accounting and stocktaking, and collation of assessment schedules and examination results.
- *Increased teacher confidence in ICT*: teachers who have hitherto been wary of computers may find that simple spreadsheets are much easier to use than they feared.
- *Emancipation*: spreadsheets can allow *modelling* and predicting to take place (the conjectural paradigm) while also taking away the drudgery of labourious calculations of rows and columns of figures.

Data-logging

Data-logging typically involves using a computer to record and process readings taken from sensors. Perhaps the simplest data-logging system is shown in Figure 1.3.4.

The sensor plays the part of a translator. It responds to some property of the environment and sends a message to the computer. The message, or signal, has the

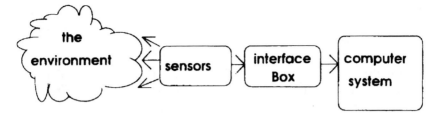

Figure 1.3.4 A basic data-logging system.

form of a voltage at one of the computer's input ports. The computer is programmed to record the value of the input signal. Temperature is an example of an environmental property which can be sensed in this way.

With modern data-logging systems, sensors can identify themselves, logging rates are automatically optimized and interfaces match the type of information given by the sensor to the type which the computer can accept. Teachers should expect many of these features in new data-logging equipment. The result should be that the 'inauthentic labour' of matching the computer to the environment is removed from the teacher and is incorporated in the hardware and software design of the system.

Here are a few practical examples of using sensors in science:

- temperature sensors to study cooling curves or insulation, e.g. heat loss from the building;
- a light sensor to study the rate of the reaction where a precipitate forms;
- light and temperature sensors as simple meters to compare habitats;
- a data-logger to measure light, temperature and oxygen readings in an aquarium, pond or greenhouse;
- light gates to measure speed, time and acceleration;
- a position sensor to monitor the movement of a pendulum;
- sensors to study current–voltage relationships.

What added-value comes from data-logging?

The following advantages have been claimed:
- *Speed.* Computers can often log much faster and more frequently than humans.
- *Memory.* Computers have enormous capacity for retaining and accessing a large body of data in a compact form.
- *Perseverance.* Computers can keep on logging – they do not need to stop for food, drink or sleep.
- *Manipulation.* The form in which data are gathered may not be the form in which we want to communicate. Computers come into their own when it comes to fast manipulation of large bodies of data.

- *Communication of meaning.* Computers can present data when gathered, in real time, using graphic display to enhance the meaning which is communicated to the observer.

Some of these advantages are aimed at transferring 'inauthentic labour' from the human to the machine (see Barton's Chapter 14 in Wellington 1998). The change of emphasis away from the routine process of logging towards the use of interpreting skills can enhance scientific thinking, creativity and problem-solving ability. However, this view is not universally shared by teachers. It has been pointed out that perseverance, ability to organize data systematically and calculating skills are part of science and that students should go through these processes in practical work.

Databases

What is a database?

In its simplest form, a database is nothing more than an organized collection of information. Thus an address book, a telephone directory, a card index and a school register are all examples of databases. They all contain data, which can convey information to people and which is organized in a more-or-less systematic way, e.g. in alphabetical order. The advantage of organizing data is partly for case of use and access to information, but it also depends on the fact that well-organized and structured data can be used to show patterns and trends and to allow people to make and test hypotheses or hunches. Therein lies the *educational value* of a database. Having an organized and clearly structured collection of data allows and even encourages users to derive information and knowledge from it.

The key skill to develop in pupils is the ability to *search* for information in a logical and systematic way. This is true not only for databases but also for CD-ROM, the Internet and spreadsheet use.

Searching skills and computer databases

The advantages of storing, organizing and retrieving information from a computer system are worth considering briefly. First, using magnetic or optical media (e.g. floppy disks, 'laser disks', CD-ROM, etc.), huge amounts of data can be stored in a relatively compact form. Second, data can be retrieved from a computer database quickly. Third, data retrieval from a computer database is relatively flexible. For example, to find a number in a paper-based telephone directory from a name and initials would be almost as quick as finding it from a computer-based directory; but consider the situation in reverse. How long would it take to find a person's name and initials with only their number? With a suitable computer database, this could be done as quickly as a search in the other direction. Fourth, changes (editions, additions and subtractions) to a computer database can be made more easily and more painlessly than to, say, a card- or paper-based database – this is, in a way, similar to the use of word processors in amending and redrafting text.

Important terms used with databases

A *file* is a collection of information on one topic, e.g. dinosaurs, planets, trees, birds. Files are organized into separate *records* (e.g. each type of dinosaur with its own name). Within each record, data might be stored on each kind of dinosaur and this can be organized into *fields*. One field might contain data on what the animal eats, another on its size, another on its weight, and so on. In setting up a file as part of a database, people can decide how many records they wish to include (e.g. how many different dinosaurs and how many fields they wish to use in storing information on each animal). Of course, they can always add records (e.g. if we hear about more dinosaurs), or more fields (if we decide to store new or more complex data). Thus records and fields can be added to, edited, or even removed. This is illustrated in Figure 1.3.5.

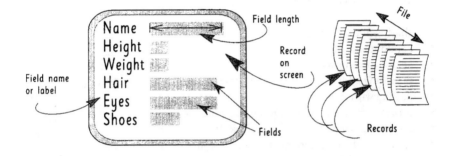

Figure 1.3.5 Database jargon.

Source: Roger Frost

Why use databases in science education?

1   *For recording data collected during an investigation or an experiment.* Data can be entered directly onto the database and stored on a computer-based medium (e.g. a disk).
2   *In allowing students to sift or browse through their own or someone else's data using the computer.* This kind of serendipitous learning (learning by browsing) can often be very valuable and is commonly underestimated.
3   *Students can explore data in a more systematic manner.* They can:

   • look for patterns
   • put forward hunches

- make predictions
- suggest and test hypotheses
- draw and discuss interpretations.

4   *Better display*. With suitable software, the computer system can be used to display and present data so that it conveys information in an attractive and clear way (cf. spreadsheets).

The use of databases in science supports and enhances many of the so-called process skills in the science curriculum such as classifying, hypothesizing and testing. It can also take away some of the 'inauthentic labour' or drudgery, discussed earlier.

Using the Internet in science teaching

The value and potential of the Internet in science teaching

The Internet provides a way of:

- sharing and exchanging information
- communicating
- accessing information
- providing a local exchange of information on resources, e.g. for pooling
- linking with industry
- giving *current* information to pupils/students
- improving study skills and search skills
- giving pupils the excitement of online computer information
- allowing collaboration in science: between pupil and pupil, school and school, teacher and teacher
- downloading material, e.g. data (particularly valuable for certain special needs pupils)
- setting up a forum for debate and queries among teachers of science.

Words of warning

Most people agree that the Internet is *potentially* a powerful resource for education – but as critical teachers, we need to avoid being carried away by the hype which often surrounds it. It certainly has educational value, which lies in three areas: in exchanging and sharing ideas and information, e.g. between teacher and teacher, pupil-to-pupil or a mixture of both; in enhancing and facilitating communication, e.g. by e-mail; and in providing a source of information for learners and teachers on almost any topic from football to photosynthesis. The value of the first two uses for schools is beyond doubt. Initiatives such as ScI-journal, for example, allow all sorts of ideas about investigational work to be shared and exchanged worldwide. But use of the Internet as a vast source of information for schools is more problematic. Yes, there is a huge supply of data on every topic – but this is at once its potential and its downfall. How much of that information has been checked and edited, or even proof-read? How accurate and reliable is the information? Who has written it and what were their motives? We should, quite rightly, treat all material on the Internet with a healthy scepticism, just as we would (or should) regard data in the national newspapers. This scepticism should be central to both the attitude of teachers and the message conveyed to learners.

Equally, the amount of information available is now so vast that it is extremely difficult for teachers to contain, or harness it, in order to meet the needs of a statutory curriculum. This is why so many teachers on courses which I run on multi-media always come up with three major, interconnected concerns: 'containing', vetting and drawing boundaries round material; similarly, structuring and guiding learners through material; and last but probably foremost, *curriculum relevance*. If learners are let loose on the Internet, where will it all end? What relevance will it have to the 'delivery' of the curriculum which, over the last 15 years, has become the classroom teacher's main driving force? And who can blame them, given the external pressures?

The Internet does have curriculum relevance. The challenge for teachers is to 'map' Internet sources onto the curriculum and then their schemes of work. [...]

Practical issues and concerns expressed by teachers

When I ask a group of teachers: 'How would you use the Internet?', their replies could be crudely summarized as: For a research tool for teachers and pupils? – almost all said 'Yes'. As a teaching aid e.g. in front of a whole class? – almost all said 'No!'

Other concerns which have been expressed to me by teachers are:

- the front end/usability;
- need for more teacher experience in using the Internet – requirement for more teacher time to get to know it;
- need to share experiences with other teachers, e.g. on a list of useful sites;
- access by pupils and teachers – will access be equal, especially as home use increases. What about the notion of entitlement?
- slowness of the system, i.e. time taken (e.g. in gaining access to something valuable);
- curriculum relevance;
- urgent need for pupils (and teachers) to develop search skills, e.g. use of search engines; discrimination/evaluation of information;
- is *more* information necessarily a good thing?
- what will happen if pupils get access to obscene or pornographic material – who will get the blame? ... probably the classroom teacher;
- ownership/copyright of material (including pupils' material);
- vetting/refereeing/filtering of material before it goes on the Internet;
- viruses;

- plagiarism, quoting without attributing;
- accuracy of information;
- partiality of information;
- vastly extended audiences for a pupil's (or teacher's) work;
- people's motives for putting material on the Internet;
- the language level of the material (most of which is text-based) and the text handling difficulties it presents;
- the 'haphazard'/uncontrolled learning which will take place if pupils are allowed free access;
- the cost, i.e. who will pay the telephone bills?

Developing students' searching skills

One of the key aims when using either a CD-ROM or the Internet is to develop in learners the ability to search a large source of information. A good search needs to be efficient and focused. There is perhaps something to be said for learning by 'browsing' (or serendipity', to use the pretentious term), and surfing the Internet is a common pastime. However, for school learning with curriculum relevance the search needs to be refined in order to maximize effectiveness in the use of valuable computer (and phone line) time. Here are some valuable strategies which have been suggested:

- *Focus* the search by making it as specific as possible, rather than using wide, general terms. For example, searching on the word 'Planet' on the Internet will produce nearly half a million 'hits'. Similarly with a topic like pollution: gradually focus it to (say) global warming (which will still produce thousands of hits) or 'acid rain'.
- *Purpose*: a good search has a specific purpose in mind with clearly framed or articulated questions.
- *Vetting*: teachers should check or 'vet' sites before a lesson (or the start of a topic). Sites can be 'bookmarked' using searching software.
- *Structure*: structuring the search and giving guidance, e.g. on the use of 'and', 'or' and 'not', will help to focus and refine. A prepared worksheet, setting out what information learners are expected to find can help, or even presenting a kind of treasure hunt/treasure trail.

Searching skills also include the higher-order skill of selecting information, i.e. deciding what is relevant and valuable (and therefore what to print); and the ability to *assess and evaluate* information for its worth and potential accuracy, i.e. to establish where the information came from, who put it there and why, e.g. do they have vested interests; or is it likely to be biased?

The teacher's role in using ICT in science

Matching teaching and learning objectives with ICT applications

One thing is certain with ICT in the future: the teacher's role will change as a result of ICT in school and in the home. My argument here is that the teacher's role is an extremely complex one – it will require flexibility and reflection and often a change of attitude. We look at the teacher's job closely in the next subsection.

However, the first issue is to clearly identify the teaching objectives in science and how they can be matched to, or *enhanced by*, the use of ICT. We have seen how several applications of ICT can help in learning and teaching science: spreadsheets, data-logging, word processing, multimedia, and so on. The first job of a science teacher is to match these applications to his or her learning and teaching objectives. For example, data-logging can help pupils to observe, study and interpret data as well as taking away some of the drudgery of manual recording and processing, such as drawing a graph with a pencil and graph paper. Spreadsheets can help to tabulate data clearly, and enable 'what if?' questions to be asked. Word processors can help pupils to produce a well-presented report, e.g. of an investigation. Simulations, on a CD-ROM for instance, can allow people to carry out experiments that are either too dangerous, too fast or too slow to do in a school.

The key question which teachers need to address is what is the authentic or important learning objective? To take a crude example, if a teacher wants pupils to learn how to use a mercury-in-glass thermometer, then using a temperature sensor and a data-logger is not a good idea! There are numerous examples like this, which classroom teachers can reflect upon for themselves. The teacher's job, not an easy one, is to ask: what can ICT do to help particular learning objectives in science? ... And (as the football managers say) to *take each one as it comes.*

The changed role of the teacher: observing, intervening, monitoring and supporting learning

The teacher's job is a tough one. As well as the educational question of matching objectives with ICT use, there are plenty of practical issues to consider too (as we saw in the earlier section on managing ICT use in school). Some of these difficulties are hard to overcome, not least the issue of having the right resources available at the right time. My own research (see Collins *et al.* 1997) shows that, even with the resources available, the teacher still has to decide: when to stand back and let the pupils get on with it, or when to intervene and steer them; similarly, how much structure and guidance should be given, e.g. worksheets to go with CD-ROMs, or free-rein learning.

The effective teacher's role seems to involve carrying out several demanding, complex and time-consuming tasks including:

- assessing proposed ICT for relevance and content (see next subsection);
- gaining a level of confidence and competence in using the material for oneself; organizing access to the technology in an equitable way; organising access to other relevant material *away from the computer* to support children's learning;
- providing a structure or a framework within which the group will work – in many cases this will be an open-ended task and discussed with the group;
- assessing pupils' ability to teach others about the workings of the machine and making the need to hand over skills explicit to the pupil expert;
- assessing the work of the group and suggesting appropriate activities which may lead to progression in students' learning;
- reflecting on the activities of the class as a whole and acting on suggestions for amendments next time round.

Central to the teacher's facilitating role is the dialogue which goes on between the teacher and the students working on the computer. This does not mean standing over the children at all times – such a task would be impossible – but it does mean engaging with learners at key moments and guiding their learning.

Reviewing and evaluating software

One of the skills which teachers need to develop with ICT is the ability to judge or evaluate items of software both *before* and *after* they have used it. Being able to assess its value *before* use is vitally important for financial reasons. If you do not like it or it won't 'work' in your department, don't buy it. Teachers also need to develop the ability and experience to *look back* on an application of ICT and evaluate its success.

Judging and evaluating software (just like assessing 'good' science textbooks) comes with intuition and experience but it can also be valuable to have a set of points or a *checklist* to aid your intuition. The points below (some obvious, others not so obvious) are designed as a framework to help in reviewing ICT, before and after you use it:

- Does it fit the curriculum? Does it support your learning goals?
- Does it fit the learners? Is the depth of treatment right for the audience? Does it suit the ability range within a class?
- Does it fit the time slot? For example, does it suit a five-minute demonstration, pupils taking short turns, or whole-lesson use in a computer room?
- Does it fit the hardware? If the software is on CD-ROM, can it be used with a network of computers? Does it need demonstrating on a large screen?
- Does it enhance science education? Can it do things better than we can normally? Does it encourage problem-solving, investigating, modelling, classifying, sorting, questioning, pattern-finding, data-exploring, researching, group work, out-of-class work?
- Does it fit the teacher? Is it easy to get started? Does the effort put in to use it produce a pay-off? Does the manual say how you are supposed to teach with it? Is it possible to customize the software to suit your approach?

The key question, of course, is what added-value does it offer in learning *and* teaching science?

The various criteria can be divided (somewhat arbitrarily) into five areas, as shown in Table 1.3.6.

Table 1.3.6 A checklist for judging ICT

Technical

- Will it run on your machine?
- Any special requirements? (e.g. extra memory, high-resolution graphics, peripherals)
- Is there valuable use of colour, graphics and animation?
- What use is made of sound? Can the sound be controlled, or even switched off?

Practical

- Is it robust?
- Can it cope with various levels and abilities?
- Does it give clear instructions?
- Is the screen well presented and laid out?
- How much text appears?
- Is it useful for individuals, small groups, or whole classes?

Subjective

- What are the reactions of teachers and pupils to it?
- Is it interesting and motivating?
- Does it get them talking?
- Do pupils find it too difficult or too easy?
- Does it build confidence ... or shatter it?

Educational

- Is the content accurate, relevant and appropriate?
- Are the program and its instructions pitched at the right level?
- What educational aims does it develop: skill and drill, factual recall, understanding, analysis, evaluation?
- Can learners use it *independently*?

Accompanying materials

- What materials come with the program: a simple users' guide; teachers' guide; documentation?
- Are there suitable and readable pupils' materials to use with or alongside the program?

Assessing work done by ICT: additional demands and teacher expectations

Using ICT can improve pupils' work (especially those with special needs), but in assessing it teachers need to be aware of new issues which have arisen as a result of ICT (both at home and at school).

Plagiarism and giving references

A number of teachers have complained to me of science homework done with the aid of Encarta (or a similar CD-ROM) or the Internet, which has gone straight from the computer and onto printer paper without any intervention by the pupil's brain. Teachers are rightly suspicious of such work, especially when the Microsoft copyright logo is still on the bottom of the page! Teachers need to demand that the work can be shown to be the pupil's own, even if a CD-ROM or the Internet was used as a source. Pupils must acknowledge the source of their work and *be taught the correct way to give references* (a skill which has rarely been taught in the past below undergraduate level).

Work enhanced by the use of ICT

Word processed work can now be spell-checked and this becomes an additional issue for teachers, especially as few of their science pupils who use word processors at home or school will be allowed to use them in the examination hall. Should some work also be presented in hand-written form, e.g. reports of investigations? Similarly, with the ability of ICT (in the right hands and using a DTP package or similar) to make a pupil's work look highly professional, how should teachers view this and assess it? Scanning in images and drawing graphs with a computer package can make some pupils' work look superb. However, is it all style and no substance?

Several pieces of research have indicated that word processed work can be of most assistance for pupils with special needs, e.g. poor writers: those who have difficulty in writing by hand. This is where ICT can be of great value to pupils who may be good at *science*, but whose writing ability does not do their scientific skill justice. However, an issue at the other extreme for teachers assessing work is whether they can be 'conned' by superbly presented work.

The first question, raised above, is: whose work is it? The second question is: what is the quality of the *content of* work which has been presented in an all-singing, all-dancing style? Teachers (more and more in future with the growth in home use of ICT) will need to make careful judgements in these two areas, that is:

- Whose work is it? Are outside sources acknowledged?
- Is the quality of the *science* work being disguised – or enhanced – by the quality of the presentation?

Collaborative work

One of the excellent features of ICT is that it permits, or rather *enhances*, collaborative group work. Pupils can often write collaboratively using a computer whereas writing collaboratively with a pen is more difficult! Increasingly, there will be assignments and coursework, at *all* levels of education, which have been done as a collaborative team effort. This trend will be fuelled by the demands of employers whose requirements of staff in new forms of employment always include 'teamwork' and 'collaboration' near the top of the list. It is interesting to observe that collaborative work is commonplace in primary school and in higher education – but it seems to be almost taboo in some secondary schools.

ICT will enhance collaborative work but the issue of how it should be assessed remains a controversial one:

- should all partners receive equal credit, or the same mark?
- have any pupils had a 'free ride?
- will pupils who (quite rightly) want a good mark avoid and exclude certain other pupils who might 'lower the grade'?

These issues will occur at all levels, from primary school to university. But they should not be allowed to prevent collaborative work from being done. Through careful observation of group work (who is doing what, when and for how long?), through record-keeping and through discussion with pupils, teachers can ensure that collaborative work will be assessed fairly and individual pupils do not see it as a soft option.

Summary

We started this chapter by considering the nature of science and science education and then asking: 'How can ICT enhance and improve it?' By looking at what computers are good at, it becomes clear that ICT can *add value* to learning and teaching in science. The chapter has outlined several applications of ICT which can be particularly beneficial (e.g. simulations, data-logging, the Internet).

One of the key jobs of the teacher is to ask what counts as *authentic* or appropriate use of ICT in science (as opposed to *inauthentic* or inappropriate use). This question can only be answered when we become clear on our *learning and teaching objectives*. For example, if our objective is to teach graph-drawing with paper and pencil then a data-logging package is not appropriate. However, using a sensor with good data-logging and graph-plotting software can remove some of the drudgery and take pupils rapidly to the higher-order skills of discussing and interpreting graphical results. The chapter has also considered the important business of *managing* ICT in a school setting. This relates closely to the *teacher's role* in using ICT, including the important issue of taking account of and managing *home use* of ICT, which is growing at a rapid rate. The use of ICT at home and at school raises vital issues for the teacher's task of ng and assessing ICT work, including work done collaboratively. Key points in essment were listed, with practical suggestions for teachers.

Finally, the teacher's role in reviewing and evaluating ICT as part of science education was discussed. The ability to review and evaluate software for its *educational value* and *curriculum relevance* is a key aspect of the teacher's repertoire of skills in using ICT. Ideas and a checklist for evaluation of ICT applications were put forward which should be valuable to teachers in a *critical* consideration of ICT in education. Indeed, the main theme of this chapter is that teachers should look forward to the use of ICT in teaching and learning where it can give *added value*. There are enough examples available of 'value-added' activities – in data-logging, in simulations, in spreadsheet and database use, and in text processing – to show that ICT can genuinely enhance science education.

References

Collins, J., Hammond, M. and Wellington, J. J. (1997) *Teaching and Learning with Multimedia,* London: Routledge.

Kahn, B. (1985) *Computers in Science,* Cambridge: Cambridge University Press.

Turkle, S. (1984) *The Second Self: Computers and the Human Spirit,* London: Granada.

Weizenbaum, J. (1984) *Computer Power and Human Reason,* Harmondsworth, UK: Penguin.

Wellington, J. J. (ed.) (1998) *Practical Work in School Science: Which Way Now?,* London: Routledge.

—— (1989) *Education for Employment: The Place of Information Technology,* Windsor, UK: NFER-Nelson.

Part 2

Designing and evaluating ICT to teach and learn science

2.1 Designing and evaluating science teaching sequences

An approach drawing upon the concept of learning demand and a social constructivist perspective on learning

John Leach and Phil Scott[1]

There is a growing body of evidence which demonstrates that students' learning of scientific concepts can be improved as a result of implementing research-based teaching sequences. In this chapter we consider some of the approaches taken to designing and evaluating such sequences and offer an alternative perspective which is based on the concept of *learning demand,* and a social constructivist perspective on learning.

In the first part, we consider the evidence base upon which claims about the effectiveness of teaching sequences are made. We argue that researchers tend to attribute improvements in students' learning to the effectiveness of the *sequence of teaching activities,* giving little explicit attention to the teacher's role in *staging* those teaching activities, in the social context of the classroom. In the second part, we present a social constructivist perspective on learning, which we use as a basis for identifying the essential elements which constitute a teaching sequence. The concept of learning demand is then introduced and developed as a tool for informing the design of teaching sequences. The chapter concludes with a brief discussion of the design and evaluation of teaching sequences.

Research on the design and evaluation of science teaching sequences

There are many studies reported in the science education literature which address the design and evaluation of teaching sequences. In these studies, researchers tend to describe the design of teaching sequences as a process of identifying teaching aims and designing instructional activities to address those aims. In the majority of cases, the effectiveness of the sequence is evaluated by comparing students' responses to specially designed test items, before and after teaching. The use of such test items allows researchers to judge the effectiveness of the teaching in meeting specific learning goals. In addition, further classroom data might be collected to evaluate whether the students' engagement with specific teaching activities matches that intended in the design of the teaching (Millar *et al.* 1999). This approach to the evaluation of teaching sequences allows researchers to comment on the extent to which a sequence is successful in meeting its initial aims.

There is, however, an increasingly influential body of opinion in the UK which suggests that both policy makers and teachers want educational research to provide information about the *most effective ways* of achieving stated learning goals (Hargreaves 1996; Blunkett 1999; Woodhead 1998). This implies some comparison of the effectiveness of different teaching approaches at achieving stated learning goals. It is clear that pre- and post-instructional testing of the kind outlined above does not allow for judgements to be made about the effectiveness of newly designed teaching sequences compared with existing, conventional approaches. Indeed, there are very few examples of research studies in science education which attempt to make this kind of comparative evaluation. This is hardly surprising, given the well-known difficulties that are involved in making valid comparisons (Brown 1992; Bassey 1986). In order to design a study to compare the effectiveness of two approaches to teaching, it is necessary to establish the extent to which the populations of students who will experience the teaching approaches are comparable and to deal with any differences. It is also necessary to have learning assessment instruments which are not biased towards the content of one teaching approach compared with the other. In addition, findings about the effectiveness of new teaching approaches in promoting learning must be interpreted in the light of how much teaching time was provided and of other costs.

There a small number of studies reported in the literature which go some considerable way towards dealing with these difficulties in providing evidence about the effectiveness of designed teaching sequences, compared with more usual teaching approaches. Two studies are referred to here, to illustrate the kinds of claims typically made from this kind of work. Viennot and Rainson (1999) describe the design and evaluation of a teaching sequence, for French undergraduate students, addressing the superposition of electric fields. They show evidence of small, but consistent, year-on-year gains in some areas by students following the 'experimental' teaching sequence compared with the 'control' sequence. Brown and Clement (1991) describe the design and evaluation of teaching sequences on gravity and inertia for US high school students. They report gains of around thirty per cent by students following the 'experimental' sequence compared with the 'control' sequence.

Both of these studies offer convincing evidence that it is possible to design teaching sequences, based on research on learning, that can be more effective in promoting student learning than the usual teaching approach. In both studies, plausible cases, based on detailed evidence, are presented as to why one teaching sequence is likely to engage with students' reasoning better than another. In each case, the research design took into account the prior attainment of students in the 'control' and 'experimental' groups, the learning assessment instruments were carefully designed not to privilege one teaching sequence over another and, in the Viennot and Rainson study, the designed teaching approach did not take any more teaching time than the usual teaching method.

In the Viennot and Rainson study, differences between the performance of students following the 'control' and 'experimental' teaching are attributed to differences in the organization of activities and content within the sequence. However, the teacher in the 'experimental' teaching sequences was also closely involved in the design and evaluation of that teaching sequence (S. Rainson), while the 'control' classes were taught by teachers who were not involved in the research study (Viennot 2000, personal communication). It is therefore possible that the noted gains in learning are due as much to improvements in the effectiveness of the teacher in engaging with students' thinking in this topic area (after prolonged consideration of the subject matter), as to changes in the teaching sequence.

The same issue arises from the report of the Brown and Clement study. Little information is given about the teachers who taught the lessons, although the text of the paper implies that the same group of teachers taught both experimental and control classes. However, the 'control' lessons were taught at an early stage in the research, before the teachers were fully immersed in the research process (Brown 2000, personal communication). It is therefore unlikely that the teachers' teaching of the 'control' classes would have been greatly influenced by their experience of being involved in the research project. Two iterations of 'experimental' teaching sequences were conducted and significant improvements in student learning were only noted after the second iteration. Brown and Clement attribute this to three factors:

1 As our team gained a more detailed understanding of the 'conceptual territory' in these areas, it allowed us to design more 'conceptually focused' examples which dealt with specific difficulties;
2 Each unit was split into two sections separated by weeks allowing for 'revisiting' of topics;
3 Many more occasions where students give oral or written explanations were included.

(Brown and Clement 1991: 383)

It is noticeable that the researchers do not make reference to the influence of the team's development of 'a more detailed understanding of the "conceptual territory"' upon the teachers' expertise in posing questions that engage with students' thinking, and responding to students' talk. It seems to us that changes in the ways in which the teachers engage with students in the classroom, as a result of their knowledge about the 'conceptual territory', go hand in hand with changes in the sequence of activities itself in accounting for the gains in learning noted in the study.

It appears that there is no explicit focus in either of these studies on the role of the teacher in terms of either the design or the evaluation of the teaching. We do not for a moment think that Brown and Clement or Viennot and Rainson are unaware of the central role of teachers in implementing teaching. Indeed, we imagine that both pairs of researchers spent some considerable time discussing between themselves how to support teachers in implementing the teaching, working with the teachers to clarify the intended teaching approach, and discussing the teaching approach with them as the lessons progressed. Rather, our claim in this chapter is that the role of the teacher, as planned by the researchers at the design stage, and the role adopted as teaching progresses, should both be addressed explicitly in any methodological account of the design and evaluation of teaching. We do not believe that it is legitimate for researchers to claim that one teaching sequence is better than another in promoting student learning, without taking into account the part played by the teacher. Although some teaching sequences are more faithful to the conceptual structure of the subject matter than others and some might well prove to be more interesting and intellectually satis-fying than others, it is certainly the case that some teachers are generally more successful in motivating and engaging their students. Although there are welcome signs that the science education research community is engaging with the method-ological problems involved in designing and evaluating science teaching (e.g. the Science Teacher Training in an Information Society Project (STTIS) 2002), the development of appropriate research methods is still at an early stage.

The argument which we are developing here, through reference to methodolog-ical accounts of the design and evaluation of teaching sequences in the science education literature, is that those sequences tend to focus upon the constituent activities and treatment of content, while giving insufficient attention to what we believe to be the key role of the teacher. Of course, there are relatively recent studies which *do* focus upon the teacher in the science classroom, particularly with regard to the ways in which the teacher acts to guide the development of the class-room talk (see, for example, Edwards and Mercer 1987; Lemke 1990; Ogborn *et al.* 1996; Roychoudhury and Roth 1996; Van Zee and Minstrell 1997; Scott 1998; Mortimer 1998), or draws upon a wider range of communicative resources to support meaning making in the classroom (Kress *et al.* 2001). In some ways, these studies present the converse situation to that outlined above, in that they offer detailed analyses of the ways in which the teacher acts to support learning in the classroom, but say much less about the subject matter to be taught and the teaching approaches taken.

In the next section, we draw upon a social constructivist perspective of learning to develop our argument for a broadly based approach to the design and evaluation of science teaching sequences, addressing issues relating both to subject matter/teaching activities and to the role of the teacher in mediating those activities.

The implications of a social constructivist perspective on learning for designing and evaluating teaching sequences

We draw upon a social constructivist perspective on learning, which has been presented in detail elsewhere (Leach and Scott 2003), to inform the development of a broader view of 'teaching sequences' than that normally found in the literature. We begin by setting out some fundamental aspects of this perspective, which draws heavily on Vygotskian and neo-Vygotskian views (Vygotsky 1987; Bakhtin 1981; Wertsch 1985; Scott 1998).

A social constructivist perspective on learning: fundamental assumptions

Central to Vygotsky's perspective on development and learning is that higher mental functioning in the individual derives from social life (Vygotsky 1978: 128). In the first instance, language and other semiotic mechanisms (such as mathematical symbols, diagrams, gesture, stance) provide the means for ideas to be talked through and communicated on the social or intermental plane and, following the process of internalization, language and other semiotic modes provide the tools for individual thinking. In this way, talk and thought are portrayed as being intimately related.

In analysing the thematic *content* of language and thought, Vygotsky (1987) distinguishes between 'spontaneous' (or 'everyday') concepts and 'scientific' concepts. Spontaneous concepts are taken as those which are learned without conscious attention, through normal day-to-day interactions, while scientific concepts are those formal concepts which originate in particular disciplines (such as physics, history or psychology) and which can only be learned through instruction. This differentiation of the content of talk and thought has been elaborated by Bakhtin (1986), who refers to the different *social languages* used by specific communities of people for particular purposes. Thus, for example, the language used by solid-state physicists in talking about the structure of ceramics forms part of one social language and the language used by potters to talk about the moulding properties of ceramics is part of another. In both cases, the development of ways of talking and thinking are fundamentally influenced by the reality of how ceramics exist in the physical world: through the scientific experiments of the physicist on the one hand and the day-to-day working practices of the potter on the other.

Wertsch (1991: 93–118) draws upon the concepts of 'social language' and 'speech genre' in suggesting that they make up a *tool kit* of ways of talking and knowing which can be drawn upon by the individual, as appropriate, in different contexts. Thus, the different social languages and speech genres which are introduced and rehearsed on the social plane of the school classroom (relating to history, geography, science and so on) offer the means for students to develop a range of distinctive modes of talking, thinking and knowing about the world. According to this perspective, scientific knowledge itself is portrayed as a social language. This statement should not be interpreted as an endorsement of a relativist ontology (Matthews 1997; Nola 1997). Rather, we use it to make the following points:

- The language used by scientists (and science teachers) to describe the world is not merely *descriptive*. Rather, entities such as genes and forces, and relationships between those entities, are created and used within communities to describe, explain and predict the behaviour of the world for specific purposes.

- Communities of scientists (and science teachers) make choices about the scientific knowledge that it is appropriate to use in different situations.

Scientific knowledge is not there to be seen in the material world. Rather, it exists in the language, practices and semiotic systems used within specific communities to account for aspects of the material world. Learners will not stumble upon the formalisms, theories and practices that form the content of science curricula without being introduced to them through teaching.

Redefining the concept of 'teaching sequence'

Drawing on the ideas set out above, science teaching can be conceptualized in terms of introducing the learner to one form of the social language of science (school science). The teacher has a key role to play in mediating the social language of school science for students. Bruner (1985) draws attention to this central role of the teacher in stating that:

> Vygotsky's project [is] to find the manner in which aspirant members of a culture learn from their tutors, the vicars of their culture, how to understand the world. That world is a symbolic world in the sense that it consists of conceptually organised, rule-bound belief systems about what exists, about how to get to goals, about what is to be valued. There is no way, none, in which a human being could master that world without the aid and assistance of others for, in fact, that world is others.
>
> (Bruner 1985: 32)

How, then, do we conceptualize the notion of a teaching sequence, the event by which the teacher assists students in learning school science? From the perspective developed in this chapter, teaching sequences involve three key features.

Staging the scientific story

The first key feature of the teaching sequence concerns the way in which the scientific point of view is made available on the social plane of the classroom. Following on from the ideas introduced earlier, we see this process as entailing a performance (involving various teaching activities) led by the teacher, in which the scientific story is gradually developed during the sequence of lessons. In referring to the scientific point of view as the 'scientific story' we have followed the lead taken by Jon Ogborn and colleagues, in their influential book, *Explaining Science in the Classroom* (Ogborn *et al.* 1996). As we see it, school science offers an account, a kind of story, of familiar phenomena expressed in terms of the ideas and conventions of the school science social language.

The performance is interactive in nature, involving both teacher and students. At different times, the teacher will be engaged in presenting new ideas, talking through ideas with the whole class and discussing ideas with individuals and small groups of students. The development of the scientific story is multimodal in nature (Kress *et al.* 2001) as ideas are communicated not only through talk but also through various images, representations, gestures and so on. The development of the scientific story is supported by a range of activities, which might involve the students in exploring particular phenomena, making measurements of certain variables, reading an account of a scientific process or watching a video.

The whole aim of the staging process (involving talk, other semiotic modes and various activities) is to make the scientific story appear intelligible and plausible (Posner *et al.* 1982) to the students. To achieve this, the teacher needs to be aware of the existing understandings of the students and to develop convincing lines of argument to engage with those existing understandings. Such arguments might involve posing key questions which get to the heart of student uncertainties, the use of particular analogies to support them in developing their thinking, or setting up conceptual conflict situations to confront different points of view. A fundamental quality of the staging process is that it is 'persuasive' (Sutton 1996) in nature as the teacher seeks to convince the students of the reasonableness of the scientific story.

In thinking about staging the scientific story, we have found it useful to draw upon the distinction made between the 'authoritative' and 'dialogic' functions of texts (see Wertsch 1991; Mortimer 1998; Scott 1997). The principle function of authoritative discourse is to introduce or make available ideas, whereas dialogic discourse involves exploration of meanings. In the classroom, authoritative discourse might involve the teacher in presenting new ideas in a transmissive mode which offers the students little or no invitation for discussion. Dialogic discourse might see the teacher asking for, and discussing, student opinions, or it might involve students in discussing ideas with each other. It seems reasonable to suggest that learning in the classroom will be enhanced through achieving some kind of *balance* between presenting information (focusing on the authoritative function) and allowing opportunities for exploration of ideas (focusing on the dialogic function). In this sense there needs to be an appropriate *rhythm* (see Mortimer 1998; Scott 1997; Scott and Mortimer 2002) to the discourse as the teaching sequence unfolds.

Supporting student internalization

The ideas set out in the preceding section focus on communication on the social plane of the classroom. There is clearly a difference between making the scientific story *available* on the social plane and having individual students make personal sense of, and become able to use, that story. Vygotsky refers to this personal sense-making step in terms of the process of *internalization*. A second key feature of the instructional process therefore concerns the ways in which the teacher can act to support students in making sense of and internalizing the scientific story. Here Vygotsky (1978) refers to the role of the teacher as being one of supporting student progress in the Zone of Proximal Development (ZPD), from assisted to unassisted competence. How might such teacher assistance appear in the classroom?

The first point to be made here is that the teacher's interventions to support internalization of the scientific story by students are made *throughout* the teaching sequence; it is not a case of making the scientific story available and then helping the students to make sense of it. In this respect, we consider that the continuous *monitoring* of students' understandings and *responding* to those understandings, in terms of how they relate to the intended scientific point of view, must be central to the teacher's role. Of course, these processes of monitoring and responding are made more difficult by the fact that the teacher is not working with one student at a time but with a whole class of students. Nevertheless, we would expect the teaching sequence to include *planned* opportunities for monitoring student under-standings (through, for example, whole-class questioning and discussion, small-group activities, or individual writing activities). We would also expect the teacher to respond to developing student understandings (by, for example, sharing partic-ular points in class, challenging particular points in class, offering comments on student written exercises, discussing issues with individual students where time allows). As teachers engage in these linked processes of monitoring and responding, they are probing and working on the 'gap' between individual students' existing understandings and their potential level of unassisted performance; they are working in the Zone of Proximal Development.

Handing over responsibility to the students

The third feature of the teaching sequence is the logical conclusion to activities to support student internalization. It involves providing opportunities for students to 'try out' and practise the new ideas for themselves; to make the new ideas 'their own'. This step of applying ideas might first be carried out by students with the support and guidance of the teacher. As the students gain in competence and confidence, the teacher gradually hands over (Bruner 1983) responsibility to them, in recognition of their increased capability for unassisted performance.

The conceptualization of 'teaching sequence' which is presented here is rather different from that commonly found in the literature, where teaching sequences tend to be conceptualized in terms of activities, with no reference to the talk which surrounds them. However, it seems to us that, central to any teaching sequence, is the way in which the teacher works with students to 'talk into exis-tence' (Ogborn *et al.* 1996) the scientific story. From our point of view, the activi-ties which are often used in science lessons (experiments, demonstrations and so on) are important, but only insofar as they can act as points of reference in the development of the scientific story. We believe that those instructional design studies which attribute increased student gains to particular sequences of activi-ties are missing a crucial point, this being that those activities are mediated or 'brought into action' by the teacher. The way that the teacher achieves this is fundamental to the teaching process and of central importance in influencing student learning.

The concept of learning demand as a tool to inform the design and evaluation of teaching sequences

Although there are many examples of how teaching sequences might be designed and evaluated in the science education literature, relatively few papers are explicit about how the available information about learners' pre-instructional ideas and the science to be taught are drawn upon in planning the teaching sequence. Notable exceptions include work in the (continental) European didactic tradition (Tochon 1999), which can be exemplified in science education by studies such as those of Tiberghien (1996) and Lijnse (1995). In this section, we develop the concept of *learning demand* (Leach and Scott 1995, 1999), which we relate to Bakhtin's notion of 'social languages' and present as a tool for theorizing the process of designing and evaluating teaching sequences.

The concept of learning demand

The point was made earlier that different *social languages* (Bakhtin 1986) are used by specific communities of people for particular purposes. Thus, a distinction can be drawn between the 'everyday' social language of day-to-day living and the 'scientific' social language which is first formally introduced in school.

From birth, each one of us is immersed in an everyday social language, which has itself been shaped by the ways in which human beings perceive their environment. It is this language which provides the means for communicating with others; it provides a way of talking and thinking about the physical and social worlds that surround us and impinge on all of our senses. In a strong sense, everyday social language acts to *shape* our view of the surroundings, drawing attention to particular features and presenting those features in particular ways. The informal or spontaneous (Vygotsky 1987) concepts which constitute everyday social language include many of those which are referred to as 'alternative conceptions' in the science education literature. Notions of 'plants feeding from the soil' and 'energy getting used up' are examples of everyday ways of thinking and talking, which are part of an everyday social language. Other 'alternative conceptions' are better viewed as products of school science learning: a social language emerges among science learners that draws upon features of everyday social language and the social language of school science, but that is different from both. From a social constructivist point of view, it is evident that it is the formal concepts of the natural sciences which provide the 'alternative' perspective to the omnipresent 'everyday' ways of talking and thinking (rather than the other way round).

A further important distinction can be made between what might be referred to as 'scientific' social languages and a 'school science' social language. It is clear that there are differences between 'real' science, as carried out in various professional settings, and 'school' science. School science has its own history of development and is subject to social and political pressures which are quite different from those of professional science. The science which is taught in schools focuses on particular concepts and ways of thinking and can therefore be thought of as constituting a social language in itself.

The concept of 'learning demand' offers a way of appraising the *differences* between the social language of school science and the everyday social language which learners bring to the classroom. The purpose of identifying learning demands is to bring the intellectual challenges facing learners into sharper focus as they address a particular aspect of school science; teaching can then be designed to focus on those learning demands.

An important point relating to the operationalization of the concept of learning demand is that a learning demand can be identified for a *group* of learners working within a specific area of scientific content. This follows from the fact that learners are immersed in a common social language in day-to-day living and will therefore arrive in school with largely similar points of view. In this respect, the concept of learning demand is linked more closely to differences between social languages and the meanings that they convey, than to differences in the 'mental apparatus' of individuals. Thus, learning demands are *epistemological* rather than *psychological* in nature (Leach and Scott 2003).

Identifying learning demands

How might learning demands for a particular conceptual area of science be specified? Here, we identify three ways in which differences between everyday and school science perspectives might arise. These relate to differences in the *conceptual tools* used, differences in the *epistemological underpinning* of those conceptual tools, and differences in the *ontology* on which those conceptual tools are based.

For example, in the context of teaching and learning about air pressure, students typically draw upon the everyday concept of 'suction' in explaining phenomena, while the scientific point of view is based upon differences in air pressure. There is a difference here in the *conceptual tools* used. In relation to plant nutrition, students commonly draw upon everyday notions of 'food' as something that is ingested, in contrast with scientific accounts which describe the synthesis of complex organic molecules within plants from simple, inorganic precursors.

Other differences relate to the *epistemological underpinning* of the conceptual tools used. For example, ways of generating explanations using scientific models and theories, which are taken for granted in school science, are not part of the everyday social language of many learners (Vosniadou 1994; Driver *et al.* 1996; Leach *et al.* 1996). For example, there is evidence that many lower secondary school students recognize the logical implications of specific pieces of evidence in relation to different models of simple series electrical circuits, but resolve logical inconsistencies by selecting different models to explain the behaviour of different circuits (Leach 1999). They do not draw upon the epistemological principle of *consistency* that is an important feature of school science. Their everyday social language does not appear to recognize that scientific models and theories ideally explain as broad a range of phenomena as possible.

Learning demands may also result from differences in the *ontology* of the conceptual tools used (Chi 1992; Chi *et al.* 1994; Vosniadou 1994; Leach *et al.* 1996). Thus, entities that are taken for granted as having a real existence in the realm of school science may not be referred to in a similar manner in the everyday language of students. For example, there is evidence that many lower secondary school students learning about matter cycling in ecosystems do not think about atmospheric gases as a potential source of matter for the chemical processes of ecological systems (Leach *et al.* 1996). There is a learning issue here which relates to the students' basic commitments about the nature of matter – initially they do not consider gases to be substantive.

Drawing on the concept of learning demand and social constructivist perspectives to inform the design of teaching sequences

Drawing upon the ideas set out in the previous sections, the following scheme offers a generalized approach to guide the planning of science teaching sequences:

1   identify the school science knowledge to be taught;
2   consider how this area of science is conceptualized in the everyday social language of students;
3   identify the learning demand by appraising the nature of any differences between 1 and 2;
4   develop a teaching sequence, as redefined earlier, to address each aspect of the learning demand.

Step 1   *The school science knowledge to be taught*

From the outset, the teacher needs to be clear about the precise nature of the 'scientific story' to be told. Thus, for a given teaching sequence, the focus of the teaching and learning might be upon descriptive accounts of phenomena, or introducing new scientific concepts, or developing and applying a scientific theory. Furthermore, each of these goals is open to different treatments in terms of the concepts used, the level of detail addressed, the complexity of the ideas used and the sequence in which those ideas are introduced. The first step in planning a teaching sequence must be, therefore, to specify in detail and to justify the science knowledge to be taught.

Experience has shown that this form of detailed analysis often leads to the identification of conceptual and epistemological themes which provide important underpinnings to the main learning goals to be addressed, but which are often overlooked, or left implicit, in the teaching approach taken.

Steps 2 and 3   *The everyday social language of learners and its relationship to school science (identifying the learning demand)*

The nature of the social language that learners bring to lessons, and the relationship of that language to the social language of school science, varies according to the scientific content area of the teaching and the age and experience of the learners. Many resources in the research literature are available to characterize students' everyday social language.

In some areas, there are striking differences between 'everyday' social language and the 'school science' social language introduced through teaching (Driver *et al.* 1994; Leach and Scott 2003). For example, in being introduced to the scientific concept of gravity, the learner is required to take on board the concept of 'action at a distance', that the gravitational force can act on a mass without being in contact with it. Here, it is quite likely that the scientific view will challenge the learner's basic assumptions about the nature of the physical world – it certainly did so for Newton – and that ontologically based learning demands will therefore arise.

There are other situations where there may be differences between school science and everyday views, but the relationship is less direct. Consider, for example, secondary school students' learning about genetics. Students are likely to have many everyday ideas to explain why offspring look similar to, or different from, other family members. However, although secondary school biology addresses heredity, its main focus is upon the structure, coding, transfer and interpretation of genetic information. These aspects of school science do not have corresponding points of reference in everyday language. Nevertheless, in the case of genetics learning, there is some evidence that students develop ways of interpreting content, introduced through school science, in terms of the fundamental assumptions developed through everyday talk. For example, the idea that 'everyone is unique' is a common everyday view. When students are taught that the genetic code is the means of coding information through the chemical structure of DNA, many therefore interpret the genetic code as providing an unique 'blueprint' for each individual, rather than appreciating the regularities in the genetic code, both within and between species (Lewis *et al.* 2000). In such cases, it appears that many learners develop a perspective which incorporates features of everyday views and the target school science.

In other cases, students may bring more general forms of everyday reasoning to school science contexts. This can be illustrated with the phenomenon of hotness/ coldness. Prior to teaching, students are surrounded by perceptual experiences that 'hotness' and 'coldness' are different, and that things get hotter as they are heated (and cooler as they are cooled). Furthermore, there is much talk where parents tell children that the nearer you get to hot fires, the hotter you get, and so on. During school science teaching, however, students encounter phenomena where more heating does not result in more 'hotness' (e.g. when heating a substance around the point of phase transition). In such cases, many students inappropriately draw upon reasoning patterns (or everyday patterns of talk) such as 'more of *x* leads to more of *y*', to offer explanations (Andersson 1986; Stavy and Berkovitz 1980; Stavy and Tirosh 2000).

Of course, there are many contexts of school science learning where there is considerable overlap between everyday and school science views. For example, basic notions of the human skeleton are unlikely to differ much between everyday and school science views, although school science will offer extra information regarding structure and function as well as a new terminology. We would suggest that it is in these areas of overlap between social languages where teachers regard topics for study as being 'straightforward' and learners think the topic is just 'common-sense'.

Step 4   Developing a teaching sequence

The step from identifying learning demands to developing a teaching sequence is one which will always involve selection and choice of teaching approaches. Although we firmly believe that identifying learning demands is a fundamental pre-requisite to developing a teaching sequence, we also acknowledge that the learning demand analysis does not lead to the unique specification of a 'best' teaching approach (Millar 1989). Nevertheless, we believe that an analysis of learning demands can inform making decisions about:

- the scientific content to be addressed during the sequence (referring to both conceptual and epistemological issues);
- the relative levels of intellectual demand made by the different parts of the scientific content, and consequently the amount of time and attention to be given to each of these;
- the way in which the scientific story is to be staged through the sequence, developing particular lines of argument to engage with students' thinking, supported by a range of different activities;
- the nature of the classroom talk (along the authoritative–dialogic dimension) that is appropriate at different points in the teaching sequence.

In practice, it is likely that the planning process will not involve a strict sequential passage through Steps 1 to 4. In particular, identification of specific aspects of the school science to be taught (1) is likely to be influenced by consideration of the ways of thinking and talking of the students (2). In other words the identification of learning demand (3) involves an iterative process moving between knowledge to be taught and students' views, and is probably consequent upon the development and refinement of both.

In making the move from identifying learning demands to planning teaching sequences, we have found it useful to start by developing 'teaching goals' which make explicit the ways in which the students' ideas and understandings are to be worked on through the intervention and guidance of the teacher. We shall now briefly illustrate such an approach to designing teaching sequences by focusing on a particular example relating to introductory work on simple electrical circuits for students in the early years of secondary schooling.

Planning a teaching sequence: an introduction to explaining the working of simple electrical circuits

In England, simple explanatory models of electrical circuits are first addressed with students in the 11–14 age range. The content to be taught is specified in the *National Curriculum for England: Science* (DfEE 1999).

Step 1   School science knowledge to be taught

In the context of the *National Curriculum for England: Science* (DfEE and QCA 1999), the school science knowledge to be taught involves developing a model of energy transfer via an electric current, where current is conserved and energy is transferred in resistive parts of the circuit. This model is developed in subsequent phases of the National Curriculum by introducing the concept of voltage. The first step in designing the teaching sequence involved an analysis of the scientific knowledge as presented in the curriculum and the identification of its conceptual structure. The brief presentation of scientific knowledge in curriculum documents often results in centrally important concepts and links between concepts not being specified (Viennot 2001). As a result of this analysis, the following conceptualizations were identified as central to the school science view to be taught to the students:

- current as a flow of charge
- current as the means of energy transfer
- current as being conserved
- the supply of energy as originating in the electrical cell
- energy being transferred in resistive elements of the circuit.

Step 2   Students' everyday views of electricity and electrical circuits

With students of this age, it is likely that significant numbers will arrive at the lessons with a variety of everyday ideas about electricity, including:

- batteries run out
- electricity makes things work
- current, electricity, volts and power are the same kind of thing
- electricity/electric current flows.

They use electrical appliances on a daily basis and take for granted that these things must be switched on, cost money to operate, can be dangerous in giving electric shocks, and so on. As teaching in this area proceeds, it is quite common for students to develop ideas such as 'the current gets used up' or 'the battery provides a fixed current' and to confuse the concepts of charge, current, energy and electricity.

In relation to broader epistemological issues, it is likely that the students will have little experience of using a scientific model which involves moving between the 'theoretical world' of the model (based on the abstract concepts of charge, current and energy) and the 'real world' of observations and measurements (Tiberghien 1996). They are also likely to have little appreciation of the fact that scientific models can be applied generally to a wide range of contexts (Driver *et al.* 1996).

Step 3   Identification of learning demands

The learning demand for a group of students studying a particular area of the curriculum is identified by comparing features of the social language of school science with the everyday social language of the students, looking for commonalities and differences. Such a comparison was carried out in terms of the features identified in the preceding sections and, in this area of the curriculum, with students of this age, the learning demand was identified as involving students in coming to:

- develop abstract scientific concepts of charge, current, resistance and energy in the context of explaining the behaviour of simple electric circuits and differentiating between the meanings of these terms.
- understand that the current carries energy in the electric circuit and that it is the energy and not the current which is 'used up' (transferred);
- be able to 'visualize' what is happening in simple series circuits, with different combinations of cells and resistances, and to predict and explain their behaviour;
- understand that the electric circuit model based on concepts of charge, current, resistance and energy can be used to predict and explain the behaviour of a wide range of simple circuits.

The first three elements of the learning demand involve conceptual issues while the final element pertains to more general epistemological matters.

The learning demand analysis for a particular topic often highlights aspects of the subject matter as being centrally important, from the point of view of teaching, which would not be identified as important from an analysis of the subject matter alone. In the case of electric circuits, for example, an analysis of the subject matter would take for granted a commitment to generalizability and consistency of explanation. By contrast, however, information about students' thinking in this area makes it apparent that this aspect of school science cannot necessarily be taken for granted with lower secondary school students. Similar issues are also raised in the studies of Viennot and Rainson (1999) and Brown and Clement (1991).

Step 4   Planning the teaching sequence

We now turn our attention to planning a teaching sequence to address the learning demands set out in the previous section.

Teaching goals

The first step in this process is to develop *teaching goals*, which make explicit the ways in which students' ideas and understandings are to be worked on through the intervention and guidance of the teacher. The teaching goals are grouped according to whether they have a conceptual or an epistemological focus:

CONCEPTUAL TEACHING GOALS

To *build on* the ideas that

- batteries make things work
- electricity/current flows.

To *introduce, and support the development of,* the ideas that

- an electric current consists of a flow of charge;
- the electric current transfers energy around the circuit;
- components such as bulbs introduce resistance to the circuit. The resistance restricts the flow of charge, reducing the current flowing around the whole circuit and resulting in the production of heat and light as the current passes through the resistance.

To *draw attention to, and to emphasize,* the idea that

- the electric current does not get used up
- rather, it is the energy which is transferred in resistances to make things work.

Progressively to *differentiate between*

- the theoretical concepts of charge, current and energy.

EPISTEMOLOGICAL TEACHING GOALS

To *introduce, and support the development of,* the idea that

- the scientific electric circuit model based on concepts of charge, current, resistance and energy can be used to predict and explain the behaviour of a wide range of simple circuits.

Staging the scientific story

In thinking about the overall shape of this teaching sequence, a fundamental issue to be addressed concerns the way in which the scientific model is introduced. It seems to us that there are two main possibilities. First, it might be decided to take an 'inductive approach' to introducing the scientific model. Such an approach would involve making observations and measurements of simple circuits and then working with the students to develop a theoretical model consistent with those data. An alternative approach is for the teacher to introduce a simple model (of charge/current carrying energy around the circuit) and check out the 'fit' of this model with observations and measurements. Either teaching route is possible, but we favour the second one. This is because the teacher can help students to develop an understanding of the concepts charge/current/resistance/energy as the model is introduced and these understandings can then be developed further through working empirically with the model. By contrast, in the first approach, it seems that the students are required to make measurements of electric current before they have an understanding of what current is.

The next teaching question concerns how the abstract model of charge/current carrying energy around the circuit might be introduced such that the students are able to 'visualize' what is happening in the circuit. Here, it is likely that the teaching would be based upon the use of an analogy, focusing on the energy-carrying function of the charge/current. We have worked with a group of teachers to develop an analogy which consists of a line of vans carrying bread from a bakery and delivering it to a supermarket (see Hind *et al.* 2001). The analogy is referred to systematically throughout the sequence and the students are encouraged to use it as a tool for their own thinking and talking about circuits. In addition, clear distinctions should be made between the electric circuit model which is being developed, the observations and data which are being explained, and the analogical picture.

As outlined earlier, the whole focus of this aspect of the teaching is on 'talking into existence' (Ogborn *et al.* 1996) the electric circuit model and its component concepts. The authoritative voice of the teacher will be heard as new concepts are introduced, developed and discussed on the social plane of the classroom.

Supporting student internalization

In addition to introducing new concepts, there must also be opportunities for the teacher to check students' developing understandings, through dialogic exchanges with the whole class, small groups, individuals and also through short written tasks. There must be opportunities for the students themselves to begin to try out these new ideas, through discussion both with the teacher and with other students. The teaching sequence is therefore planned not only to include particular practical activities (in which the students work with apparatus, collecting data) but also to specify opportunities for talk and various forms of interaction around those activities. These are planned in advance and form an integral part of the teaching sequence.

Handing over responsibility to the students

Following the model-building phase, students are given the opportunity to work with it in a number of familiar and new contexts. We see working with the electric circuit model as being crucial to enabling the students to make the model their own. Sutton makes the point that 'the teacher's personal voice is important but learners must also have some freedom of re-expression' (Sutton 1996: 149). Here, the teacher plans opportunities for students to talk through their developing understandings both with the teacher and with each other. The teacher is thereby able to monitor student progress and to intervene as necessary to scaffold (Wood *et al.* 1976) the learning of individuals and small groups. This phase of the teaching is planned around a series of contexts progressively differentiated in terms of the demands made in applying the model. As well as providing the opportunity for students to take responsibility for applying the scientific model, the teaching of this phase also addresses the epistemological teaching goal of appreciating the generalizability of scientific models. [...]

Designing and evaluating teaching sequences: an agenda for future work

In this chapter, we have set out an approach to designing teaching sequences which is based on a social constructivist perspective of learning and the concept of learning demand. This approach emphasizes the importance of explicitly addressing not only the development of teaching activities in the design process but also the key role of the teacher in mediating those activities. We have demonstrated that the role of the teacher is very often neglected in research reports of teaching approaches, possibly due to a lack of theoretical tools to describe and evaluate that teacher activity. We have drawn upon the concepts of authoritative and dialogic discourse as tools which can be used to identify the different kinds of communicative approach used by the teacher and these ideas are in process of further development (Scott and Mortimer 2002).

Our approach to the design of teaching sequences also has clear implications for the way in which we think about their evaluation. As we saw when discussing research in this area, the usual approach to evaluating teaching sequences is to carry out some kind of assessment of student learning against the learning objectives addressed by the teaching. Such approaches are clearly valid, as the primary aim of teaching sequences is to promote student learning. However, such methods can say very little about the cause of any learning gains that are observed, because no data are collected about how the teaching was conducted. The claim that learning gains can be attributed to the sequence of activities that constitute the teaching sequence, rather than a particular set of activities which were staged in a certain way, remains problematic. Furthermore, if researchers only have data about learning gains and the sequence of teaching activities used, in the absence of information about how those activities were staged, their communication of the teaching sequence to other teachers will be very limited. It would certainly come as no surprise if different teachers achieved very different outcomes in terms of student learning, with comparable groups of students, by following the same sequence of activities without any attempt to stage those activities in the same way.

Given our rationale and approach to designing teaching sequences, their evaluation must involve measurement of student learning outcomes *together with* an account of how the activities were staged in the classroom. The staging of the teaching would be evaluated in terms of the extent to which classroom discourse had followed the pattern proposed in the design of the teaching sequence. For example, classroom data would be collected to evaluate how the teacher changed the balance of authoritative and dialogic classroom talk in introducing new scientific ideas, in supporting student internalization, in responding to student questions and so on.

In order for research on the design and evaluation of teaching sequences to inform the practice of science teachers in general, it is necessary to be clear about the circumstances in which particular teaching approaches – including both activities and their staging – lead to learning gains and are therefore worth communicating to teachers. At the beginning of this chapter we indicated that the teachers of the 'experimental' teaching sequences reported in the research literature are not typical of others in the teaching community because of their involvement in the design and implementation of the research. However, this should not be taken as indicating a belief on our part that those teachers are in some way *special* or *superior* to other teachers. Rather, we believe that those teachers have developed particular insights into the teaching of a topic that serve them well in their teaching. The ongoing challenge for designing and evaluating teaching sequences is to identify the aspects of the teaching activities and their staging that were instrumental in promoting students' learning and to consider how these can be passed on to other teachers who were not involved in the research process.

Acknowledgement

The work reported in this paper was conducted as part of the ESRC Research Network *Towards Evidence Based Practice in Science Education* (Award L139251003). Together with the authors, Andy Hind and Jenny Lewis developed the teaching sequence referred to in the paper. A version of this paper was first presented at an invited symposium arranged by Martine Méheut and Dimitris Psillos, and we gratefully acknowledge feedback from the symposium participants on our work. We also acknowledge valuable discussions with the following colleagues on earlier drafts of this paper: Hilary Asoko, Christian Buty, Andy Hind, Jenny Lewis, Robin Millar, Andrée Tiberghien and Laurence Viennot.

Note

1   This paper is a work of joint authorship.

References

Andersson, B. (1986) 'The experiential gestalt of causation: a common core to pupils' preconceptions in science', *European Journal of Science Education* 8(2): 155–71.
Bakhtin, M. M. (1981) *The Dialogic Imagination: Four Essays by M. M. Bakhtin*, ed. Michael Holquist, trans. Caryl Emerson and Michael Holquist, Austin: University of Texas Press.
—— (1986) *Speech Genres and other Late Essays,* ed. C. Emerson and M. Holquist, trans. V. W. McGee, Austin: University of Texas Press.

Bassey, M. (1986) 'Pedagogic research: on the relative merits of search for generalisation and study of single events', *Oxford Review of Education* 7(1): 73–94.

Blunkett, D. (1999) *Introduction to the Consultation on the Proposed Changes to the National Curriculum*, London: Qualifications and Curriculum Authority.

Brown, A. (1992) 'Design experiments: theoretical and methodological challenges in creating complex interventions', *Journal of the Learning Sciences* 2(2): 141–78.

Brown, D. and Clement, J. (1991) 'Classroom teaching experiments in mechanics', in R. Duit, F. Goldberg and H. Niedderer (eds) *Research in Physics Learning: Theoretical and Empirical Studies* (pp. 380–97), Kiel, Germany: IPN.

Bruner, J. (1983) *Child's Talk: Learning to Use Language*, New York: Norton.

—— (1985) 'Vygotsky: a historical and conceptual perspective', in J. Wertsch (ed.) *Culture, Communication and Cognition: Vygotskian Perspectives* (pp. 21–34), Cambridge: Cambridge University Press.

Chi, M. T. H. (1992) 'Conceptual change within and across ontological categories: examples from learning and discovery in science', in R. Giere (ed.) *Cognitive Models of Science: Minnesota Studies in the Philosophy of Science* (Vol. 15, pp. 129–86), Minneapolis: University of Minnesota Press.

——, Slotta, J. and deLeeuw, N. (1994) 'From things to processes: a theory of conceptual change for learning science concepts', *Learning and Instruction* 4: 27–43.

DfEE (1999) *Science: The National Curriculum for England*, London: QCA.

Driver, R., Asoko, H., Leach, J., Mortimer, E. and Scott, P. (1994) 'Constructing scientific knowledge in the classroom', *Educational Researcher* 23(7): 5–12.

——, Leach, J., Millar, R. and Scott, P. (1996) *Young People's Images of Science*, Buckingham: Open University Press.

Edwards, D. and Mercer, N. (1987) *Common Knowledge: The Development of Understanding in the Classroom*, London: Methuen.

Hargreaves, D. H. (1996) *Teaching as a Research-based Profession: Possibilities and Prospects*, The Teacher Training Agency Annual Lecture 1996, mimeo.

Hind, A., Leach, J., Lewis, J. and Scott, P. (2001) 'Teaching science for understanding: electric circuits', available on the Web at <http://edu.leeds.ac.uk/projects/lis/EpseTeachResources.html> (accessed 1 February 2002).

Kress, G., Jewitt, C., Ogborn, J. and Tsatsarelis, C. (2001) *Multimodal Teaching and Learning: The Rhetorics of the Science Classroom*, London: Continuum.

Leach, J. (1999) 'Students' skills in the co-ordination of theory and evidence in science', *International Journal of Science Education* 21(8): 789–806.

—— and Scott, P. (1995) 'The demands of learning science concepts: issues of theory and practice', *School Science Review* 76(277): 47–52.

—— and —— (1999) 'Learning science in the classroom: drawing on individual and social perspectives', paper presented at the meeting of the European Association for Research on Learning and Instruction (EARLI), Gothenburg, Sweden, August 1999.

—— and —— (2003) 'Individual and sociocultural views of learning in science education', *Science and Education* 12(1): 91–113.

——, Driver, R., Scott, R. and Wood-Robinson, C. (1996) 'Children's ideas about ecology 2: ideas about the cycling of matter found in children aged 5–16', *International Journal of Science Education* 18(1): 19–34.

Lemke, J. L. (1990) *Talking Science. Language, Learning and Values*, Norwood, NJ: Ablex Publishing.

Lewis, J., Leach, J. and Wood-Robinson, C. (2000) 'All in the genes? Young people's understanding of the nature of genes', *Journal of Biological Education* 34(2): 74–9.

Lijnse, P. (1995) '"Developmental research" as a way to an empirically based "didactical structure" of science', *Science Education* 79(2): 189–99.

Matthews, M. (1997) 'Introductory comments on philosophy and constructivism in science education', *Science and Education* 6(1): 5–14.

Millar, R. (1989) 'Constructive criticisms', *International Journal of Science Education* 11(5): 587–96.

——, Le Maréchal, J.-F. and Tiberghien, A. (1999) '"Mapping" the domain – varieties of practical work', in J. Leach and A. C. Paulsen (eds) *Practical Work in Science Education: Recent Research Studies* (pp. 33–59), Dordrecht: Kluwer.

Mortimer, E. F. (1998) 'Multivoicedness and univocality in classroom discourse: an example from theory of matter', *International Journal of Science Education* 20(1): 67–82.

Nola, R. (1997) 'Constructivism in science and science education: a philosophical critique', *Science and Education* 6: 55–83.

Ogborn, J., Kress, G., Martins, I. and McGillicuddy, K. (1996) *Explaining Science in the Classroom*, Buckingham: Open University Press.

Posner, G. J., Strike, K. A., Hewson, P. W. and Gertzog, W. A. (1982) 'Accommodation of a scientific conception: toward a theory of conceptual change', *Science Education* 66(2): 211–27.

Roychoudhury, A. and Roth, W.-M. (1996) 'Interactions in an open-inquiry physics laboratory', *International Journal of Science Education* 18(4): 423–45.

Scott, P. H. (1997) 'Teaching and learning science concepts in the classroom: talking a path from spontaneous to scientific knowledge', in *Linguagem, Cultura e Cognicao Reflexoes Para o Ensino de Ciencias* (pp. 110–28), Belo Horizonte, Brazil: Faculdade de Educacao da UFMG.

—— (1998) 'Teacher talk and meaning making in science classrooms: a Vygotskian analysis and review', *Studies in Science Education* 32: 45–80.

—— and Mortimer, E. E. (2002) 'Discursive activity on the social plane of high school science classrooms: a tool for analysing and planning teaching interactions', paper presented at the 2002 AEPA Annual Meeting, New Orleans, USA, as part of the BERA invited symposium: *Developments in Sociocultural and Activity Theory Analyses of Learning in School*.

Stavy, R. and Berkovitz, A. (1980) 'Cognitive conflict as a basis for teaching quantitative aspects of the concept of temperature', *Science Education* 64(5): 679–92.

—— and Tirosh, D. (2000) *How Students (Mis-)understand Science and Mathematics: Intuitive Rules*, New York: Teachers College Press.

Science Teacher Training in an Information Society Project (STTIS) (2002) downloaded from <http://blues.uab.es/-idmc42/sttis.html> (accessed 3 May 2002).

Sutton, C. (1996) 'The scientific model as a form of speech', in A. G. Welford, J. Osborne and P. Scott (eds) *Science Education Research in Europe: Current Issues and Themes* (pp. 143–52), London: Falmer.

Tiberghien, A. (1996) 'Construction of prototypical situations in teaching the concept of energy', in A. G. Welford, J. Osborne and P. Scott (eds) *Science Education Research in Europe: Current Issues and Themes* (pp. 27–47), London: Falmer.

Tochon, F. V. (1999) 'Semiotic foundations for building the new didactics: an introduction to the prototype features of the discipline', *Instructional Science* 27(1–2): 9–32.

Van Zee, E. H. and Minstrell, J. (1997) 'Reflective Discourse: developing shared understandings in a physics classroom', *International Journal of Science Education* 19(2): 209–28.

Viennot, L. (2001) *Reasoning in Physics: The Part of Common Sense*, Dordrecht: Kluwer.

—— and Rainson, S. (1999) 'Design and evaluation of a research based teaching sequence: the superposition of electric fields', *International Journal of Science Education* 21(1): 1–16.

Vosniadou, S. (1994) 'Capturing and modelling the process of conceptual change', *Learning and Instruction* 4: 45–69.

Vygotsky, L. S. (1978) *Mind in Society: The Development of Higher Psychological Processes,* Cambridge, MA: Harvard University Press.

—— (1987) *The Collected Works of L. S. Vygotsky,* Vol. 1, R. W. Rieber and A. S. Carton (eds), N. Minick (trans.), New York: Plenum.

Wertsch, J. V. (1985) *Vygotsky and the Social Formation of Mind,* Cambridge, MA: Harvard University Press.

—— (1991) *Voices of the Mind: A Sociocultural Approach to Mediated Action,* London: Harvester Wheatsheaf.

Wood, D. J., Bruner, J. S. and Ross, G. (1976) 'The role of tutoring in problem solving', *Journal of Psychology and Psychiatry* 17: 89–100.

Woodhead, C. (1998) *Educational Research – A Critique. The Tooley Report* (introduction), London: Ofsted.

2.2 Designing multimedia e-learning for science education

Tom Boyle

There are at least three major types of participant in the process to design multimedia e-learning: the original designers, the local tutors and trainers, and the learners. Design is concerned with the principled shaping of an artefact, event or experience. A traditional model is for the designer to act as producer and the user to act as a consumer – a model that may be applied to e-learning. However, the dynamic, interactive nature of computer and Internet technology opens up new possibilities. Modern pedagogies provide design principles to take advantage of these possibilities. This productive intersection has led to new conceptions of e-learning design as more dynamic, open and participative; it offers the users, both tutors and learners, the chance to become not just consumers but participants in the design process. This theme provides a central leitmotiv in the following discussion.

This chapter traces, and critically comments on, approaches to the design process that range from traditional instructional systems design to the new wave of options opened up by work on reusable learning objects. The aim is not didactically to sort the sheep from the goats. Well thought-out design strategies and tactics from radically different approaches often have something valuable to offer. The aim is rather to contribute to the understanding of users, which in turn contributes to their empowerment as informed participants in the design process (for further discussion of informant design, see, for example, Scaife and Rogers 2001). For the purposes of this chapter the main user audience is the course tutors, although at all stages the ultimate criteria for the design choices made are the benefits received by the learners.

This chapter is organized in four major sections:

- Strategic approaches to multimedia e-learning design
- Dealing with complex, abstract domains
- Design for access
- Learning objects and the opportunities they open to the tutor as designer.

The first section deals with strategic approaches to e-learning design. The strategic approach adopted has a profound influence on how learning is conceptualized and thus on the nature of the learning environment created by the design team. This choice has a powerful influence on the degrees of freedom opened up for intermediaries in the design process – tutors and course designers – and the learners. It is thus important to start at this level. The second section then focuses on how these strategic principles can be mapped to deal with two central challenges in science education: complexity and abstraction. The chapter reviews how multimedia design incorporating pedagogical principles, such as scaffolding and visualization, can help tackle these problems.

The third section discusses the issue of accessible design. Making sure the multimedia experience is accessible to all is a fundamental challenge. After these central design issues have been discussed, the final section examines an increasingly influential way to view the architecture of learning environments. Modern developments, focused on learning objects and standards, are opening up new possibilities for tutors, and indeed learners, to participate as creative designers of the learning experience.

Strategic approaches to educational multimedia design

The most obvious strategic divide in educational multimedia is between instructivist and constructivist approaches. An instructivist approach regards the computer essentially as a teaching machine. The constructivist approach regards the technology as a basis for constructing learning environments. This divergence has a marked influence on the nature of the learning experience and the degree of freedom given to tutors and learners for creative participation.

Instructional systems design

The instructivist approach was developed most systematically in traditional instructional systems design. This approach had its roots in the behaviourist psychology of Skinner, who believed that we could optimize human learning by systematically ordering the selection and scheduling of learning events. By selectively rewarding (or reinforcing) successful actions and giving negative reinforcement to unsuccessful actions, we could optimally shape learning behaviour. The earliest 'teaching machines' were based on these principles.

This suggestion of a systematic approach to the design of 'programmed learning' was taken up by Gagné (1965), who extrapolated beyond the limited theoretical base of the time to provide a systematic description of types of learning. From these roots the systematic approach to the design of computers as optimized teaching systems was developed over the next decades (for example, see Gagné and Briggs 1979; Price 1991). This approach became known as instructional systems design.

Instructional systems design takes a formal, disciplined approach to the design of 'computer-based training'. It provides prescriptions of procedural sequences that are applied to achieve instructional goals. The initial computers on which these systems were based were text-based and line-oriented. However, the ethos and influence of this approach is still evident in many multimedia systems. Fenrich (1997), for example, follows this type of approach in his book on developing instructional multimedia applications. The influence of this systematic instructional approach is especially noticeable in multimedia training systems developed for industry. This approach has strongly influenced the design of 'integrated learning systems' – multimedia packages that enlist drill and practice as a major pedagogical tool to aid the attainment of clearly specified educational targets (Underwood *et al.* 1996).

From the tutor's point of view, these systems offer replacement or augmentation for didactic instruction. Thus the huge market for information technology (IT) certification, such as the European Computer Driving Licence, has led to the marketing of products developed along these general instructional lines. Systems like these may enable hundreds or even thousands of students to be presented with systematic multimedia instruction that provides animated demonstrations and testing of the material to be learned. These systems enable the tutor to begin to move towards being a manager of learning rather than a source and transmitter of content.

Constructivism

The central tenet of constructivism is that knowledge of the world is constructed by the individual. Constructivism rejects the concept of knowledge as a commodity that can be transmitted from teacher to student (or computer to student). Knowledge is a cognitive construction, produced through interaction with the world, that people use to make sense of the world (Cunningham *et al.* 1993; Grabinger and Dunlop 2000; Boyle 1997). The role of educational multimedia then becomes to foster and support these constructive processes. Support for learning rather than teaching becomes the focal issue.

Constructivism has grown in influence to become the dominant approach for those designing learning technology. This influence extends beyond educational multimedia to other rapidly expanding areas such as electronic conferencing where ideas concerning the social construction of knowledge have proved very popular.

To facilitate these constructive learning processes the emphasis in design is placed on:

- Rich interaction
- Authentic learning tasks
- Empowering the learner, especially through experience of the knowledge construction process
- Collaborative learning
- Engaging in cognitive process rather than acquisition of cognitive product
- Developing self-awareness of the knowledge construction process.

Constructivism changes the roles of the learner and tutor. The knowledge transmission model is downplayed or totally rejected. The role of the tutor is not to ensure the efficient transmission of a body of knowledge. It changes to being a facilitator, coach, organizer and supporter of the learner. The learner may be engaged in problem-based learning where the problems are placed in as authentic a context as possible. Science education becomes viewed not as the delivery of the science curriculum, but as engaging the learners in the processes of scientific thinking.

It is beyond the scope of this chapter to go into a detailed review and critique of constructivism. Such a review is provided in Boyle (1997). It should be noted, however, that the application of appropriate constructivist principles for science education needs to be clarified and supported by evidence, and that the complexity and abstraction of scientific and mathematical knowledge may prove particularly challenging. The key challenge for those designing multimedia e-learning is therefore to address how to best produce authentic, rich interaction in abstract domains.

The discussion now moves on to consider how the design principles generated by constructivism impact on designing multimedia e-learning for science. In particular, it looks at the challenges provided by the complexity and abstract nature of much scientific knowledge.

Tackling abstraction and complexity in science education

Science is often about producing abstract explanations that frequently seem far removed from the everyday experience of the student. These ideas may be expressed in a form that commonly seems complex to the learner. The problem is exacerbated because the tutor is very familiar with these concepts and may fail to appreciate the problems faced by the learner. Educational multimedia can have a great deal to offer in tacking these twin problems.

It has been argued that strategic approaches to educational multimedia design operate at a high level in that they provide a sense of the direction to be taken. There is also a need for a set of design principles and techniques that map from strategic guidance to the construction of real, usable systems. The chapter now focuses on two important design techniques elaborated in constructivist approaches to dealing with the problems of abstraction and complexity. The first technique is 'interactive visualization', a way of making abstract knowledge more accessible. The second is 'scaffolding' – the provision and timely removal of transitional support in dealing with complex learning tasks. These techniques have supported and extended the constructivist emphasis on rich, authentic interaction. The application of these pedagogical principles enables us to create systems that bring science alive for the learner.

Papert, interactive visualization and transitional objects

An initial entry into these design principles is provided by the work of Papert (1980), who developed pedagogically informed approaches to constructive computer-supported learning. Papert worked for two years with Jean Piaget, the father of developmental cognitive psychology. Papert, a leading mathematician, explored how these ideas could help children learn about mathematics and science. He developed, in his words, a series of 'powerful ideas' to facilitate the child's cognitive development. These ideas were implemented in a computer language called Logo. The use of this computer language reflects the technology of the day, but the design ideas resonate through to modern developments.

Papert was particularly concerned with how children could make the transition from everyday familiar experience to the abstract world of mathematics, as he was concerned that many mathematical concepts seem too abstract, removed and alien for children to grasp. He used a transitional object, the Logo 'turtle', together with turtle graphics to facilitate this transition.

The Logo turtle is initially a small robot that moves across the floor and is controlled from a computer. This transitional object enables the child to make sense of the task in everyday terms and facilitates moving into the world of the abstract. The Logo turtle can be controlled by entering familiar-sounding commands on the computer, like 'forward', 'left' and 'right'. These commands are used to get the turtle to draw shapes. Later, and more abstractly, the turtle becomes a cursor on a computer screen. The shapes are then drawn on the monitor screen using the same commands.

Learning about geometric problem-solving is then extrapolated from knowledge of the child's familiar, intuitive knowledge of body geometry. Thus, when children are asked to draw a circle on a computer using Logo commands, one child may be encouraged to tell another how to walk in a circle. The commands, which are basically 'forward' and 'turn', become the basis for a program for the turtle. As a consequence of this approach, one eight-year-old boy argued with Papert that a circle is really a pentagon with lots of little sides. This is a quite profound mathematical insight, but it also derives from the child's own knowledge because he or she discovered this insight through working with Logo. The idea of transitional objects, or transitional contexts, is a crucial one for the design of interactive learning environments for complex, abstract skills.

Papert developed another idea, which is highly relevant to modern multimedia e-learning – the concept of 'microworlds'. These provide virtual environments where learners can actively explore certain abstract concepts. For example, in a 'Newtonian' world, children can manipulate objects and see how they behave under different gravitational conditions. The learner can change the size or direction of gravity in the microworld and explore the effects. Papert argued that this provides a better basis for coming to terms with Newtonian physics than do abstract descriptions in textbooks. Multimedia technology provides the basis for much more sophisticated microworlds than could be created in Logo, but it is the concept of microworlds that provides a very powerful technique for constructing sophisticated interactive learning environments.

Papert's approach does not provide teaching regimes but child-centred learning environments, where learning is treated as an active constructive process (Papert 1980, 1993). The power of interactive visualization has become a staple feature of modern multimedia e-learning. Systems such as 'Interactive Physics' allow both teachers and pupils to manipulate simulations of physical phenomena and observe the results. Science-oriented educational multimedia often encourage active participation and provide graphic feedback to the learner. Figure 2.2.1, for example,

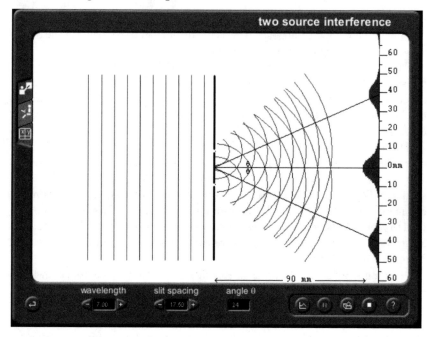

Figure 2.2.1 Oscillations and waves: two-source interference.

Source: Fable™ *Multimedia Oscillations and Waves* CD-ROM

provides an illustration of a system where students can manipulate parameters in the study of wave patterns and observe the result.

Scaffolding

Scaffolding is the provision and timely removal of transitional support in dealing with learning tasks. It is a powerful technique that was initially revealed in studies of child learning. From the early to mid-1990s, scaffolding was increasingly embodied as a design feature of multimedia learning environments for science. The use of scaffolding was originally revealed by studying how parents naturally support their children's learning (Bruner 1975). It took a while for this principle to become translated into a design feature in online learning environments. The principle then became particularly salient in systems dealing with learning in science and technology.

This design principle has been strongly emphasized in the work of Linn (1996) and her colleagues. Linn has used an instructional framework called 'scaffolded knowledge integration' to construct a learning environment for middle and high school students to learn about science. The process of conducting a school scientific project is systematically analysed into a series of activities. These activities include: students stating their initial position on the topic; gathering evidence on this topic (from the Internet and other sources); reflecting on the evidence and

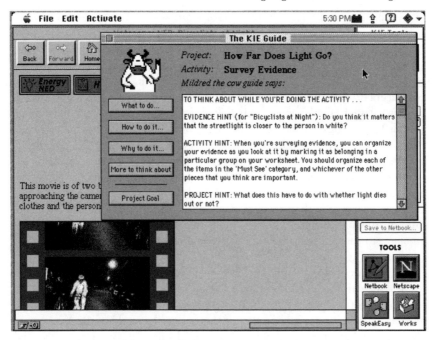

Figure 2.2.2 The *Knowledge Integration Environment*, illustrating scaffolding support for learning activities.

engaging in group discussions to clarify alternatives; and integrating the evidence to form a scientific argument. Linn and her colleagues developed a set of tools to support and scaffold learner activities in these major activities. The activity of reflecting on the evidence, for example, is supported by a tool that provides prompts, hints and examples to help students engage in reflective practice. This is illustrated in Figure 2.2.2, in the form of the *Knowledge Integration Environment* (KIE). The original KIE project has been succeeded by a similar project, the *Web-based Inquiry Science Environment* (WISE) project. The aims of this project echo those of the KIE approach, but the software is completely web-based.

Jackson identifies 'key scaffolding strategies' in supporting high-school children in modelling scientific problems (Jackson *et al.* 1996). One scaffolding strategy is to ground the 'abstract' task in terms of familiar objects and relationships. For example, a photograph of a stream that the children studied is used as a background in a project on the study of pollution. This 'personalized representation', Jackson argues, grounds the learning in a familiar, supportive context.

A key challenge in science is how to bridge between familiar and new forms of representation. In studying scientific problems, learners are exposed simultaneously to familiar and new representations of the 'same' information (Jackson *et al.* 1996). For example, the English statement 'stream quality decreases as phosphate is added' is juxtaposed with a graph providing a mathematical representation of this relationship. The students use English phrases, such as 'a lot', to construct expressions describing scientific relationships. These phrases are selected from lists provided in dialogue boxes. These again support the transition into using mathematical terms. The association of the new representation with the familiar base of experience aids the transition to understanding new, more mathematical means of representation. Jackson also emphasizes the role of immediate visual feedback contingent on the learner's actions to support students in testing their hypotheses.

Guzdial used a similar approach to help engineering students learn about design (Guzdial *et al.* 1996). Authentic problems are often complex; if they are to be used effectively in learning, students must be supported in handling this complexity. Software support was provided for three main types of activities: expressing and visualizing ideas; access to problem-solving resources; and collaboration through electronic discussion groups. The learners could access a case library, for example, to obtain examples of the experiences and outcomes of others involved in similar problem solving situations Guzdial claims that the features of this environment emulate, to some extent, 'how a professional chemical engineer might support (scaffold) an apprentice or intern' (Guzdial *et al.* 1996: 45).

The use of appropriate multimedia systems greatly enhances the opportunities for dealing with the problems of abstraction and complexity that are inherent in learning about science. Multimedia e-learning can support the visualization of abstract knowledge, scaffolding the transition into the world of the abstract and empowering the learner as a problem solver in rich virtual environments. The challenge for those designing educational multimedia is to know how and when to use scaffolding to achieve these ends and also what to use as transitional objects.

Design for accessibility

Rich environments are no use to a student who cannot access the learning environment. The issue of design for accessibility is therefore a crucial one. Apart from the moral considerations, educational institutions are under a legal obligation to provide accessible learning environments. Rather than being considered as an 'add-on' to the normal design process, accessible design should be built in from the start. Design for accessibility should thus benefit everyone and not just users with disabilities. This is part of a movement towards 'universal design', defined as:

> The design of products and environments that can be used and experienced by people of all ages and abilities, to the greatest extent possible, without adaptation.
>
> (Banes and Seale 2002: 3)

The move towards accessible design has been given considerable extra impetus by increased legal requirements. In the UK, the Special Educational Needs and Disability Act (SENDA) (2001) extends the provisions of earlier legislation to cover educational services, including e-learning. SENDA makes it an offence to discriminate against a person for reasons relating to their disability (HMSO 2001). There is also an anticipatory requirement built into the legislation. This places an onus on educational institutions to anticipate and pre-empt the needs of potential students. E-learning materials must thus be designed to meet the needs of students with disabilities.

Legal pressure has led to improvements in the authoring tools available for e-learning and multimedia development. For example, in the USA, Section 508 of the Rehabilitation Act requires federal agencies procuring information technology to ensure that the technology is accessible to people with disabilities. This has put accessibility high on the agenda in the USA, where many of the software tools are developed, and companies have placed a strong emphasis on supporting accessibility in their authoring tools. The most important aspect of design for accessibility, however, is not the tools but the principles that guide the design process.

A key target area for accessible design is systems developed for the World Wide Web. The World Wide Web consortium (W3C) is responsible for the Web Accessibility Initiative (WAI) (W3C 2003). It has developed principles within a wider context that ensure web technologies support accessibility, while developing tools to evaluate and facilitate accessibility. These principles affect content, navigation and page layout. The WAI-DA (Web Accessibility Initiative Design-for-All) project in Europe has complemented this work with activities relevant to the European context (ICTSB 2000). A similar set of precepts has been advocated by TechDis, a UK-based service providing advice and resources for disability and educational use of ICT (TechDis, n.d.).

Educational multimedia designers should not only address the issues of making material accessible but also should find innovative ways of using technology to support students with disabilities. The challenge of accessibility should enrich, not impoverish, educational multimedia design. As Banes and Seale point out, the application of these principles should not involve reducing design to some lowest common denominator:

> It is important to acknowledge that increasing accessibility does not mean compromising the impact and creativity of design, it is a matter of awareness and sensitivity to the issues involved.
>
> (Banes and Seale 2002: 4)

The design principles have to be mapped onto existing technology. The designer therefore needs to be aware of the strengths and limitations of assistive technologies used to help people with various disabilities to access computers and the Internet.

There is a wide range of assistive technology products. The one of which most people are most aware is the screen-reader. The TechDis database, however, contains over 2,500 assistive technology products. The TechDis Accessibility Database (TAD) can be used to identify suitable technology and sources of supply (TechDis 2003). TAD supports several forms of search including one by 'learning and teaching' approach. By selecting a disability and then a teaching and learning situation, the user can retrieve information on the products suitable for that disability and educational context. In many cases, there are linked case studies that illustrate the use of the technologies.

The use of assistive technologies may lead to situations requiring consideration in the broader design process. Thus, screen-readers provide a different experience of a web page to users with visual impairment. Instead of seeing the page as a whole, the user has to work through the features sequentially. If the screen is divided into columns or frames, care has to be taken in design that the screen-reader does not follow the wrong sequence, leading to garbled text. A screen-reader will read all of one column before proceeding to the top of the next. If the text was arranged to be read across the rows in a table then the output of the screen-reader will be highly confused. This does not mean that tables, for example, cannot be used in web pages, but care needs to be taken in anticipating how a screen-reader will access the text. To this end, there are a number of validation tools available that check for possible problems with websites.

The use of appropriate tools in itself, however, cannot ensure that web material is accessible. It requires 'deliberate development, testing and evaluation informed by human judgment' (Witt and McDermott 2002: 44). Witt and McDermott provide a good overview for developing accessible websites. The book in which their chapter appears provides articles on a wide range of accessibility issues (Phipps *et al.* 2002). It also provides extensive sets of web links to relevant information and services.

Learning objects

The concept of learning objects is having an increasing impact on how educational multimedia are produced, disseminated and used. There are at least two conceptions of learning objects. Both these views are relevant to science education. The first approach is concerned with producing standardized, interoperable learning 'packages' where educational resources from any computer-based learning environment ought to be transferable and usable in any other environment. The second approach is to view a learning object as a relatively small, self-contained 'chunk' of learning. In this approach, the emphasis in creating educational multimedia shifts from creating monolithic systems to creating repositories of learning objects. These objects can then be selected and organized to meet the needs of the particular courses and learner cohorts.

The implications of these developments for users of educational multimedia are potentially immense. However, there are challenges to be met, not least in ensuring that learning objects are standardized in order to create an open environment where users can select and mix resources from different vendors and run them within the managed learning environment of their choice. Users will no longer be locked into proprietary systems. The second potential advance is even more striking. E-learning systems could be composed of reusable and preferably re-purposable components (learning objects). Instead of being presented with finished systems, the user will be able to configure and 'design' the learning environment to suit his or her needs and preferences.

This section will briefly review the international work on learning object standardization. This will be followed by a discussion of learning objects as 'chunks' of learning that provide the flexible building blocks for larger systems.

Standardization and learning objects

Standardization provides an important base for the efficient interchange of ideas in science. Standards in terminology, measuring systems and modes of structuring journal papers enable the efficient communication and critique of ideas that is so central to scientific progress. It has been argued strongly that e-learning would benefit in a similar way from standards that support the efficient structuring, retrieval and reuse of 'learning objects'. These standards aim to provide an environment where the user can select and combine the best e-learning objects, rather than being tied to specific vendor systems.

A number of major international bodies have been involved in extensive work to create standards for the packaging and interchange of learning objects. The IMS (originally Instructional Management Systems) Global Learning Consortium, for example, has been prominent in developing specifications for a number of standards (for a view of how IMS and other bodies work to produce these standards, see Duval 2001). These specifications are submitted to standardization bodies, such as the Institute of Electrical and Electronics Engineers (IEEE), for acceptance and ratification as accepted standards. The two areas of most immediate concern to this discussion are learning object metadata and learning object packaging.

One aim is to provide a basis for searching repositories of online learning objects in order to retrieve objects suitable for a particular purpose. An example of such a repository is the Universitas 21 learning resource catalogue (Koppi and Hodgson 2001). To aid these searches 'metadata' are attached to the e-learning object. Metadata are 'data about data'. They involve descriptions that are attached to learning objects that specify information required to catalogue and retrieve these objects. Different specification bodies have produced their own variants of metadata descriptions. One of the fullest descriptions for learning objects was developed by the IMS and, in June 2002, this was accepted and ratified by the IEEE as an international standard (see IEEE 2002 for a draft of this standard).

Metadata have to be attached in some way to the learning object. Specifications have also been developed for 'packaging' learning objects. The IMS has produced a specification in this area that specifies a standard structure which contains two main subparts – a 'manifest', to which the metadata and other required information are added in a standard format, and the learning object files themselves (for example, a series of HTML files giving a lesson on a topic in physics). This structured information can be compressed in one container file and transported between systems.

The main aim of standardization is to achieve interoperability between components created in different authoring environments. As Duval points out:

> Standardisation is a requirement of larger-scale deployment of learning technologies, as it prevents users from being locked into proprietary systems.
>
> (Duval 2001: 485)

When we buy an electrical plug, we do not worry who produced it; we expect it to plug into any of the power outlets in our house. The standardization initiatives aim to achieve the same basis for the universal, flexible use of learning objects. We will be able to retrieve the learning objects we want (with searches based on the standardized metadata), then download the objects, and 'plug' them into our learning system.

It is beyond the remit of this chapter to explore in detail the full range of standardization activity. Calverley (2002) provides a good guide to the relevance of this work to creating reusable learning materials. The main specification and standardization bodies all maintain active websites. The main organizations involved are: IMS, Dublin Core consortium, Aviation Industry Computer-based Training Committee and Advanced Distributed Learning Initiative. The main accreditation bodies, that is the bodies that ratify these proposals as international standards, are the IEEE and the International Standards Organization. For those who wish to explore these issues further, the Centre for Educational Technology Interoperability Standards provides an informative website for activity in these areas.

Objects as chunks of learning

Standardization is making a significant impact on the development of e-learning. However, in order to provide a non-contentious basis for standardization, a learning object is defined to be almost anything. Thus, the IEEE LOM draft standard defined a learning object as:

> any entity, digital or non-digital, that may be used for learning, education or training.
>
> (IEEE 2002)

Even this broad wording was not retained in the published standard. Despite the thrust of this statement, there is a widespread perception that learning objects are relatively self-contained 'chunks' of learning. This view is not incompatible with wider standardization work. These 'chunks' can be packaged and described using the standards. However, it does reflect a narrower and more precise view of 'learning objects'. A representative collection of multimedia learning objects, covering chemistry, physics, mathematics and life science, is found on the National Learning Network website (see NLN 2003).

The 'learning chunks' approach can provide a productive basis for opening up questions that are bypassed in wider standardization work. This theoretical exploration reveals the potentially revolutionary impact that standardized learning objects may have on the production, distribution and use of educational multimedia resources.

Boyle and Cook (2001) argue that the main approaches to standardization have taken a theoretically weak approach to solving the problems of reuse and recombination, in part because learning object standards are described as 'pedagogically neutral' (IEEE 2002). The packaging and metadata therefore provide ways of locating objects and linking them like pieces in a jigsaw, but:

There is no guarantee, however, that the jigsaw will make pedagogical sense.
(Boyle and Cook 2001: 103).

Boyle and Cook (2001) argue for a pedagogically informed approach to the description of learning objects. They also propose that, for learning objects to be truly reusable, they need to be designed with that intent in mind. Adding packaging and metadata after the event may be all that is possible for extant systems. However, learning resources in the future should be authored for reusability. This requires a clear conceptual basis for how a pedagogically sound, reusable learning object might appear.

Boyle (2003) proposes a set of principles based on a synthesis from software engineering and pedagogy. Software engineering is concerned with the design, development and maintenance of large, complex software systems. A major challenge in software engineering has been the issue of developing systems that can be updated and adapted over a period of time. To achieve these goals, software engineering has developed principles to guide the construction of the components within the system. The first principle is that of *cohesion* – each unit should do one thing and only one thing (Sommerville 1996; Pressman and Ince 2000). A direct link can be made to the idea of learning objectives in pedagogical theory. This mapping suggests that each learning object should be based on one clear learning purpose or objective.

In order to provide this freedom to order learning objects, a further design principle is important. This is the principle of *minimized coupling*, which states that the unit should have minimal bindings to other units. Thus, the content of one learning object should not refer to and use material in another learning object in such a way as to create necessary dependencies. In a web application, for example, the text should not have embedded URLs that point to necessary information in other objects. Boyle (2003) argues that links to other objects should be managed on a separate area of the screen. He argues that learning objects should be cohesive units based around clear learning goals with managed coupling to other learning objects.

Repositories of cohesive, de-coupled objects provide maximum freedom for the local tutor to select and order learning objects to suit the needs of the learners they serve. The local tutors do not have to choose from off-the-shelf learning programs. They are provided with the building blocks to create their own learning programs. The same materials may be used to augment traditional class-based instruction or to create specially tailored courses, such as short, intense commercial courses. The role of the tutor is thus enhanced from one of informed selection of multimedia to the tailored construction of multimedia learning or training courses.

Learning objects have to be developed to facilitate this goal. One way of achieving this is to create compound learning objects (see Figure 2.2.3). Compound objects are structured collections of individual objects. Boyle (2003) points to examples developed at London Metropolitan University. A base object is created as a standard web page. The only significant difference is that, following a

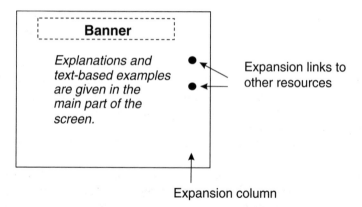

Figure 2.2.3 Schematic layout for a compound learning object.

design pattern suggested by Lyardet *et al.* (1998), all expansion links are organized in a separate expansion column on the right of the screen. These links then point to other independent objects.

The shaping or 're-purposing' of the compound object through the addition and deletion of links is straightforward. The local tutor can thus enrich the default object by adding his or her own links, or shape the object by deleting and adding 'replacement' links. The main text content of the base object is written so as to provide a self-contained learning object that will operate even if no links are present. Since it relies on text, this learning object may not be very exciting. However, access to multimedia objects through the expansion column can provide a very rich learning experience.

Compound objects provide a mechanism for providing alternative objects for a wide range of learners. The same material can be explained in text form in one object and through an interactive animation in another. This approach also provides an enriched environment for a broad base of students. Providing multiple perspectives on the same task or knowledge domain is advocated by many constructivists (Swan 1994; Grabinger and Dunlop 2000).

Higher-order objects, such as syllabus lists, may contain an ordered set of pointers to the learning objects. This is easily implemented on the Web. This provides greater flexibility in courseware organization, because the two layers of course organization and learning resources have been separated. Different syllabuses or course structures can then easily be generated, based on the same repository of learning objects.

The implication of this type of approach is to empower the local tutor. We can move from a situation where the course tutor selects a prefabricated multimedia learning environment to one where the tutor is empowered to construct and individually tailor courses based on repositories of reusable multimedia learning resources. The concept of learning objects is driving educational multimedia in new, exciting directions. The users of the multimedia may become actively involved in shaping the nature of the educational experience in ways that previously were seldom possible.

Pedagogical quality and learning objects

What ensures the pedagogical quality of learning objects? The learning objects standardization work says little on this crucial issue. Rather, this has been about agreeing the broadest possible consensus about descriptive and packaging structures. It has not been about pedagogical quality. In designing and evaluating learning objects, the pedagogical principles discussed in the earlier sections of the chapter come into play. We want learning objects that are not only cohesive, decoupled and packaged, but also are pedagogically exciting. Design principles, such as rich interactive visualization and scaffolding, should inform the design and evolution of learning objects.

There is a danger of structuring learning objects as mini 'knowledge acquisition' exercises. Here the multimedia may have a limited 'click and show' functionality, with quizzes to test the knowledge gained. The surface media presentation is fine, but the structuring of learning interactions remains limited. Many of the science learning objects currently (2003) in the NLN learning objects repository, for example, seem broadly to follow this format. Higher-order, constructive use of the resources has to be supplied by the teacher. By contrast, the 'Colour Harmonies' object in the agriculture section of the same NLN repository supports richer user-oriented interactivity. It encourages user-centred exploration of the colour wheel and provides contextual relevance through examples of flower border schemes that implement the 'abstract' harmonies of the colour wheel (see NLN 2003). Learning objects thus provide a structuring format that provides many advantages for reusability, but there is no guarantee of pedagogic quality. That depends on the critical application of the kind of principles discussed earlier in the paper.

Summary

The leitmotiv of this chapter has been the increasing empowerment of 'users' in the design process. The first half examined strategic approaches to educational multimedia design and the application of design principles to deal with the issues of complexity and abstraction. It argued that traditional instructional systems design aimed to provide more efficient means for the acquisition of knowledge. This provides tools and resources to enable the tutor to become a more effective organizer and manager of learning. Constructivism changes the emphasis to engaging learners as active, critical participants in the knowledge construction process. In this approach, skills acquired in critical thinking, problem-solving and communication are emphasized. This approach has had a strong influence in multimedia e-learning design that provides resources and tools to support tutors in facilitating these active learning processes.

The constructivists emphasize the need to 'engage' the learner. However, this is clearly impossible if the learner cannot access the e-learning material. The central part of the chapter discussed the issue of designing accessible learning resources and making them available. There are several sources that provide clear guidelines in this area. However, in the end, this provides a challenge for the creative design and deployment of multimedia e-learning.

The final section has dealt with learning objects and standards. The development of national and international repositories of learning objects, based on agreed standards, provides a basis for the specialization and tailoring of multimedia education that is new. This has the potential to greatly enhance the creative, constructive role of tutors in the design process. It also opens up possibilities for learners to choose tailored learning environments that suit their needs. This is a development that will take several years to develop fully, not least because there is an ongoing need to clarify the theory, both pedagogical and technical, which will provide a firm basis for portable, pedagogically effective learning objects.

References

Banes, D. and Seale, J. (2002) 'Accessibility and inclusivity in higher education: an overview', in L. Phipps, A. Sutherland and J. Seale (eds) *Access All Areas: Disability, Technology and Learning*, JISC, TechDis Service and Association for Learning Technology.

Boyle, T. (1997) *Design for Multimedia Learning*, Harlow: Prentice Hall.

—— (2003) 'Design principles for authoring dynamic, reusable learning objects', *Australian Journal of Educational Technology* 19(1): 46–58.

——. and Cook, J. (2001) 'Towards a pedagogically sound basis for learning object portability and re-use', paper prepared for the *ASCILITE 2001* conference, available on the Web at <http://www.ascilite.org.au/conferences/melbourne01/pdf/papers/boylet.pdf> (last accessed 14 March 2003).

Bruner, J. S. (1975) 'The ontogenesis of speech acts', *Journal of Child Language* 2: 1–19.

Calverley, G. (2002) 'Distributed learning project guide: creating reusable materials', unpublished paper, available on the Web at <http://www.cetis.ac.uk/groups/20010809144711/FR20020618103339> (last accessed 14 March 2003).

Cunningham, D. J., Duffy, T. M. and Knuth, R. (1993) 'The textbook of the future', in C. McKnight, A. Dillon and J. Richardson (eds) *Hypertext: A Psychological Perspective*, New York and London: Ellis Horwood.

Duval, E. (2001) 'Standardized metadata for education: a status report', in C. Montgomerie and V. Jarmo (eds) *Ed-Media 2001*, World Conference on Educational Multimedia and Hypermedia, AACE, Tampere, Finland.

Fenrich, P. (1997) *Practical Guidelines for Creating Instructional Multimedia Applications*, Fort Worth: Dryden Press.

Gagné, R. M. (1965) *The Conditions of Learning*, New York: Holt, Rinehart and Winston.

—— and Briggs, L. J. (1979) *Principles of Instructional Design*, New York and London: Holt, Rinehart and Winston.

Grabinger, R. S. and Dunlop, J. C. (2000) 'Rich environments for active learning: a definition', In D. Squires, G. Conole and G. Jacobs (eds) *The Changing Face of Learning Technology*, Cardiff: University of Wales (Cardiff).

Guzdial, M., Kolodner, J., Hmelo, C., Narayanan, H., Carlson, D., Rappin, N., Hubscher, R., Turns, J. and Newsletter, W. (1996) 'Computer support for learning through complex problem solving', *Communications of the ACM* 39(4): 43–5.

HMSO (2001) *Special Educational Needs and Disability Act 2001*, London: The Stationery Office.

Information and Communication Technology Standards Board Project Team (ICTSB) (2000) *Design for All – Final Background Report*, available on the Web at <http://www.ict.etsi.org/Activities/Documents/ICTSB%20Main%20Report%20.pdf> (last accessed 14 March 2003).

Institute of Electrical and Electronics Engineers (IEEE) (2002) *Draft Standard for Learning Object Metadata*, New York, IEEE, available on the Web at <http://ltsc.ieee.org/doc/wg12/LOM_WD6_4.pdf> (last accessed 14 March 2003).

Jackson, S. L., Stratford, S. J., Krajcik, J. and Soloway, E. (1996) 'A learner-centred tool for students building models', *Communications of the ACM* 39(4): 48–9.

Koppi, T. and Hodgson, L. (2001) 'Universitas 21 learning resource catalogue using IMS metadata and a new classification of learning objects' (pp. 998–1001), in C. Montgomerie and V. Jarmo (eds) *Ed-Media 2001, World Conference on Educational Multimedia and Hypermedia*, AACE, Tampere, Finland.

Linn, M. C. (1996) 'Key to the information highway', *Communications of the ACM* 39(4): 34–5.

Lyardet, F., Ross, G. and Scwabe, D. (1998) 'Using design patterns in educational multimedia applications', In T. Ottmann and I. Tomek (eds) *Ed Media and Ed Telecom '98, Proceedings of the 10th World Conference on Educational Multimedia and Hypermedia*, AACE, Freiburg, Germany.

National Learning Network (NLN) (2003) *Materials, Development and Implementation*, Coventry: BECTA, Available on the Web at <http://www.nln.ac.uk/materials.asp> (last accessed 14 March 2003).

Papert, S. (1980) *Mindstorms: Children, Computers and Powerful Ideas*, New York: Basic Books.

—— (1993) *The Children's Machine*, New York: Basic Books.

Phipps, L., Sutherland, A. and Seale, J. (2002) *Access All Areas: Disability, Technology and Learning*, JISC, TechDis Service and Association for Learning Technology.

Pressman, R. S. and Ince, D. (2000) *Software Engineering: A Practitioner's Approach* (5th edn), Boston and London: McGraw-Hill.

Price, R. V. (1991) *Computer-aided Instruction: A Guide for Authors*, Pacific Grove: Brooks/Cole.

Scaife, M. and Rogers, Y. (2001) 'Informing the design of a virtual environment to support learning in children', *International Journal of Human-Computer Studies* 55: 115–43.

Sommerville, I. (1996) *Software Engineering* (5th edn), Wokingham: Addison-Wesley.

Swan, K. (1994) 'History, hypermedia and criss-crossed conceptual landscapes', *Journal of Educational Multimedia and Hypermedia* 3(2): 120–39.

TechDis (n.d.). *Welcome to the TechDis Web Site*, York: The Technologies Centre, available on the Web at <http://www.techdis.ac.uk/> (last accessed 14 March 2003).

—— (2003) *The TechDis Accessibility Database*, Brighton: University of Sussex, available on the Web at <http://www.niad.sussex.ac.uk/> (last accessed 14 March 2003).

Underwood J., Cavendish, S., Dowling, S., Fogelman, K. and Lawson, T. (1996) 'Are integrated learning systems effective learning tools?', *Computers and Education* 26(1–3): 33–40.

Witt, N. A. J. and McDermott, A. P. (2002) 'Achieving SENDA compliance for an academic web site: an art or a science', in L. Phipps, A. Sutherland and J. Seale (eds) *Access All Areas: Disability, Technology and Learning*, JISC, TechDis Service and Association for Learning Technology.

World Wide Web Consortium (W3C) (2003) *Web Accessibility Initiative*, available on the Web at <http://www.w3.org/WAI/> (last accessed 12 March 2003).

2.3 Evaluation of ICT

An overview for learning and teaching science

Martin Oliver

Evaluation has, in recent years, become an integral part of education. It is a requirement for funded research into the use of information and communications technology (ICT) in education and an expected part of institutions' ongoing activities, for example. But what exactly is evaluation and how is it relevant to learning and teaching science?

This chapter will introduce the idea of evaluation, considering how different assumptions about what it is, and what it is for, shape the way that it is planned and carried out. This will provide the necessary groundwork for the consideration of specific issues in evaluating ICT in the context of science learning.

What is evaluation?

One unavoidable issue is that evaluation, like so many complex social practices, is hard to define because what 'counts' as evaluation is contested. Typically, however, evaluation involves both describing and judging, in terms of both merit and worth (Guba and Lincoln 1981). These concepts need explanation. As described by Guba and Lincoln (1981), both are conceived as being part of a broader concept of 'value', but with merit referring to intrinsic qualities while worth refers to extrinsic or contextual value. These definitions are made problematic, however, by recent thinking about social practice (for example, Potter and Wetherell 1987), which calls into question whether we can talk of things as having intrinsic properties when all we can access is our experiences of them. The alternative to talking about intrinsic properties is to take the position that our understanding of things is socially constructed – in other words, we understand things (including concepts) by using them, seeing others use them and talking about this. If this is the case, then all aspects of an object's value are extrinsic and contextual. For this reason, it makes sense to talk in a less precise but more intuitive way about things having worth if their value can be determined in terms of input/output efficiency (for example, if they are financially effective) and merit if their value arises from moral or philosophical positions (for example, if a particular science initiative encourages independence and reflection, whether or not it is cost-effective).

This emphasis on judging may be typical, but it is not universal. Not all evaluators feel that evaluation should both describe and judge; those who position themselves in the ethnographic tradition, for example, argue that their work should be non-judgemental, concentrating instead on providing credible and plausible accounts of observed practice (Jones 1998a).

A brief history of evaluation

It is reasonable to wonder why there is such debate and how these different positions have emerged. Guba and Lincoln (1981) chart a brief history of educational evaluation from the use of achievement tests in the 1890s onwards. Initially, 'evaluation' was a subsidiary concept to measurement and the emphasis was on the scientific testing of individual differences using standardized tests, often with little reference to the curriculum (or wider context) from which the students were drawn. However, in the early 1960s, educational evaluators began expressing their dissatisfaction with this approach, arguing that studies needed to support refinement and improvement, not simply provide judgements that endorsed or condemned courses.

Another particularly important shift came with the rejection of the established evaluation format (which was described as the 'agricultural-botany paradigm', reflecting the idea that curricula were 'applied to' students like chemical fertilizers on plant crops) as being unable to meet its own criteria of objectivity or to help educational practitioners. Moreover, it was argued that the model of hypothesis testing was simply not the best way to understand complex real-world situations which, unlike laboratory settings, were not amenable to control. Instead, a more open-ended, exploratory approach was proposed (for example, Parlett and Hamilton 1972). Their approach emphasized the need to follow up unexpected developments, to show an awareness of the influence of context (which traditional methods had sought to eradicate through controlled experiments) and thus to 'illuminate' the focus of the study.

The rise of a new approach did not lead to the old being abandoned; indeed, both remain visible in educational research today and the controversies over method and meaning that led to the split remain unresolved (Hammersley 1997). There have been numerous attempts to unify the two schools; although none has been successful, these attempts have given rise to yet other approaches. Patton (1997), for example, has suggested that the argument between the two traditions has distracted evaluators from a more important issue: that no matter how closely a study adheres to the principles of its tradition, if the report that is produced sits on a shelf unread, then the investigation was pointless. His writing characterizes utilization-focused evaluation, which starts from the premise that a good evaluation is one that enables people to do things. Usefulness is thus privileged over rigour, and any method can be used so long as the audience of the report will find it credible. However, the importance of rigour is not ignored and utilization-focused evaluators still aspire towards it. When a 'quick and dirty' evaluation will be helpful, they will make compromises, however, in order to ensure that their study is timely and useful.

Another important trend in educational evaluation has been the rise of 'action research'. This has its roots in the work of the psychologist Kurt Lewin, who sought to understand and model how individuals acted in society (Lewin 1952). He emphasized the importance of working with the people being studied in order to effect change, an approach that resonated with the problems facing teachers who sought to evaluate what took place in their own classrooms (McNiff 1988). Action research has developed into a movement within education that places great value on the ideas of democracy, emancipation and collaboration; that evaluation should not be something done to subjects, but done with participants (Kemmis 1996). The evaluation process thus develops iteratively: it moves through cycles of planning, acting, observing and reflecting which build upon each other, sometimes progressing (for example, by developing and refining a model of classroom practice, or taking an increasingly detailed focus on a particular issue), sometimes diverging (for example, by highlighting an important but previously neglected issue that the evaluator considers worthy of investigation), depending on the interests and values of those involved (McNiff 1988).

While these different schools of thought seem to imply that educational evaluation has moved steadily away from its roots in experimentation, this is not always the case. Particular forms of evaluation based on quantitative methods and aspiring to scientific status have come to the fore in the current era of educational accountability, even though it has been noted that policy-based, outcomes-driven audits of practice run the risk of distorting rather than reporting the practice they seek to describe (Blalock 1999). Additionally, over the past decade or so, the idea of evidence-based practice has arisen in medicine and there are now calls from policy makers to adopt similar approaches in education (Davies *et al.* 2000). This approach places great emphasis on the idea of systematic review, which involves drawing together disparate research studies and summarizing their findings in order to make recommendations to policy makers. In order to do this, a hierarchy of evidence has been drawn up that states explicitly the degree of faith that the method places in different methodologies. Randomized controlled trials sit at the top of the hierarchy as a gold standard, with qualitative methods (such as all those advocated by Parlett and Hamilton 1972) relegated to the level of anecdotal evidence, either discounted entirely or, at best, given a role in supporting the findings from favoured types of study. As a reaction against 'unsystematic' research, it appears that educational evaluation has come full circle.

The current situation is thus rich but complicated, with some defining evaluation in terms of adherence to particular methods, others explaining it as a process embodying specified values and yet others as social performance that should support the audiences' ability to act. In the next section, the process of evaluation will be outlined, drawing primarily on this final point of view.

The strategy and politics of evaluation

Although the concept of evaluation remains contested, this has not stopped people from evaluating. For this simple reason, it is possible to provide advice and support to those who are interested in undertaking evaluation by drawing on a model of professional evaluation practice (Conole and Oliver 2002).

As part of the creation of an online evaluation tool kit (Institute for Learning and Research Technology (ILRT) n.d.), a model of evaluation design was developed that split the process into a sequence of steps. Of course, this is an idealized representation of practice; in reality, progress through these steps is unlikely to be linear and not all studies or evaluators will follow every step.

According to this model, evaluation consists of the following stages:

1　Identification of the audience(s) for the evaluation
2　Selection of an evaluation question
3　Choice of an evaluation methodology
4　Choice of data collection methods
5　Choice of data analysis methods
6　Selection of the most appropriate format(s) for reporting the findings to the audience.

These steps can be thought of as a combination of contextual (1, 2 and 6) and mechanical (3, 4 and 5) or, alternatively, as strategic and tactical choices. Placing the audience and their needs above methodology locates this model firmly in the school of utilization-focused evaluation; in other traditions, the methodology would influence the kinds of questions that were considered to be acceptable – so, for example, experimental studies would require well-defined hypotheses, whereas illuminative studies would typically involve open-ended questions.

In order to explore this model in more detail and to illustrate issues such as those which arise when designing a study, each of these steps is explored in the following sections.

Identification of the audience(s) for the evaluation

The first step in an evaluation, it is proposed, is to identify its audience (Box 2.3.1). Making this assertion positions evaluation as a political and social activity (Patton 1997). Typically, the identity of an audience will be clear – in funded studies, for example, whoever has commissioned the work will expect to be an audience. Traditionally, this group might have been considered to be the *only* audience for the work. However, more recently, evaluation has been reconceived as being about more than simply answering policy makers' questions; instead, it has been repositioned and reconceptualized as a process that can contribute to both organizational learning (Preskill and Torres 1999) and individuals' learning (Patton 1997). Patton has also argued that this process of learning need not be restricted simply to receiving information (for example, by being told the outcome); it can consist of

Box 2.3.1   **Examples of identifying an audience**

Few published papers include a section describing how the audience for the study was selected so, by way of an example, a project's dissemination strategy has been selected. The Dissemination of Information Technology for the Promotion of Materials Science (DoITPoMS) project sought to make learning resources that had already been created by the consortium members more widely available (DoITPoMS 1999). The audience identified consisted of the materials science course tutors in the participating universities, together with contacts from specific institutions in the USA and Europe. There is no record of an attempt being made to find out from this audience what aspects of teaching material provision most concerned them; this may be because the project team consisted of people who were also teachers in this discipline and so were confident that they knew what their audience wanted.

In addition, the project team identified the relevant Learning and Teaching Support Network (LTSN) subject centre as an audience. The LTSN is a nationally funded initiative whose role is to undertake further dissemination, allowing the project to cascade its findings out to a much wider audience than it could have reached alone. One of its stated aims is to disseminate good practice in teaching – it is therefore safe to assume that being given examples of such practice would be of interest.

learning from the experience of taking part in the process of the study, as a participant, or as part of the evaluation team, or as someone involved in steering the investigation.

In this expanded view of the role of evaluation, studies typically have multiple audiences. These might include the participants in the study (and, in the case of children, their guardians), anyone responsible for commissioning the study, managers responsible for an area of work, technicians involved in supporting the technology involved and, of course, the evaluators themselves.

Each of these audiences may have its own interests and concerns. Some of these might be obvious, or could easily be found out; others might require a preliminary study in themselves. Identifying these concerns will help to direct the study by providing a frame of reference that allows decisions to be made about what might prove to be useful or interesting to do.

Interestingly, few research studies appear to question who their audience might be. In part, however, this is likely to be a consequence of the genre of research writing: the scientific style of writing that dominates research articles plays down the role of the researcher and presents the work as general truth, rather than as an account written for a particular group (Brew 2001). However, it may also result from the fact that many researchers work as part of a community, defined by its position within a tradition or discipline; their audience remains unspecified because it consists of their peers.

Selection of an evaluation question

Just as research papers are largely silent on the matter of the audience of the evaluation, the selection of the question to be addressed by a study is also frequently glossed over (Box 2.3.2). However, it has also been argued that it is an important part of the research process and also a particularly difficult one (Oliver and Conole 2000). There is a tendency in evaluation to ask the simplest or most obvious question, rather than one that is useful and answerable (Patton 1997). Several things can be done to counteract this tendency. One approach involves starting from the concerns expressed by stakeholders and then using these to generate a shortlist of questions. In order to help evaluators expand their list of questions and then select one question as the focus for their study, the evaluation tool kit (ILRT n.d.) prompts users to think about rephrasing their questions so that they are:

- exploratory ('how …?', 'when …?', 'under what conditions …?', 'for whom …?');
- comparative ('… better or worse than …', '… compared with other students, with the class last year, with the class in another school, etc.?');

Box 2.3.2   **Choosing an evaluation question**

As with the selection of audience, few published studies directly address this issue, so hypothetical illustrations are given instead.

A teacher might wonder if the Internet can support their pupils' learning, but this is probably not a good evaluation question. If a study is undertaken and the answer to this question is 'yes', this is reassuring but uninformative; if the answer is 'no', then the study will have provided no guidance on how to resolve this problem.

Taking the Internet and student learning as a starting point, a series of questions that might be of interest is then generated. It might have been better to ask how the Internet can support pupils' learning, whether it seems to be better than not having access to the Internet, how long pupils spend on the Internet or even whether there any ways in which having access to the Internet might hinder learning (for example, by making it easy to find spurious information). Finally a decision is made that what the study really wants to find out about is what students use the Internet for when they are set some homework, so that a decision can be made about whether it would be useful to make support available more widely.

- about measurement ('how much ...?', 'how often ...?', 'how long ...?', 'how many ...?');
- based on contrasting or even contradictory assumptions (for example, instead of 'how much better?', 'how much worse?'; instead of 'what are the benefits?', 'what are the problems?'; instead of 'who fails', 'who succeeds?').

This process tends to help the users of the tool kit to identify the elements of the questions that are most important to them. Next, users are prompted to try various combinations of their new questions (for example, a comparative with a measurement question, an exploratory with a contrasting assumptions question, etc.). Finally, users go back over the list of questions they have generated in order to pick the one (or ones) that they most want to have answered.

Another useful strategy for determining whether a question warrants a study involves posing possible answers to the audiences involved to see what they find credible or useful. If the answers do not seem to be helpful, this might suggest that a different question might be better as the focus for the study.

Choice of an evaluation methodology

The process of posing questions reveals all sorts of assumptions about what we consider valuable; the type of question that is selected also influences how we might go about answering it (Box 2.3.3). For example, asking whether using ICT helps students learn typically reflects a positivist view of the world, such as that of evidence-based practice, wherein the 'scientific method' serves to reveal truths about things that happen 'out there' (Davies *et al.* 2000). Asking what students' experiences of using ICT are, on the other hand, reflects a phenomenographic view, wherein what is important is individuals' subjective experience (Kvale 1996). Equally, someone may not care what students might or might not know or feel, so long as their exam performance improves; this reflects a behaviourist position, wherein what happens 'in the head' is considered unknowable so the researcher focuses exclusively on what can be measured (Skinner 1950). Alternatively, they might seek not to judge what they see at all; they might, instead, just describe it in order to understand social behaviour from the point of view of the people who are involved, as in the ethnographic tradition (Jones 1998b).

These different positions are methodologies: theoretical frameworks that shape the way in which a researcher understands his or her engagement with the world. Since few teachers or academics will have received training in or opportunity to reflect on approaches to educational evaluation, recent research has sought to develop techniques or tools that prompt them to consider a selection of key methodological issues. What is aspired to is not that such newcomers become 'instant experts', but simply that, if they locate themselves within a particular tradition that they find comfortable. They should, nonetheless, pause to think about the question being addressed in order to consider whether it fits naturally within the style of the study being undertaken (Oliver 2000).

Box 2.3.3 **How questions relate to methodologies**

Oliver *et al.* (1999) carried out a study to address the question of whether introducing a piece of software called C-Cubed helped undergraduate chemistry students to perform better on mid-term assessments. This was an essentially behaviourist study, following a quasi-experimental method; the assumption was that there would be an interplay between observable characteristics (for example, gender) and the use of software, and this was measured using standard sets of assessment questions. However, no attempt was made to compare what was observed against a specially designed control group.

In contrast, the study by Scanlon *et al.* (1999) of collaborations in a primary classroom sought to investigate teachers' and children's perceptions of a task. Because this element of the study concerns the subjective experience of events, it can be described as a phenomeno- graphic study; it sought to describe phenomena as they were experienced by the participants in the study.

Choice of data collection methods

Once the context for the study is established, the practical question arises of how best to gather the data required (Box 2.3.4). Certain types of study lend themselves to particular methods; for example, an open-ended exploration of the variety of ways in which people conceptualize evolution would probably be best served by interviews, while a study of the prevalence of these conceptualizations among a given population might involve a questionnaire. To some extent, this relationship can be illustrated by looking at the kinds of methods typically associated with particular methodologies, such as standardized tests or observation for experiments and interviews for phenomenography.

An important consideration for evaluation is the convenience of gathering data. In certain circumstances, suitable data arise as a by-product of existing activities. For example, most educational systems keep records of progress; similarly, studies of web-based learning are often able to utilize the 'trace' of online learning represented by system usage or postings to bulletin boards. However, legislation such as the Data Protection Act in the UK imposes restrictions on the ways in which data such as these can be reused. Under such legislation, care must be taken to meet certain obligations such as not identifying the individuals who provided the data, and evaluators must consider whether they need to contact the people described to ask permission for their data to be used for this new purpose.

The techniques best suited to gathering data will depend on the nature of the study. Some formats, such as closed-answer ('tick box') questionnaires, provide focused data in a convenient format and are well suited to studies involving large

---

Box 2.3.4 **Choosing data collection methods**

In the study by Scanlon *et al.* (1999) of primary school children collaborating to learn about the water cycle, the researchers wanted to explore participants' experiences of working collaboratively to produce dynamic documents. They collected existing data, such as the documents and storyboards that had been used to create the dynamic documents. They also used a variety of methods to gather new data, such as interviews with teachers, questionnaires about students' views of science, video recordings of the collaborative process, and before and after interviews with the children. In their account of this study, the data collection is described as 'extensive'. While it provided a rich resource from which to explore the 'multi-layered, interactive, shared social experiences' in which they were interested, many evaluators would find such a body of data overwhelming.

Oliver and Shaw (2003) set out to study how undergraduate students used an online discussion forum to learn biochemistry. A questionnaire was used to provide an overview of students' perceptions of this process, and this was contrasted with an analysis of what students had actually posted to the board. (These messages were used for analysis and were cited from, once suitably anonymized, with the students' permission.)

---

numbers of people. Observation can reveal unanticipated issues, but it can be intrusive and there is no guarantee that interesting things will happen within the time allotted. Interviews allow people to explain their view of the world and permit interesting developments to be investigated as they arise. However, in addition to the time taken by the discussion itself, many hours may be required for transcription.

Two issues are particularly important when considering how to collect data. First, different kinds of data can be collected to answer the same question, or the same kind of data can be gathered from different sources, in order to allow a process of triangulation (judging the consistency of conclusions from multiple perspectives) during the analysis, which will result in greater confidence in the results (Breen *et al.* 1999). Second, it is relatively easy to collect data; this often results in a mass of unfocused data being gathered which then overwhelms the evaluator.

Choice of data analysis methods

No matter how data are collected, they can always be analysed in a number of different ways (Box 2.3.5). Interviews, for example, are normally analysed qualitatively – but there is no reason why the utterances cannot be coded and counted, why pauses cannot be measured, why turn-taking cannot be modelled. In fact, all of these techniques are used to analyse interviews by researchers interested in linguistic analyses. Similarly, there is no reason why a mathematical model derived from quantitative data cannot be judged by qualities such as its elegance, or its assumptions interpreted in order to understand its rhetorical power, and so on (Kvale 1996).

However, certain kinds of analysis lend themselves naturally to particular forms of data. Counts, measured intervals and other quantitative data are typically analysed statistically, assuming that certain basic conditions are met. These conditions vary according to the type of data collected – so, for example, if the data that are gathered are numerically measurable and continuous (such as how long someone took to complete an assessment), a different test is needed from that for data that are about categories (for example, yes/no judgements about whether someone passed the assessment). These distinctions are well described elsewhere (for example, Greene and d'Oliveira 1999) and so will not be dwelt upon here.

Measurement and classification is only possible, however, once we have made certain assumptions about what is important in the data. With many types of data (such as video recordings of classrooms), it is often hard to tell in advance what will prove to be important. In such situations, it is usually more useful to analyse the data in terms of the qualities that are observed, rather than the quantities in which they occur. This process of analysis can be completely subjective, relying solely on the intuition and integrity of the evaluator, but typically it will follow a formalized, systematic process in order to develop a deeper understanding of the data (see, for example, the discussion of methods by Kvale 1996).

Box 2.3.5   **Choosing data analysis methods**

Oliver and Shaw's (2003) study, described in Box 2.3.4, involved analysing undergraduate students' responses to a survey. Inferential statistical methods were used because it was believed that students' previous educational experience would shape their willingness to take part in discussions of biochemistry online. In fact, the evidence did not support this hypothesis. What did prove to be important, however, was the teacher's ability to inspire the students to debate and discuss the issues.

Issroff (1999) investigated secondary school students studying the periodic table, looking in particular at how the task design (working alone, in a pair but not cooperatively, or as a cooperative pair) influenced learning. A range of data analysis methods was used, including timing certain activities (leading to bar charts, tables and graphs) and categorizing certain exchanges (as being about the topic, about what to do next, about who should control the hardware and about anything else). Issroff argues that each of these methods only reveals a limited aspect of how task design influenced learning and that it was by triangulating multiple methods that issues such as dominance (who took control of the learning process) could be fully understood.

This might involve classifying data, seeking further evidence to confirm or revise the classification, then further analysing the relationships between categories in order to build a grounded theory of what has been observed (Glaser and Strauss 1967). Alternatively, it could involve the close reading of individual texts, such as an interview transcript, in order to list the subjects and objects mentioned and record how each is talked about. Then this could be used to analyse how various discourses are used in order to achieve political or social ends, or to create a particular sense of identity (Banister *et al.* 1994).

Importantly, however, the perceived value of analytical methods varies depending on the beliefs of the person viewing the analysis. Evidence-based practice, for example, dismisses all qualitative research as being unreliable, relegating it to a supporting role along with anecdotes and other informal research (Davies *et al.* 2000). Meanwhile, some educational researchers see the kinds of analysis that take place in evidence-based practice as assuming a positivist view of the world that is inappropriate in education, and that the need to control variables means that its ecological validity (that is, its relevance to real situations, which in education are typically complex and messy) is minimal (Hammersley 2001).

There are several ways to deal with these ongoing debates. Leaving aside the possibility of ignoring them (consigning the evaluator to a position of naivety), it would be possible to take a position (locating oneself within one tradition and following their rules for what 'counts') to try and appease several groups (often achieved by using multiple methods of analysis in order to triangulate results, giving greater confidence in what is found). Alternatively, it would be possible to follow the utilization-focused approach of using the analytical techniques that will find greatest favour with the intended audience (so long as these are not felt to be entirely inappropriate). Which of these is the most appropriate approach must be determined by the beliefs of the evaluator.

Selection of the most appropriate format(s) for reporting the findings to the audience

A central premise of utilization-focused evaluation is that studies that do not communicate effectively with an audience are worthless. Consequently, it is important to plan how the findings of a study can be communicated (Box 2.3.6).

The selection of reporting format depends largely on practical or political considerations. In small-scale studies that are primarily of local interest, informal discussion and word-of-mouth dissemination are appropriate and effective. However, the long-term impact of these approaches may be limited. By contrast, an international journal article may never be read by immediate colleagues, but it may influence practice around the globe and could be cited for years.

Each format has its own strengths and weaknesses and, as with data collection and analysis methods, it is often useful to combine more than one approach in order to balance these. For example, colleagues could be briefed with a short presentation in a lunch break; a manager could be sent a one-page executive summary; an article could be sent to a national newsletter; and a report describing

> *Box 2.3.6* **Selection of methods for communicating findings**
>
> As with the first two steps, the strategic step of communicating with the audiences of a study is rarely discussed in research papers. This is partly because they themselves are an example of reporting findings to an audience. Returning to the dissemination strategy mentioned earlier (DoITPoMS 1999), the project used informal contact with staff in each institution, a project flier (available from a national subject centre), institutional workshops, e-mails to relevant mailing lists and the creation of a website. While these methods cover formal and informal, quick and more enduring formats, and known as well as general audiences, there was little in the strategy about disseminating detailed information about any studies conducted. A detailed report on the website or a journal article describing such activity might represent good ways of addressing this.

the work could be made available on the Internet by a relevant educational organization, such as a subject centre. This would form an effective mix because:

- the informal briefing is a fast way of communicating the findings, which could be covered thoroughly, although there is no guarantee who would attend;
- the manager could be sent the note, rather than relying on he or she taking the initiative to ask for it, although such a summary could only ever present the study superficially;
- the newsletter would reach people that the evaluator does not know (and thus could not send information to), but might take a while to be published and might also suffer from being brief;
- the report could cover the study thoroughly and would enable people to seek out the information over the next few years (at least), rather than the evaluator having to know who is (and will become) interested and send them the information.

In other words, these approaches differ in terms of whether they are quick, whether they are 'push' or 'pull' media, whether they are formal or informal, the level of detail they impart, their endurance as a resource and whether the evaluator knows the intended audience individually or as a general group.

Discussion: issues for evaluation

Thinking through the steps above can help with planning a study, or critiquing a process that is well documented; however, as was noted, the strategic elements of this process (relating to audience, question and dissemination) are rarely addressed explicitly in published papers. In order to be able to read research papers critically then, it is worth exploring issues that arise within the middle three steps (selection of methodology, data collection method and analysis) in greater detail. To do this, issues have been grouped as relating to technical, ethical or philosophical concerns. However, this list of issues is illustrative, not exhaustive.

Technical issues

Any given evaluation technique has its limits; each was designed with a particular task in mind, and thus each can be used inappropriately. Understanding the limitations of each approach is an important step in ensuring that the conclusions that might be drawn from any given study are warranted.

For example, experimental designs rest on the ability to draw comparisons between conditions. There are questions about whether this is possible in education. Since educational innovations often change the nature of what is learnt, it can be argued that comparative studies of any type are inherently flawed. Such arguments often draw the analogy of trying to compare apples and oranges. Ironically, this same analogy can be used to show the problem with this argument. Apples and oranges are easily compared – their calorific value, hue, weight and people's opinions towards them can all be described and contrasted. Similarly, with educational innovations, students' preferences, pace and performance in tests or exams (which in practice rarely change as a result of innovation) can all be used as the basis for comparison.

A more pertinent criticism, and one which must be addressed on a case-by-case basis, is whether or not these measures reveal anything of educational importance. If performance on some assessment remains unchanged between two conditions, what does this mean? Does this mean that what pupils have learnt is identical? Is it that students in the computer-related condition have learnt things that the existing form of assessment fails to assess? (For example, are they able to do the same questions but understand certain principles more thoroughly, or visually, or differently, in some other way?) Are both equally worthwhile, or is one better because, for example, it provides pupils with the opportunity to practice computer-related literacy skills? The fundamental issue here is not whether a difference between conditions can be identified – it is what that difference *means* that is problematic.

When the need for control is added to comparative designs, as in the case of experiments, yet further issues arise. The purpose of inferential statistics is that they allow causes to be identified. In authentic educational settings, however, clear causes are hard to find. Other contextual elements (such as access to supportive peers, parents or paid tutors) can affect performance; changes to computing access policies, teaching staff or resources and infrastructure can all change the nature of an innovation as it is studied; students who experience bad teaching often work harder as a result, hiding possible negative effects; and, of course, educational contexts are social settings, so there is often nothing to stop those with access to an innovation sharing with those who do not. Thus control can be hard to achieve and studies that do not address this issue explicitly should be treated with caution.

Another common problem, also related to inference, concerns the nature of proof. In qualitative studies, it is often clear that the evidence presented is partial. However, many quantitative studies present their findings in a way that seems general and universal. There are two problems with this.

First, experiments cannot prove hypotheses; they can only support them. With all experiments, there is a chance that a result is untrue and has been caused by inaccurate measurement, an unrepresentative sample of participants, or some other type of error. As a result, findings are always presented with a measure of significance, which indicates the percentage chance that the effect was caused by one of these errors.

Second, there is the issue of sampling. With any study, irrespective of methodology, the question must be considered as to how widely the conclusions can be generalized. Again, qualitative methods often make this concern explicit, valuing 'rich' descriptions of contexts so that the reader can decide upon the extent to which this case resembles his or her own (Stake 1994). In experimental studies, however, the reader must infer from any demographic information given whether or not the participants in the research are in any way similar to the pupils who might be involved in some learning development. These demographic data represent a model of what the researcher believes is significant: for example, that the important variation between individuals can be described in terms of classification according to age and gender. Since pupils vary from year to year, school to school (let alone country to country), as well as in terms of what might be described as their social class, it can easily be argued that a model such as this neglects important variables. If the model is incomplete in these potentially important ways, then the confidence with which conclusions can be generalized must be called into doubt. Indeed, it has been argued that, rather than trusting the general conclusions of experiments over the provisional conclusions of case studies, experiments ought to be doubted and questioned in exactly the same way as the tentative findings of qualitative studies (Holt and Oliver 2002).

Finally, any study is only as good as the data upon which it draws (Patton 1997). This observation is particularly important in the context of studies involving children, although some researchers would argue that the same concerns hold true for data concerning any individual's experience of education. Issues such as whether young children fully understand what they are being asked, whether they are able to communicate what we want to know, and whether we are in a position to appreciate what they might mean, are all open to question. In such a situation, finding simple ways of eliciting data becomes important, as does triangulation.

Ethical issues

Cohen and Manion (1994) provide a thorough guide to the ethical issues associated with educational research, all of which hold true for evaluation more generally. These include the following:

- Getting access and gaining acceptance. For example, securing permission from a school's headteacher and chair of the board of governors as well as from the teacher, pupils and their parents before commencing a study.
- Privacy. Is it justifiable to ask for sensitive personal information? With whom can this information be shared?
- Anonymity. There is an inevitable tension between providing an audience with enough information about research participants and ensuring that they cannot be identified.
- Confidentiality. This involves hiding the fact that a particular person is involved in research, in case, for example, subsequent publication might allow them to be identified.
- Deception. In some cases, information that might distort or pre-empt the study is withheld.

The cornerstone of addressing these issues, Cohen and Manion argue, is informed consent. This principle is based upon the idea that each individual has the right to freedom and self-determination. Participants in research should thus have the right to understand what they are taking part in and to end their involvement at any point. However, as they point out, there are many problems with this principle. In some studies where deception is necessary (such as studies involving covert observation), providing a full explanation is impractical. Similarly, there are many debates about whether the rights of individuals can ever be compromised to further the good of the many. Because these tensions must be interpreted on a case-by-case basis, it is not practical to provide definitive rules; instead, bodies have drawn up guidelines that evaluators are encouraged to follow (for example, British Educational Research Association (BERA) n.d.).

Comparative studies are faced with particular problems. Many initiatives are introduced because it is considered that they will improve learning. If this is believed, even cautiously, can one group be denied access to these opportunities, particularly if this might give the favoured group an advantage on formally assessed work that could influence opportunities open to them later in life? One solution to this problem involves piloting initiatives within non-assessed areas of the curriculum. This remains problematic, however, because assessment has such a profound effect on how pupils act (Biggs 1999). The situation may change dramatically once assessment is reintroduced. Other alternatives include crossover designs, in which the group experiencing the innovation swaps with the group who do not have access to it after some mid-point measurement or observation, or simply providing access to the resources for revision purposes once the study is complete.

Designing studies around the interests of various audiences positions evaluation as being a practical and political activity. It is not, like studies in the illuminative or experimental schools, a search for truth; instead, it is a process that seeks to advise and educate in order to inform subsequent action (Patton 1997). This raises important ethical questions for evaluators. If evaluation enables action, whose actions will be supported? Whose agendas will be served? Traditionally, evaluators have answered the questions of those who commission the study; the people in the study are positioned as research subjects, and are treated as sources of data. Other forms of evaluation (such as action research or utilization-focused evaluation) have tried to subvert this situation, treating people as research participants rather than subjects to be 'treated'. Like many emancipatory ideals, this renaming can be done cynically, so that the terms change but practice remains unaltered. Alternatively, though, the process of evaluation can alter to reflect this new mindset. Participants can be allowed to give their point of view, not just answer pre-specified questions; they can be invited to discuss the agenda of the study, the appropriateness of the methods used to carry it out and may be involved in reporting the findings to the people who instigated it rather than having their stories reinterpreted by the evaluators. Whether any of this is a useful or important thing to do will depend on the specific situation being evaluated. What is important is that the evaluators should remain aware of the different political agendas that their study might be used to support so that they can take a principled position about which groups' agendas they will work to support (Oliver and Harvey 2002).

Philosophical issues

Initially, it might seem strange to refer to philosophical issues when evaluation often appears to be a highly pragmatic activity. However, without some philosophical perspective on learning, it is impossible to determine the appropriate scope of a study.

What, for example, counts as learning? The very idea remains contested and, while various forms of assessment (such as standardized tests) are often used as a proxy for learning, this remains problematic for several reasons. Perhaps most importantly, it is assumed that what has been learnt can be performed; that there is a direct correlation between learning and assessment. This is evidently not the case. Similar problems arise when considering whether the introduction of some new form of teaching 'causes' learning, or judging how a student's actions should be interpreted (Oliver and Harvey 2002).

These complexities are neatly discussed by Martin (1999), who has developed a model that shows the interplay between various elements of the educational situation. According to her model, there is an interplay between perceptions of the teaching environment and the teacher's approach to teaching; between the approach to teaching and students' perceptions of the learning environment; between students' perceptions and their approaches to learning; and between their approach and the learning outcomes they achieve. Each step in this model is a two-way process, much of which may remain tacit.

Unlike many of the technical issues that face evaluation, these philosophical problems are ones for which there is no solution. Instead of seeking answers, evaluators need to take a position, being honest about the theoretical perspectives, assumptions and values they bring to the study, so that the influence of these can be appreciated by their audience and their implications understood (Oliver and Harvey, 2002).

Conclusions

This chapter has discussed how the use of ICT in science learning and teaching can be evaluated from an historical and social perspective. This perspective reveals how pragmatism has arisen as a guiding principle for evaluation, it illustrates the steady accumulation of different approaches to this practice and it explains why it is impossible to provide a definitive description of what 'counts' as evaluation. It also reveals evaluation to be a social and political activity. This highlights the need for evaluators to remain sensitive to issues of power in their studies, as there are potential conflicts of interest between addressing the concerns of pupils and the need for powerful audiences to legitimate the study by acting on it, and between student-centred rhetoric and the tendency towards treating participants in a study as little more than sources of data.

The ambiguity and ambivalence inherent in this viewpoint place evaluators in a difficult position. On the one hand, evaluation becomes simply whatever it is that evaluators do. This perspective has been used here to provide an outline of the process of evaluation. This can be adopted and followed in a straightforward way by teachers and other practitioners who are seeking to become evaluators of science learning. However, on the other hand, the same situation makes it clear that any approach to evaluation is open to criticism; evaluation remains a contested practice, not a precisely definable skill to be acquired.

A balance must be struck between these two extremes. Following 'recipes' for evaluation may serve as a good introduction to this activity, but unless the evaluator progresses beyond this point, his or her studies can only ever be naive. At the same time, incessantly debating the niceties of different forms of practice can prevent the evaluator from acting at all. Instead, an evaluator must develop a familiarity with techniques and practical issues, acquiring a sound basis for action, while also taking a theoretical (and philosophical) stand that provides a clear framework from which to interpret the meaning of the outcomes of his or her actions.

References

Banister, P., Burman, E., Parker, I., Taylor, M. and Tindall, C. (1994) *Qualitative Methods in Psychology: A Research Guide*, Buckingham: Open University Press.

Biggs, J. (1999) *Teaching for Quality Learning at University*, Buckingham: Open University Press.

Blalock, A. (1999) 'Evaluation research and the performance management movement: From estrangement to useful integration?', *Evaluation* 5(2): 117–49.

Breen, R., Jenkins, A., Lindsay, R. and Smith, P. (1999) 'Insights through triangulation: combining research methods to enhance the evaluation of it based learning methods', in M. Oliver (ed.) *Innovation in the Evaluation of Learning Technology*, London: University of North London Press.

Brew, A. (2001) *The Nature of Research: Inquiry in Academic Contexts*, London: RoutledgeFalmer.

British Educational Research Association (BERA) (n.d.) *Ethical Guidelines*, available on the Web at <http://www.bera.ac.uk/guidelines> (last accessed 11 October 2002).

Cohen, L. and Manion, L. (1994) *Research Methods in Education* (4th edn), London: Routledge.

Conole, G. and Oliver, M. (2002) 'Embedding theory into learning technology practice with toolkits', *Journal of Interactive Media in Education*, available on the Web at <http://www-jime.open.ac.uk/2002/8/conole-oliver-02-08.pdf> .

Davies, H., Nutley, S. and Smith, P. (2000) 'Introducing evidence-based policy and practice in public services', in H. Davies, S. Nutley and P. Smith (eds) *What Works? Evidence-based Policy and Practice in Public Services*, Bristol: Policy Press.

Dissemination of Information Technology for the Promotion of Materials Science (DoITPoMS) (1999) *Dissemination Strategy*, unpublished project document, available on the Web at <http://www.msm.cam.ac.uk/doitpoms/docs.html> (last checked 13 March 2003).

Glaser, B. and Strauss A. (1967) *The Discovery of Grounded Theory: Strategies for Qualitative Research*, London: Weidenfeld and Nicholson.

Greene, J. and d'Oliveira, M. (1999) *Learning to Use Statistical Tests in Psychology* (2nd edn), Buckingham: Open University Press.

Guba, E. and Lincoln, Y. (1981) *Effective Evaluation*, San Francisco: Jossey-Bass.

Hammersley, M. (1997) 'The relationship between qualitative and quantitative research: paradigm loyalty versus methodological eclecticism', in J. Richardson (ed.) *Handbook of Qualitative Research Methods*, Leicester: British Psychological Society.

—— (2001) 'On "systematic" reviews of research literatures: a "narrative" response to Evans and Benfield', *British Educational Research Journal* 27(5): 543–54.

Holt, R. and Oliver, M. (2002) 'Evaluating Web-based learning modules during an MSc programme in dental public health: a case study', *British Dental Journal* 193(5): 283–8.

Institute for Learning and Research Technology (ILRT) (n.d.) *Evaluation of Learning and Media Toolkit*, Bristol: University of Bristol, available on the Web at <http://www.ltss.bris.ac.uk/jcalt/> (last accessed 13 March 2003).

Issroff, K. (1999) 'Time-based analysis of students studying the periodic table', in K. Littleton and P. Light (eds) *Learning with Computers: Analysing Productive Interaction*, London: Routledge.

Jones, C. (1998a) 'Evaluating a collaborative online learning environment', *Active Learning* 9: 31–5.

—— (1998b) 'Evaluation using ethnography: context, content and collaboration', in M. Oliver (ed.) *Innovation in the Evaluation of Learning Technology*, London: University of North London Press.

Kemmis, S. (1996) 'Emancipatory aspirations in a post-modern era', in O. Zuber-Skerritt (ed.) *New Directions in Action Research*, London: Falmer Press.

Kvale, S. (1996) *Interviews: An Introduction to Qualitative Research Interviewing*, Thousand Oaks, CA: Sage.

Lewin, K. (1952) *Field Theory in Social Science: Selected Theoretical Papers*, London: Tavistock Publications.

Martin, E. (1999) *Changing Academic Work: Developing the Learning University*, Buckingham: Open University Press.

McNiff, J. (1988) *Action Research: Principles and Practice*, London: Routledge.

Oliver, M. (2000) 'An introduction to the evaluation of learning technology', *Educational Technology and Society* 3(4): 20–30.

—— and Conole, G. (2000) *Using the ELT Toolkit to Evaluate a Professional Development Programme* (BP ELT Report No. 16), London: University of North London.

——, —— and Spillane, D. (1999) *A Comparison of Traditional and Computer-based Tutorials for Chemistry Students Learning Factorisation* (BP ELT Report No. 8), London: University of North London.

—— and Harvey, J. (2002) 'What does "impact" mean in the evaluation of learning technology?', *Educational Technology and Society* 5(3): 18–26.

—— and Shaw, G. (2003) 'Asynchronous discussion in support of medical education', *Journal of Asynchronous Learning Networks* 7(1): 56–67.

Parlett, M. and Hamilton, D. (1972) *Evaluation as Illumination: A New Approach to the Study of Innovatory Programmes* (Occasional Paper 9), Edinburgh: Centre for Research in the Educational Sciences, University of Edinburgh.

Patton, M. (1997) *Utilization-focused Evaluation: The New Century Text*, London: Sage.

Potter, J. and Wetherell, M. (1987) *Discourse and Social Psychology: Beyond Attitudes and Behaviour*, London: Sage.

Preskill, H. and Torres, R. (1999) 'Building capacity for organizational learning through evaluative inquiry', *Evaluation* 5(1): 42–60.

Scanlon, E., Issroff, K. and Murphy, P. (1999) 'Collaborations in a primary classroom: mediating science activities through new technology', in K. Littleton and P. Light (eds) *Learning with Computers: Analysing Productive Interaction*, London: Routledge.

Skinner, B. (1950) 'Are theories of learning necessary?', *Psychological Review* 57: 193–216.

Stake, R. (1994) 'Case studies', in N. Denzin and Y. Lincoln (eds) *The Handbook of Qualitative Research*, London: Sage.

2.4 Evaluating information and communications technology

A tool kit for practitioners

Martin Oliver and Grainne Conole

This chapter describes a tool kit which can help practitioners evaluate the use of information and communications technology (ICT) in their courses. This tool kit is being developed as part of the BP *Evaluation of Learning Technology* (ELT) project. The aim of this project is to create, test and refine a research tool which will help practitioners with little or no prior experience of evaluation work to carry out studies of their own uses of ICT.

The chapter starts by outlining some of the problems associated with evaluations in this area. It goes on to look at some of the methodologies which have been developed for assessing the educational effectiveness of ICT use. Then, the tool kit is described, looking in turn at each of three key elements: selecting a methodology, choosing methods of gathering data, and identifying appropriate data analysis techniques. An application of the tool kit is presented briefly, in order to illustrate how it can be used. The chapter concludes by addressing some of the issues raised by such a resource and points to further work required in this area.

Background

There is a strong move nationally towards integrating ICT into the curriculum (Dearing *et al.* 1997), much of which has been motivated by the view that ICT offers many educational advantages over traditional teaching (Atkins 1993). However, few studies have been able to demonstrate the kind of advantages which have been promised, showing, rather unsurprisingly, that there are both pros and cons to ICT use. For example, there are variations in its success across age or subject grouping (Hammond 1994), ability (Atkins 1993), and prior computing experience. Furthermore, pragmatic concerns such as access to resources (Draper 1997) and the effective integration of ICT into courses (Hammond 1994; Gunn 1997) can also prove to be critical factors in whether or not the use of these resources is effective.

The lesson to be learnt from this is that evaluations have an important role to play in identifying the issues involved in integrating ICT into courses. Indeed, even a cursory review of the literature reveals that it is very rarely that a study is unable to show scope for improvement in the design or use of ICT resources. Related motivation for evaluating ICT use can be drawn from the increasing need for quality assurance. Practitioners are being required to provide such assurance as part of their job. However, few teaching staff have the skills required to carry out evaluations of ICT use and fewer still are aware of the range or scope of methodologies available to them. This has resulted in a comparatively small amount of evaluation work in this area and a superficial and naive use of ICT in courses.

Finally, it is worth clarifying what the term 'evaluation' covers in the context of this chapter. Evaluation of ICT has been used to describe a range of activities, ranging from simple checklists for reviewing software, such as that of Blease (1988), to extensive evaluation methodologies including tools and notes for users, such as those produced by the *Teaching with Independent Learning Technologies* (TILT) project (Draper *et al.* 1994). While principled reviews are important, work describing a pedagogic tool kit allowing practitioners to select and integrate ICT resources has been described elsewhere (Conole and Oliver 1997, 1998). This chapter will concern itself purely with evaluations that involve empirical studies. The next section will review a selection of methodologies of this type.

Existing methodologies for evaluating ICT use

A wide variety of methodologies for evaluating ICT use already exist; a general review of these has been provided elsewhere (Oliver 1997). For this chapter, it suffices to describe four methodologies which illustrate the diversity of approaches available.

Even a superficial review of methodologies shows that no single approach to evaluating the use of ICT is best suited to all the needs or situations which arise. Instead, each has its own strengths and weaknesses and has been designed with specific evaluation needs in mind. Controlled experiments (Light and Smith 1970) for example, are ideally suited to testing well-defined hypotheses, a prerequisite for designing and planning studies. They also allow results to be generalized. However, by definition, they require the ability to identify and control factors that might influence outcomes, something which can raise practical and ethical problems in an educational setting and which can limit the scope of the findings generated.

By way of contrast, illuminative evaluations (Parlett and Hamilton 1987) provide an ethnographic exploration of educational programmes. They set out without predefined aims and seek to identify and explain problems, issues and features during the course of the study. Their primary concern is to describe and interpret events, whereas experimental approaches aim to measure or predict.

Other methodologies fall between these extremes. The approach adopted by The Open University (Jones *et al.* 1996) gathers data mainly through questionnaires and computer logs, supplementing these with interviews and contextual documents such as the course designers' aims, meeting records, and so on. Typically, this leads to a rich qualitative explanation of the educational and affective successes of the uses of ICT, supplemented by descriptive statistical analysis to summarize measurable factors. The emphasis on questionnaires and the use of statistics make the approach well suited to large-scale programme evaluations.

Atkins (1988) also proposes a hybrid style of evaluation. Here, qualitative and quantitative techniques are used to complement each other, with the additional cross-checking that improves confidence in results. However, this approach is better suited to moderately small groups since the qualitative analysis it advocates requires all the data to be sifted, categorized, rechecked as new data is added, then verified by an independent researcher. While thorough, this approach is time intensive and can prove inappropriate for large-scale evaluations.

As noted, these four methodologies are far from being the only approaches to the evaluation of ICT use. However, they are diverse enough to illustrate the range of approaches available. The next section will describe a tool kit that supports practitioners trying to select and apply one or more of these methodologies.

The tool kit

In order to support staff in the process of selecting and applying a methodology, a tool kit is being developed as part of the ELT project which guides them through the stages of an evaluation. This removes the need for a detailed understanding of each of the approaches, rather providing a method that guides them through the selection and application process. The tool kit consists of three stages: selecting a methodology, gathering data and analysing the data. Each of these will be discussed in turn.

Selecting a methodology

Practitioners are rarely aware of the range of methodologies available for evaluations, let alone which is best suited to a particular requirement. Because of this, the first element of the tool kit consists of a resource which supports the decision-making process.

This chapter proposes that evaluations can be described in terms of three qualities, referred to as *authenticity, exploration* and *scale*. It should be noted that this is not necessarily a complete or an exhaustive set of descriptors, and neither are these necessarily independent qualities. However, their selection does allow a pragmatic distinction to be made between types of evaluation. Each of these qualities will be described in turn.

Authenticity describes the notion of how closely an evaluation captures the context of an existing course. An evaluation of an entire course, looking at a whole student cohort and looking at influences such as institutional policy, would be considered to be highly authentic. One which considered a single hour-long educational exercise set up as a controlled experiment would have a low level of authenticity.

Exploration refers to whether the study has well-defined initial hypotheses or is tackling an open problem. A study which aimed to see how much a piece of software improved students' performance on algebraic manipulation would involve a

	Authenticity		Exploration		Scale	
	Low	High	Low	High	Low	High
Experimental	x		x			x
Illuminative		x		x		x
Open University		x	x			x
Atkins's methodology		x	x	x	x	

Figure 2.4.1 A comparison of four different evaluation methodologies in terms of their qualities.

low degree of exploration; one which tried to discover the ways in which the software improved performance would be more explorative.

Scale is concerned with the number of participants involved in the study. A case study of two students is obviously of a different scale to an evaluation of a cohort of 200 students on a course.

A consideration of the study's aims in terms of these three qualities can help practitioners to select an appropriate methodology. If some of these characteristics are fixed, then the range of methodologies available will be reduced, making the choice far simpler.

Figure 2.4.1 illustrates how these qualities can be used to shortlist and compare appropriate methodologies from the four described earlier. Each has been described in terms of the types of evaluation they are well suited to supporting. To this extent, each is a caricature; clearly, individuals familiar with a particular methodology may be able to adapt it to support a broader range of possibilities than those indicated here. This emphasizes the fact that the framework is intended to be supportive, rather than prescriptive, and that practitioners with expertise in this area will be able to adapt the tool to suit their style of evaluation.

It should be noted also that for some of these qualities, methodologies have been described as both *high* and *low*. This reflects the fact that they are versatile enough to support a range of evaluation designs.

The design of a study may determine some or all of these qualities in advance. A practitioner who is required to assess the effectiveness of the use of technology on their course of 150 students will have the level of authenticity and scale fixed for them, for example. What remain are choices about the aims of the study and the selection of a methodology which best meets these requirements. The practitioner may, for example, decide that he or she will focus on whether or not certain benefits, seen to occur on a similar use of a piece of software, are having an effect on students' learning. This would suggest a study with a fairly low level of exploration. Since both authenticity and scale are required to be high by the constraints already imposed upon them, consideration of the classification shown in Figure 2.4.1 suggests that The Open University's approach would be a good methodology to adopt.

If one or more of the criteria are left open by the experimental design, the table allows a shortlist to be prepared and options compared. In the above example, fixing authenticity and scale produced a list of two options (an illuminative approach or that of The Open University). These could then be compared in terms of other listed qualities, the difference being in terms of the degree of exploration they support.

While comparisons between four approaches are fairly trivial, the advantages of this method become clear when looking at a broader range of options. The review of methodologies mentioned earlier lists eleven methodologies, for example, and is not exhaustive (Conole and Oliver 1998). The process of making sensible and informed comparisons between these is eased considerably by adopting the criteria and table format used in Figure 2.4.1.

Gathering data

Many methodologies for evaluating ICT use have associated procedures for gathering data. In some cases, these are implicit; in others, guidelines are given, but the precise methods are left to the evaluator to select. As before, the tool kit allows several options to be considered, illustrating at a simple level the implications of each.

In the case of The Open University method, a table has already been provided which suggests methods of data capture (see Figure 2.4.2) (Light and Smith 1970). This is subdivided into potential areas of analysis and includes a rationale, the type of data that will be gathered, and the methods that can be used to obtain them.

This closely resembles the approach adopted by the tool kit described in this chapter, and has, indeed, been used to inform its development. However, as with the selection of methodologies, the choice of data collection methods can be informed through the use of criteria such as those described in the previous section. In this case, the main criterion is time required: how great is the time requirement associated with gathering each type of data? This quality takes into account only the time required from the researcher, not the participant. This means that using a diary or learning log, for example, has a low time requirement, since all that the researcher will be required to do is prepare a master document and instruction sheet. Very little subsequent input is required from the researcher, although the amount of time each student puts in to completing the log may be considerable.

The objectivity required by a hypothesis can have considerable impact on the selection of a data capture method. As with the other qualities, this is not a matter of more being better but of achieving a balance. In determining the attitudes of students towards ICT use, low objectivity is clearly appropriate; when attempting to measure the educational impact of introducing ICT, a highly objective form of data capture would be better.

Focus is a concept which considers the state of the data which is gathered. An unstructured interview or a naturalistic observation could generate almost anything. Structured questions restrict responses to a narrower range of topics, concentrating responses on a limited set of options. A multiple choice test merely

	Context	*Interactions*	*Outcomes*
Rationale	Past evaluations and litarature suggest that context must be considered	Need to look at interactions in order to focus on the learning process	Learning outcomes and affective outcomes (e.g. changes of perception or attitude) must both be considered when assessing effectiveness
Data	Course/computer-assisted learning (CAL) designers' aims, policy documents and meeting records	Records of student interactions, student diaries, and online logs	Measures of learning, changes in attitude and perceptions
Methods	Interviews with CAL designers, analysis of policy documents	Observation, diaries, video/audio and computer-use records	Interviews, questionnaires, tests

Figure 2.4.2   A framework for evaluation used at The Open University.

offers the chance to opt for one of a predetermined set of answers. In this sense, the multiple choice test is more focused than structured questions, which in turn are more focused than a truly open interview. The degree of focus will have clear implications in terms of the analysis of data, with a highly focused set of data being easier to analyse than an unfocused set, but often leading to a more limited finding.

Note that some data capture methods are capable of supporting both low and high degrees of focus, for example, and that, as with the criteria in the preceding section, classification systems using these criteria will represent common usage rather than a theoretically ideal justification.

Restricting this discussion to the methods suggested in Figure 2.4.2, the comparison can be made as shown in Figure 2.4.3.

Importantly, selection of data capture procedures is not an exclusive process. It may be appropriate to use several methods, depending on the aims of the evaluation. The recommended data collection methods in Figure 2.4.2, for example, can be seen to represent a spread across objectivity and focus, allowing a broad range of evaluation aims to be tackled. These could include the measurable impact of using software, the effect on students' study practice, students' opinions on the introduction of ICT resources, and so on. What also becomes clear from the table is that, while selecting multiple data capture methods broadens the range of aims that can be supported, it will have clear implications in terms of the time required to gather the information.

Analysis of data

Just as the previous stages have involved comparisons, so different analytical methods can be described and considered. Here, there are two main comparison criteria: the degree of abstraction of the results and the time required to reach them.

	Time required		Objectivity		Focus	
	Low	High	Low	High	Low	High
Interview		x	x		x	x
Access to policy documents	x			x		x
Observation		x		x	x	
Student diaries	x		x		x	
Video logs	x			x	x	
Audio logs	x			x	x	
Computer-based logs of interaction	x			x		x
Questionnaire	x		x		x	x
Tests	x			x		x

Figure 2.4.3 A comparison of data capture methods.

Abstraction captures the notion of the *distance* between the data and the way the findings are presented. Simple presentation of transcripts, for example, imposes no interpretation on the data. Codification of comments, leading to a chi-squared comparison between groups of respondents, gives a finding which is far harder to relate to the raw data. Text supported by comments falls between these extremes. The choice of how synthetic or processed the findings are will be determined by the audience to whom the evaluation will be presented.

Time required is closely related to the depth of analysis that a method provides. A superficial reading of transcripts provides few detailed results, but is quick to carry out. Developing a grounded theory will lead to far deeper insights, with associated implications in terms of time (and possible further data collection). Such a quality is clearly of pragmatic concern to practitioners.

To illustrate how methods can be compared, Figure 2.4.4 lists some of the options available to a practitioner who has chosen to use an interview to gather data.

In this case, choice of methodology could be influenced by the other analyses which are carried out. A reflective narrative would complement a very abstract statistical analysis of test scores, for example, while generating categories would be useful for gaining insight into common problems such as interface design. As with the other comparison tables, the important aspect of this tool is that it enables practitioners to make informed and balanced choices, rather than predetermining one course of action.

Although not included here, the final tool kit will also include information on how to apply the selected methods of analysis, pointers to theoretical discussions

	Abstraction		Time required	
	Low	High	Low	High
Categorization	x		x	
Categorization and statistical comparison		x	x	
Grounded theorizing	x			x
Reflective narrative	x		x	

Figure 2.4.4 A comparison of data analysis methods.

of the methodology and examples of case studies where the method has been applied.

General comments on the tool kit

The previous sections have outlined the key elements of the tools provided for practitioners to guide them in the selection and application of methodologies for evaluating educational uses of ICT. Several further comments are also worth noting.

The tool kit is viewed as a supportive, not a prescriptive, resource. As mentioned before, it would be entirely appropriate for practitioners with experience in evaluating ICT use to modify or skip sections. It would be easy, for example, to create a new methodology piecemeal from the different data capture and analysis options available, rather than selecting a prepackaged selection in the form of a named methodology. This would have the advantage of producing a tailor-made methodology, but would preclude the possibility of reference to case studies illustrating the approach in practice.

Another aspect of its flexibility is that practitioners can reclassify methodologies in line with their own experience. The classifications presented in the previous sections are based on a review of the methodologies and case studies which apply them, together with personal experience. This approach could clearly be repeated by practitioners in order to *personalize* the tool kit.

Similarly, the tool kit is considered to be a starting point, not a complete resource. Figure 2.4.1 lists only four methodologies and Figure 2.4.3 only nine forms of data capture. It would be a simple matter to extend these tables by taking a new method, considering it in terms of the qualities used for comparison, and adding it alongside the others. This makes the tool kit an adaptive, dynamic and flexible resource, capable of coping with new methodologies as they are created.

The next section presents an illustration of the application of the tool kit which demonstrates how these comparisons can be used to support principled and informed decisions on the choice of methodology for the evaluation and analysis.

An application of the tool kit

An example application of the tool kit will illustrate how the tools can be used and how this can influence the design and implementation of an evaluation study.

The context

The course to be evaluated was a first-year programme covering mathematical methods for chemistry. Staff teaching this course were aware of several computer-assisted learning (CAL) packages which covered this material and wanted to know the impact that replacing a tutorial with a computer-supported session would have on students' learning. There were sixty-two students on the course.

Selection of methodology

Discussion with the staff identified two aims for the study: identification of the impact CAL-based tutorials would have on students' learning and an analysis of the problems facing students trying to learn factorization. Each of the aims was considered separately.

Several qualities of the evaluation were fixed by the context. The scale, while not huge, is moderate. Additionally, the degree of authenticity is fixed. As this is an evaluation of the impact of CAL on a course, a high degree of authenticity is required. Consideration of Figure 2.4.1 suggests that The Open University methodology would be appropriate.

A similar comparison was made for the exploration of problems facing students learning factorization. The same scale and level of authenticity apply; essentially, where this evaluation aim differs is in terms of the degree of exploration. For this reason, an illuminative approach was adopted.

Gathering data

In order to address both aims of the evaluation, a number of complementary methods of data collection were employed. These were selected to cover a variety of types of data, in terms of objectivity and focus. Importantly, these were also selected so as to provide a reasonable load in terms of the time required to gather data.

To assess the impact of the CAL-based tutorial, data were gathered in the form of test results (objective, focused), surveys of use and attitudes (subjective, focused) and observational records (objective, unfocused). Information on context was gathered through interviews with practitioners delivering the course (subjective, unfocused).

The data on problems facing students learning factorization were drawn from two sources: observation of the tutorials (objective, unfocused) and working notes and answers on the tests (objective, focused). Although these data gathering methods also carry high time requirements, the observation for each of these study aims can clearly be carried out at the same time.

Choice of data analysis methods

Having identified suitable methods for data capture, the next step is to specify how the data will be analysed. Again, this is a case of balancing abstraction and time requirements. Figure 2.4.5 shows how this has been achieved for the data gathering methods identified above.

This provides a balanced review of data on the impact of CAL-based tutorials, chosen so as not to impose excessive time demands. It also provides a preliminary understanding of the problems students face when learning factorization, providing an analysis which is detailed yet concrete, and clearly illustrated in terms of the mistakes and confusion that arose as students attempted to complete the test.

Evaluation aim	Data capture method	Data analysis method	Abstraction	Time required
Impact of CAL-based tutorial	Test results	Analytical statistics	High	Low
	Survey	Descriptive statistics	High	Low
	Observation	Categorization	Low	Low
	Interviews	Categorization	Low	Low
Problems learning factorization	Observation	Categorization	Low	Low
	Test results	Grounded theorizing	Low	High

Figure 2.4.5 A summary of the data analysis methods selected.

Summary

This chapter has presented an application of the tool kit. An evaluation was required which considered the impact of CAL-based tutorials on a first-year course teaching mathematics to chemists and it also identified the problems students face when learning factorization. Appropriate evaluation methodologies were chosen. Based on these, a well-balanced mix of methods for gathering and analysing data was selected, resulting in a detailed plan of the steps required by the study. This serves to illustrate both the process of applying the tool kit and the sort of outputs that can be generated.

Conclusions and further work

This chapter has described a new tool kit which enables practitioners to choose a methodology for evaluating their use of ICT. It also allows them to compare and select methods for gathering and analysing data. In order to illustrate the use of this tool kit and the kind of outcomes it leads to, it was then applied to the design of a study of the impact of CAL-based tutorials.

In addition to this demonstration of the tool kit, further empirical support for its usefulness is being provided by a series of studies carried out as part of the BP ELT project. These will be used to inform a reflective analysis of use of the toolkit, leading to revisions to its design. Further insights will be gained through a series of case studies of practitioners working with the toolkit.

Other related work includes the extension of the tables used in the tool kit, allowing it to cover a broader range of methods, and the inclusion of more detailed support notes, guiding the process of data gathering and analysis. However, care has been taken to make the tool kit flexible enough to allow its customization by users. There is clearly scope for it to be developed or revised by practitioners through use, making it a dynamic and adaptive resource.

References

Atkins, M. (1993) 'Evaluating interactive technologies for learning', *Journal of Curriculum Studies* 25(4): 333–42.

—— (1988) 'Practitioner as researcher: some techniques for analysing semi-structured data in small-scale research', in A. Jones (ed.) *Computers in Education*, Milton Keynes: Open University Press.

Blease, D. (1988) 'Choosing educational software', in A. Jones (ed.) *Computers in Education*, Milton Keynes: Open University Press.

Conole, G. and Oliver, M. (1997) *A Pedagogical Framework for Embedding C&IT into the Curriculum* (BP ELT Report No. 2), London: University of North London.

—— and —— (1998) 'A pedagogical toolkit for improving the quality of teaching using learning technologies', in S. White (ed.) *Proceedings of the Implementing Learning Technologies: Strategies and Experience Conference*, Birmingham: Staff and Educational Development Association (SEDA) in association with the Teaching and Learning Technology Support Network.

Dearing, R. *et al.* (1997) *Higher Education in the Learning Society: Report of the National Committee of Inquiry into Higher Education*, London: HMSO and NCIHE Publications.

Draper, S. (1997) 'Prospects for summative evaluation of CAL in higher education', *Association for Learning Technology Journal* 5(1): 33–9.

——, Brown, M., Edgerton, E., Henderson, F., McAteer, E., Smith, E. and Watt H. (1994) *Observing and Measuring the Performance of Educational Technology* (TILT Report No. 1), Glasgow: University of Glasgow.

Gunn, C. (1997) 'CAL evaluation: future directions', *Association for Learning Technology Journal* 5(1): 40–7.

Hammond, M. (1994) 'Measuring the impact of IT on learning', *Journal of Computer Assisted Learning* 10: 251–60 .

Jones, A., Scanlon, E., Tosunoglu, C., Ross, S., Butcher, P., Murphy, P. and Greenberg, J. (1996) 'Evaluating CAL at The Open University: 15 years on', *Computers in Education* 26(1–3): 5–15.

Light, R. and Smith, P. (1970) 'Choosing a future: strategies for designing and evaluating new programs', *Harvard Educational Review* 40: 1–18.

Oliver M. (1997) *A Framework for Evaluating the Use of Educational Technology* (BP ELT Report No. 1), London: University of North London.

Parlett, M. and Hamilton, D. (1987) 'Evaluation as illumination: a new approach to the study of innovatory programmes', in R. Murphy and H. Torrance *Evaluating Education: Issues and Methods*, London: Harper and Row.

Part 3

Extending access to science learning

3.1 Extending access using ICT

Issues and prospects

Martyn Cooper

Many students at all levels of education now use computers in their learning. This is particularly the case in science learning. Increasingly significant elements of courses, at higher education level in particular, are mediated by computer. Lecture notes, seminar topics, practical instructions, etc. are posted on course websites. The computer is used not only for reporting work, as a tool in research and for data analysis, but also in laboratories to control experiments. There is increasing use of multimedia learning activities (for example, virtual science approaches). Computers are used to support communications between students and between students and their teachers by e-mail, discussion lists and online forums. People with disabilities must be enabled to use ICT to help them participate fully in the computer-based activities of both their courses and the wider context of their educational institution.

Many countries are developing legislation making it illegal to discriminate against disabled people in education. In the UK, the key legislation is the Special Educational Needs and Disability Act (SENDA) 2001 (HMSO 2001). This states that education providers must not treat a disabled person less favourably for any reason that relates to the person's disability. Further, the education provider is required to make reasonable adjustments to enable a person with disabilities to participate in its courses. Access to the ICT facilities and computer-related elements of its courses is an important area where, by considering the needs of students with disabilities, discrimination can be prevented. If necessary, reasonable adjustments can readily be made to meet the needs of individual students with disabilities.

In response to the imperative that students with disabilities need to be fully enabled to use ICT, this chapter sets out to:

- Give an overview of how different disabilities may impinge on a student's use of a computer and what tools are available to facilitate the access of students with disabilities to ICT.
- Give pointers to what responses (reasonable adjustments) an educational institution and its individual teaching and support staff need to make to

ensure that the computer-mediated sections of the curriculum are accessible to students with disabilities.

* Indicate some additional resources, sources of information and services that may assist in ensuring that an institution and individual members of its staff carry out their responsibilities in meeting the ICT-related needs of current and future students with disabilities.

Scope

This chapter focuses on the use of computers and does not cover other technological support that it may be necessary to make available to students with disabilities, such as loop systems in classrooms or lecture theatres for users of hearing aids. Nor does it consider where human support may be more appropriate (for example, note takers or sign language interpreters). It focuses on learning in science subjects, but many of the issues affect education more broadly.

Information and communication technology and the learner with disabilities

For students with disabilities to fully access the science curriculum, they need access to the computer, because this is now so much a part of curriculum delivery. This section outlines the different means that can be employed to enable students with a range of special educational needs to make effective use of a computer, while the following section outlines the principles that must be applied in developing educational software or web-based content to ensure that it is accessible to students with disabilities.

Enabling effective use of a computer

Some students with disabilities use accessibility features provided by the operating systems of the computer, or specialist software or hardware to facilitate their use of the equipment. These software or hardware tools are often referred to collectively as 'assistive technology'. If it is to be accessible to students with disabilities, any software or content mediated by the computer has to be developed so that it is compatible with these tools. This section provides an overview of the range of assistive technology available and the types of student that they may benefit. It is, however, beyond the scope of this chapter to provide detailed guidelines on supporting an individual student in selecting the most appropriate assistive technology to meet specific needs.

It is generally unhelpful to consider medical classifications of disability when seeking to identify the means of enabling people with disabilities to make efficient use of the computer. It is preferable to consider the abilities, and disabilities, of the individual with respect to what they need to do to make most effective use of the computer; in other words, to take a functional approach. The functions to be considered fall into two broad categories:

- How the person may best input commands and information into the computer (for example, most computer users use the keyboard and mouse).
- How the person receives the output from the computer (for most computer users this will generally be the monitor, but it may also include loudspeakers and printers).

The way in which these functions can be supported by mainstream and specialist tools is described in the following sections.

Computer input methods

Computer input methods cover any way that a person using the computer is able to interact with the computer's operating system or any software running on the computer. This includes navigating through and selecting options, or directly entering text and data. For most people, most of the time, computer input is facilitated by the keyboard and mouse and many people with disabilities also choose to use a conventional keyboard, as it generally presents no problem to, for example, people with a visual impairment, who normally readily learn to touch-type. A simple key-guard (a rigid sheet with finger holes for each key laid over a conventional keyboard), can help those with a tremor or weak hands or arms, preventing them from hitting keys in error. However, for those who find a conventional QWERTY keyboard difficult or impossible to use, there are a great many alternatives available, some of which are listed below:

- Alternative keyboard configurations are available, for example, larger and smaller sized versions, keyboards configured for single-handed use, and keyboards designed to reduce repetitive strain.
- Virtual keyboards for switch users. Some people with severe physical disabilities elect to use a single switch or a combination of a small number of switches, which can be operated with any body movement over which they have consistent control. To enable them to type, switches can be used as inputs to a variety of virtual keyboards. These virtual keyboards are software applications that run on the computer being controlled. They usually display a layout of letters and numbers on the computer monitor and offer a range of scanning and word prediction features to facilitate efficient typing. Some communication aids that non-speakers use, often controlled by switches in a similar way, can act as direct replacements for computer keyboards.
- Speech recognition. Since the mid-1990s speech recognition software has become readily available. Words spoken by the user are translated into typed input for any application on their computer, or into the commands to control the application. With practice, efficient input can be achieved through speech recognition. There are drawbacks, however. For example, in many speech recognition programs it is necessary for the user to announce each word individually and users must also correct mis-translations, which will probably occur more frequently than typos for an average keyboard user. However,

continued technological developments are improving the situation, so that the user can speak more naturally and the computer's accuracy of recognition improves with use.

- Alternatives to the mouse. There is a wide variety of pointing devices that can be used instead of the mouse. These include joysticks and trackballs, which can offer different benefits. Some can, for instance, be operated by foot, while others minimize the effect of tremor on cursor movement. For those who cannot or choose not to use any of these, then effective control can be enabled via the keyboard alone. The action of a mouse can be emulated by use of the arrow keys but it is normally preferable to use keyboard shortcuts that achieve the same functionality as pointing and clicking a mouse at a menu, button on the display, or a 'hot spot'.

Notes on the implications of alternative keyboards

A consideration when working through the implications of using different keyboard alternatives is the distinction between direct and indirect alternatives.

- Direct alternatives to conventional keyboards are ones that connect to the computer via the keyboard port (for example, single-handed, Braille or chord keyboards).
- Indirect alternatives to conventional keyboards do not use the keyboard port (for example, on-screen virtual keyboard, voice recognition software or touch-screen software).

Because indirect alternatives depend on software running on the computer being used by the students, there can be issues of compatibility between this software and the programs that the students need to use. A direct alternative does not, in general, give rise to any such problems. However, indirect alternatives may offer features that are important to improve the speed of entry for the user, such as scanning strategies or word prediction.

Some students with disabilities are only able to 'type' at speeds which are significantly slower than would be expected of most students. This has implications for how these students are best supported in their studies and can have particular implications for examinations. Such students will generally require more time to give a fair account of themselves.

Computer output methods for different needs

Computer output methods encompass the different ways users receive information from the computer or any software running on it. In most cases, this simply refers to the images presented via the computer's display monitor and sound played through its speaker system. However, the importance of print as an output method should not be neglected. There are also some more specialized output methods for particular applications, and some developed specifically to meet the needs of computer users with disabilities. Some examples are outlined below.

Screen-readers and Braille displays

In order to access computer output, individuals with no useful sight use software known as a 'screen-reader'. This presents the textual content of the screen either to a speech synthesizer or a Braille display. A speech synthesizer can be either hardware or a software component and can produce a range of synthetic voices. A Braille display consists of an array of plastic 'pins' that move up and down to create the dot pattern of a line of Braille dynamically. The user reads the Braille by passing his or her finger(s) over the characters as the line of text is 'scanned'. Fewer people use Braille displays than speech synthesizers. There are several possible explanations for this, not least the high cost of Braille displays and the fact that less than 20 per cent of people who are blind are fluent Braille readers (this percentage may be higher among blind students).

People who are blind are usually unable to use a mouse or similar pointing device because they cannot see the position of the cursor on the screen. Screen-readers enable the user to navigate the screen in a systematic way in order to read the contents of windows, dialogue boxes, menus, etc. To enable blind people to access screen-reading software, it is essential that all functions are available to this software and that they can be accessed from keyboard commands. In addition, all graphical elements must have meaningful text labels.

However, ICT is not the only answer here. For example, additional approaches exist that can provide access to those without sight to graphical material, including tactile diagrams (for example, see National Centre for Tactile Diagrams 2003) and haptic displays that rely on the sense of touch. There are challenges here too. For example, dedicated design is required for the former and the use of the latter by students who are blind is still largely the object of research rather than common practice.

Screen magnification and display formatting

Those with partial sight have differing needs in terms of accessing a computer. Some require high levels of magnification, which can be provided by screen magnification software. This can magnify the whole screen, or act as an on-screen magnifying glass, magnifying only the area surrounding the cursor, and it can also provide different levels of magnification. Some screen magnifiers can be used in conjunction with a speech synthesizer, providing speech output as an additional support.

As well as magnification, people with partial sight may benefit from other adaptations to the way in which information is presented. For example, high contrast between text and the background and the use of different colour combinations can make text more readable. Screen magnifying software and the ability to select preferred character sizes and contrasting colour schemes is also provided as standard on Windows and Mac computers. The user can select the viewing conditions, which will then be applied to most programs running on that computer, without the need for separate adjustments in each program.

A large screen (for example, 21"/ 53 cm) can also be of benefit to those with partial sight. For input to the computer, most partially sighted people can use a mouse and large-print keyboard labels exist to render the keyboard more visible for those who are unable to touch-type.

Auditory outputs and hearing impairment

In general, people who are deaf or have impaired hearing do not require any specific assistive technology in order to use a computer effectively. Those who have some useful hearing may require control over the volume and tone of audio outputs or coupling to their hearing aids. However, if an educational software application makes extensive use of sound, alternatives need to be provided for users who are hearing-impaired. This normally consists of a transcript of the recorded speech. In such cases, the software developer needs to consider how a person who is deaf would navigate to, and access, the text alternatives.

Deaf-blindness

People who are deaf-blind can access computers using a standard keyboard for input and a Braille display to access the output in the same way as some people with visual impairment.

Dyslexia

Students with dyslexia may use a wide range of display modifications and assistive technologies. In general, such students have difficulty reading on-screen text and they may also have difficulty in composing and physically typing their own work. This group can be supported by assistive technology for both input and output. For those who have difficulty with inputting information into the computer, voice recognition can be useful to compose written work. Those who have difficulty reading on-screen text can use software to change the presentation of the text. The type of presentation depends on the specific needs of the individual, but many find it useful to change the size, character spacing, line spacing, and line length of text on the screen. In addition, different combinations of text and background colour can make text more readable. People who have difficulty reading may also find it useful to have text read aloud by text-to-speech software.

Software configurations and adaptations

Over the past ten years or so, operating systems have increasingly incorporated features that enable people with disabilities to use the computer more readily. For example, you can access these optional features on a Windows 2000 PC under Start/Programs/Accessories/Accessibility. Similar functionality was also made available on Windows 95/98 through the accessibility icon in the control panel. Further examples here include 'sticky keys', which enable features that would normally require more than one key to be depressed simultaneously to be accessed by pressing keys sequentially (for example, Ctrl/Alt/Del). Basic screen magnification is also usually provided. The options available may not always be obvious to students, however, and support may be needed in selecting which of these tools are helpful and also in configuring them to work with relevant software applications.

Another facility that has become increasingly important is the use of personal style sheets. These define, for example, in what size and colours text and background should be displayed when viewing a web page in a browser. For these to be used, the content provider needs to configure the pages so that the user's own style sheets can override the default presentation style.

For students on campus, where a variety of university-provided computers are used at different times, there is much to be gained by implementing individual user profiles, with configuration files being accessed by any machine at login. This greatly reduces the effort required in providing effective ICT support to large numbers of users. Where this is done, the provision should also include any accessibility features or assistive technology the particular student uses in the profile. The technological developments in this area are positive, as most network technologies and operating systems now provide for such features. Thus, this is often more a policy issue than a technical one.

Issues with some software packages when using assistive technologies

Problems may occur when students need to use a particular software package for their course and this proves to be incompatible with the assistive technology they use. This incompatibility can arise for two main reasons:

- The assistive technology and the software package make competing demands on the resources of the student's computer.
- The software package does not provide the 'hooks' needed for the assistive technology to interact with it.

Since basic computing power and the functionality of all components of the standard desktop computer are nowadays substantial, the first problem is less common. However, one example of this type of problem is where the student uses a software-based speech synthesizer package that uses the computer's sound card to produce the speech output as it 'reads aloud' the selected text. Some sound cards can only process one channel of audio at a time. Hence, there may be a clash if the student is using the synthesizer to read text presented in a software package when the same package is also trying to play audio messages.

One simple example of the second type of problem is where a student does not use a mouse or equivalent pointing device and the controls of the software package are presented only for mouse interaction, with no keyboard equivalents. However, there are also more complex issues relating to whether a software package is compatible with accessibility functions in the operating system. These are commented on further in the section 'Software packages and educational multimedia' (p. 165).

When a computer is for a student's personal use, the best way of dealing with these problems is at the specification stage for the computer and the assistive technology. These issues must also be considered when selecting software packages to be used as part of a course. By ensuring that appropriate expertise is brought to bear at the time of specifying the student's computer and assistive technology, many of the problems resulting from the first reason above can be averted. An important part of this process should be a review of the software packages required for courses. As a way of meeting its obligations under SENDA (HMSO 2001); that is, to make its courses accessible to students with disabilities, an educational institution should set essential accessibility criteria for selecting any software package for use in its courses, as matter of policy.

Solving these problems at the specification stage is an ideal approach, but practical compatibility problems between particular assistive technologies and different software packages will still arise. Usually these can be overcome but this often requires experience and technical skills. Educational establishments therefore need to make appropriate support staff available. This would normally mean equipping specialist student support teams with appropriate ICT support skills, or ensuring that the main computer support teams include sufficient numbers of people with adequate expertise and experience relating to accessibility.

Assessing the needs of students with disabilities

The above overview of assistive technologies and approaches for making the computer accessible is intended only as a generic introduction. The selection of a particular piece of equipment to support an individual student with disabilities should be carried out in consultation with a suitably experienced needs assessor. In the UK, government grants, called Disabled Students Awards (DSAs), are available to most students with disabilities in higher education. The equipment element of these grants includes a provision for assessment of need. Some universities offer their students support by providing needs assessments. Many such centres also offer these services to students from other institutions. The principle providers of needs assessments for equipment provided under the DSA scheme belong to the National Federation of Access Centres (for example, see NFAC n.d.). At school level, equipment may be provided for the individual student in response to the educational statementing process. Alternatively, these resources may be part of the ICT provision of special needs schools, or as part of mainstream schools with designated provision for pupils with special needs.

Making the curriculum accessible

Conventional university education, in some respects, has changed little over the years in terms of how it delivers the curriculum. In most subject areas and institutions, the lecture, seminar and tutorial remain the principal modes of delivery, with laboratories and fieldwork supplementing these, particularly in science and engineering subjects. However, even where these traditional approaches are maintained, computers are increasingly used to support them. A more comprehensive use of computers in delivering curricula is being adopted in some institutions that are seeking to make the Web central to their course delivery, both in campus-based and distance-learning contexts. This is often achieved using commercially available integrated suites of software called Managed Learning Environments (MLE) or Learning Management Systems (LMS). These combine administrative functions, such as course registration and student records, with mechanisms for creating and delivering web-based courses. It is not the purpose of this chapter to comment on the relative merits of the different ways of using computer technology in curriculum delivery. However, it is a matter of fact that virtually all university courses use computers to a greater or lesser extent. This section gives some pointers to actions that academics, programmers, web authors and technical support teams can take to ensure that the computer-based aspects of their courses are accessible to students with disabilities.

In essence, making the computer-based elements of the curriculum accessible means:

- ensuring that the educational content is authored according to established accessibility guidelines;
- ensuring that the computer systems used to mediate this content to students are compatible with assistive technology the students may use;
- where that content cannot be made accessible using ICT, ensuring that reasonable alternatives are made available.

The accessibility guidelines, referred to above, are discussed further here. These guidelines essentially ensure that the user can control, to some extent, the way that content is presented to them and that the delivery system can exploit the benefits of assistive technology. Hence, where earlier in this chapter pointers were given as to how a student can be enabled to use the computer, the following sections outline how those charged with delivering the curriculum should do so in a way that is accessible to students with disabilities.

Principles for accessibility

There exist some basic, well-established principles for accessibility that apply to all computer software. How these principles are realized in a particular piece of software or online content depends very much upon the authoring tools, programming language or development environment used. The choice of authoring environment can have a significant impact on how readily accessibility criteria are met.

General principles of software accessibility

- *Allow for user customisation.*
  (Particularly of text size and style, background and foreground colours.)
  This enables different students to select how text is displayed so that they can most easily read it.

- *Provide equivalent visual and auditory content and interface elements.*
  (Text descriptions for images and video, transcription of auditory content, text labelling of interface elements, etc.)
  This gives students with sensory impairment access to multimedia elements within the software.

- *Provide compatibility with assistive technologies.*
  This recognizes that not everyone interacts with their computer by keyboard and mouse.

- *Allow access to all functionality from the keyboard alone.*
  (This means ensuring that the software can be fully used without a mouse.)
  This accommodates the many people with physical disabilities or visual impairments who are unable to use a mouse.

- *Provide context and orientation information.*
  (This requires sufficient navigation support by informing the user of where they are in the program. It should take into account that some users may be using screen-readers.)
  This is a good design principle for all users, but poor navigation design is particularly problematic for screen-reader users.

World Wide Web-based content and learning activities

The World Wide Web Consortium (W3C) creates web standards (for example, see W3C 2003a). Under its Web Accessibility Initiative (WAI), it has drawn up extensive guidelines for creating web pages that are accessible to many people with a disability (for example, see W3C 2003b).

At first sight, the WAI guidelines can appear complex. It is therefore worth noting that a good starting point is the WAI's own online training package, which is referred to as 'Curriculum' (W3C 2000a). The WAI also provides a 'Techniques' document (W3C 2000b) and useful 'Checklists' (W3C 1999) for web developers. There are several guidelines, each of which is associated with one or more checkpoints describing how to apply that guideline to particular features in web pages. Each checkpoint is assigned one of three 'priority' levels, reflecting the impact on accessibility if it is not followed. Levels of conformance are then specified against these priorities. It is recommended that an educational website seeking to meet the needs of students with disabilities should aim for 'Double-A' conformance, which means meeting all priority one and two checkpoints.

Most websites and pages are produced using authoring tools rather than 'hand crafting' HTML. There is a high degree of variability in how readily these tools support authoring in a way that conforms to the accessibility guidelines. However, in response to US legislation, most of the major suppliers of such tools are seeking to address this issue in recent and planned releases.

It is important not merely to follow guidelines for accessibility when creating web content, but then to test it for accessibility. Ideally, this would be done by people with a range of disabilities viewing the pages with their usual assistive technology. Where this is not possible, however, several automated validation tools are available, both for validating the HTML mark-up language and for accessibility. Further, it is good standard practice to check web pages with more than one browser. By including a text-based browser in this procedure, key problems in accessibility can be detected.

Notably, it is not usually good practice for web developers lacking experience of accessibility to use some of the more sophisticated screen-readers intended for people with visual impairment. Unless significant time is invested to learn and practise using these packages, problems with a website may be reported that are, in fact, due to a lack of understanding of how to access the range of features of the screen-reader.

Key principles to ensure accessibility when designing content for the World Wide Web

1   Follow the established standards and guidelines. This includes the standards for HTML as well the Web Accessibility Guidelines. Text browsers or other assistive technology could misinterpret non-standard HTML.
2   Keep designs clear and simple. This will promote the readability and usability of your pages. Good design for people with disabilities is good design for all!
3   Test and validate your designs. This is preferably done by asking people with disabilities who use different ways of accessing the Web to review your pages. Pages should at least be tested with a text browser and automatic validation tools.

Issues for virtual learning environments

The use of integrated software suites to support and manage the learning process in higher education is becoming widespread. The terminology used here is various and used in different ways by different communities. Broadly, however, the term Virtual Learning Environment (VLE) is used to refer to software that supports various online interactions between students and their tutors. As we have seen, the terms LMS and MLE are also used to describe an integration of the whole range of information systems employed by an educational establishment. This may include a VLE as well as, for example, course registration and student record systems. Since this chapter is concerned with students' interaction with ICT, the term VLE is used here.

A VLE usually provides access via a web-publishing tool that enables tutors to present curriculum material (notes, presentations, assignments, reading lists, etc.) to their students. This is normally combined with mechanisms which control when this material is made available to the students and also enables their activity and progress to be tracked. A VLE supports communication between the student and tutor and their peer-group by, for example, e-mail conferences. The VLE also usually provides access to learning support material and services.

This brief statement of the functionality of a VLE illustrates how its accessibility has the potential to enable students with disabilities to participate in courses. Since VLEs are designed to impact across the presentation of an entire course (and in some cases across an institution), tackling accessibility issues must be a strategic priority.

There are two broad areas for accessibility consideration in a VLE:

1   Access to, and navigation around, the student interface of the VLE itself.
2   Access to content presented by the VLE.

The first of these is an issue for the suppliers of the VLE. Indeed, all the major suppliers of VLEs are seeking to address the issues of accessibility in their products, mainly in response to the power of Section 508 of the USA's Rehabilitation Act (1998) in affecting universities' purchasing decisions. SENDA in the UK can also be reasonably expected to have a similar impact here. If an educational institution seeks to introduce a VLE, it should ensure that a key feature of the specification will be accessibility for students with disabilities. Otherwise, it could be judged to be significantly disadvantaging such students.

The second area of concern is that content presentation may also be affected by the design of a VLE, particularly with regard to the authoring tools it might offer teaching staff for creating content that will be presented to students via the VLE. These should ideally promote accessibility and certainly not introduce barriers to students with disabilities. Much of the responsibility for the accessibility of the content will, however, fall on authors, who are usually the teaching staff. The task of authoring accessible content need not be an onerous one, but it is a key staff development issue. In most cases, the content will consist of web pages, so the accessibility issues apply which were outlined under 'World Wide Web-based content and learning activities' (p. 162). Much of the content will be text-based and require little special response. However, all teaching staff authoring content for presentation on a VLE need to be made aware of the accessibility issues, especially where they seek to include diagrams or multimedia elements.

Software packages and educational multimedia

Where an institution, department or individual lecturer writes, commissions or purchases a piece of software to be used by students as part of their studies, they must, from the outset, specify the accessibility criteria and confirm that these are then met. It is far easier and less costly to incorporate accessibility features at the beginning rather than requesting 'fixes' once prototypes are in an advanced stage of development. Typical examples of the sort of packages being considered here are simulations such as 'virtual science' packages, or computer programs that offer students access to multimedia material. As long as the software used is accessible, the increasing use of computers in laboratory work has the potential to enable students with disabilities to be active participants rather than passive observers. For example, some universities have demonstrated the use of simulations and other computer-based activities as alternatives to fieldwork that may otherwise have been inaccessible to some students with disabilities.

JAVA is currently a popular programming language for developing such educational software. Pointers to developer's guidelines for achieving accessibility are available on the Web. These guidelines direct the developer to program in such a way as to meet the principles of accessibility given above. Following these guidelines may constrain a programmer to work in an unfamiliar way, particularly when creating user interfaces, and this may slightly increase the development time required. Helping the developer to understand why accessibility is important is, therefore, an integral part of the process of specifying and developing such software. Note that for some accessibility features, such as those requiring an integration of the software of the assistive technology and the JAVA program (for example, screen-reader access to interface commands), the assistive technology must be produced in such a way as to enable this. This is increasingly the case with recent products but it should be recognized that, even if developed according to the JAVA accessibility guidelines, whether a piece of educational software is indeed accessible to a student with disabilities may depend on the assistive technology they employ.

Much educational software is developed not by programming as such, but by using multimedia authoring tools. Different tools promote to differing degrees, or even prevent, the creation of accessible educational software. It is beyond the scope of this chapter to survey these and, indeed, this is a rapidly changing situation. Again, largely in response to US legislative pressure, many producers of these authoring environments are incorporating features in recent versions of their products to promote accessibility. It is therefore important that the educator or institution commissioning software applications for students not only specifies the accessibility criteria, but also questions what development environment will be used and how this will enable these criteria to be met.

As in all other developments where accessibility is a requirement, its achievement should be tested for. Ideally, this should be done as soon as early prototypes are available, as well as at the end of the development period.

Alternatives to print

The computer can prove an enabling technology for those who, for various reasons, find the use of printed material problematic or impossible. This group can include those with a visual impairment or dyslexia, who have problems reading, or those whose physical disabilities make handling a book difficult. If set texts and other courseware normally presented in printed form can be made available electronically, then these students can use their usual assistive technology to access them. The challenge for the curriculum providers is to make the appropriate texts available in a suitable electronic form. There are technical issues here, but it is copyright considerations, in fact, that present some of the biggest barriers to exploiting this enabling opportunity. Recent UK legislation was designed to address this issue (HMSO 2002). If these issues could be overcome, it would be possible to make all texts specifically written for a course available electronically. Indeed, there are many text resources already available in this form. The emerging area of e-books may accelerate the availability of electronic texts over the next few years and this will then raise the issue of accessibility in e-book readers.

Computers in practical work

Computers are increasingly a part of practical work in science education. For example, in data collection and analysis and in some experiments which have been controlled by computers. Provided this is done in a way that is accessible for students with disabilities, the use of computers in practical work has the potential to enable full participation for many students with disabilities.

Educational assessment

Assessment of a student's progress is a fundamental part of their participation in education. For students with disabilities, it is important that they are assessed in such a way that neither disadvantages them nor gives them an advantage over their peers. This is predominantly an issue of policy and good practice within the institution and is outside the scope of this chapter. However, there are two important areas relating to the use of ICT in examinations by students with disabilities, which are briefly mentioned here.

Computers, assistive technology and examinations

First, it is important here to restate the individual nature of need. In examinations, there is no one set response to facilitating all students with a similar disability; rather, the best solution will depend on the coping strategies of individuals. However, where the normal coping strategies of a particular student with disabilities relating to reading and writing includes the use of a computer, this facility must also be extended to them in their examinations. If, for example, the preference for a student who is blind is to use a computer with a screen-reader to access text and to write by typing, it would be appropriate to enable him or her to take their examination at a computer. There has been some reservation in the past about making computers available to students in examinations. An institution may wish to ensure that a student taking an examination at a computer has no access to information that would not normally be made available to others taking the same examination. This may mean providing a dedicated machine for the examination that is not networked. Care must be taken in such cases, however, to ensure any assistive technology the student normally uses is installed and configured as normal.

Computer-aided assessment

The second area to consider is the increasing use of computer-aided assessment (CAA) in higher education. Here, students may undertake computer-based tests as preliminary assessments prior to undertaking a course, to provide them with feedback on progress, or as a summative assessment at the end of a course.

Potentially, CAA can enable many students with disabilities to be assessed in the same manner as their peers, which can help to reduce any feelings of special treatment. Clearly, to do this, the presentation of the CAA tests must be compatible with any assistive technologies used. There is a wide variety of CAA systems used, some based on commercial products and others developed as bespoke solutions by particular institutions. However, virtually all of these use a web-based approach for both the presentation of questions and the receiving of student responses. Hence, the guidelines referred to under 'World Wide Web-based content and learning activities' (p. 162) apply equally here. Particular care is needed when considering, for example, how a screen-reader user is able to navigate to the fields used to answer a given question. If check boxes are used to select from multiple-choice answers, it must be clear which box refers to which answer in the way that the question is read out.

As in the case of VLEs discussed previously, clear accessibility criteria should be stated when an institution is considering purchasing or commissioning CAA software.

Conclusion

For many people with disabilities, computers are tools that enable them to participate in education, and they are being used increasingly in the delivery of the curriculum at all educational levels. Issues of access to ICT must form a key part of policy and practice. These must be considered in the design of the curriculum, the way it is to be delivered and the provision of support services. These issues affect all teaching staff and many with roles in management, strategic planning and service provision within education.

This chapter set out to inform the development of policy and practice in this area. It has provided an introduction to how people with disabilities may be enabled to make effective use of computers. It has gone on to give an overview of the implications of the differing ways the computer may be used for meeting the needs of students with disabilities. Educational institutions in the UK now have a legal as well as moral obligation not to discriminate against students on the grounds of their disability. In nearly all cases, enabling access for students with disabilities to computer-mediated services and elements of the curriculum falls within the description of reasonable adjustment used in this legislation.

Acknowledgements

With thanks to the many people who have informed my understanding of the practical issues of assistive technology and software accessibility over the past fifteen years and in particular to my colleagues in the Accessible Educational Media group at The Open University for their assistance in writing this chapter. Special thanks are owed to Dr Chetz Colwell and Dr Hazel Kennedy.

References

HMSO (2001) *Special Educational Needs and Disability Act 2001*, London: The Stationery Office.

—— (2002) *Copyright (Visually Impaired Persons) Bill*, London: The Stationary Office.

National Centre for Tactile Diagrams (2003) *What are Tactile Graphics?*, Hatfield: University of Hertfordshire, available on the Web at <http://www.nctd.org.uk/WhatareTGs.asp> (last accessed 12 March 2003).

National Federation of Access Centres (NFAC) (n.d.) *Using the National Federation of Access Centres Network*, Plymouth, University of Plymouth, available on the Web at <http://www.nfac.org.uk/nfac2003.pdf> (last accessed 12 March 2003).

World Wide Web Consortium (W3C) (1999) *Checklist of Checkpoints for Web Content Accessibility Guidelines 1.0*, available on the Web at <http://www.w3.org/TR/WAI-WEBCONTENT/full-checklist.html> (last accessed 12 March 2003).

—— (2000a) *Welcome to the Curriculum for Web Content Accessibility Guidelines 1.0*, available on the Web at <http://www.w3.org/WAI/wcag-curric/> (last accessed 12 March 2003).

—— (2000b) *Techniques for Web Content Accessibility Guidelines 1.0*, available on the Web at <http://www.w3.org/TR/WAI-WEBCONTENT-TECHS/> (last accessed 12 March 2003).

—— (2003a) *Leading the Web to its Full Potential*, available on the Web at <http://www.w3.org/> (last accessed 12 March 2003).

—— (2003b) *Web Accessibility Initiative*, available on the Web at <http://www.w3.org/WAI/> (last accessed 12 March 2003).

3.2 Redesigning practical work

Web-based remote experimentation

Terry Di Paolo and Eileen Scanlon with
Chetz Colwell, Martyn Cooper,
Victoria Uren and Anne Jelfs

In this chapter we discuss the provision of practical work in higher education informed by our experience of working on a project aimed at developing remote access to laboratory work over the Internet: the *Practical Experimentation by Access to Remote Learning* (PEARL) project. This chapter begins by looking at practical work in higher education and the constraints placed upon it in the academic setting. The remainder of the chapter concentrates on remote experimentation, focusing on the experience at The Open University of developing and implementing a remote physics experiment. It ends by outlining some of the findings from an educational evaluation of the remote experiment and its implications for the future of remote experimentation.

Practical work in higher education

The role of practical work in the university curriculum is undeniably important yet there is considerable variation among institutions in terms of the amount of time a student will spend in the laboratory and the number of activities he or she will perform in the course of his or her degree. Jervis (1999) claims that even though practical work has been a component of European degree-based study since the nineteenth century, there is no formal pedagogy that informs science educators as to what proportion of practical work on the undergraduate curriculum contributes to an effective science education.

Figure 3.2.1 presents an adaptation of the Hegarty-Hazel (1990) model of practical work in the undergraduate curriculum. The original Hegarty-Hazel model is one of the few models of practical work in tertiary education that highlights that practical work is part of a broader landscape of teaching on a course.

The model in Figure 3.2.1 suggests that a course involving some form of practical work will go through three developmental stages: an initial planning phase, a

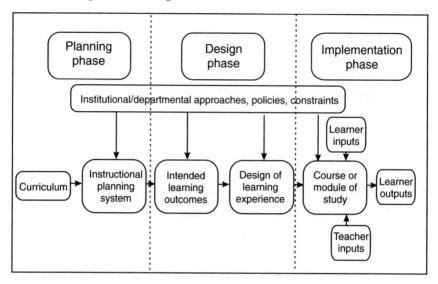

Figure 3.2.1 Model of practical work in science adapted from Hegarty-Hazel (1990).

design phase and, finally, an implementation phase. The various factors that are considered in each of these stages often mean that two universities, which seemingly offer a similar course to students, may attribute different resources and learning outcomes to the same practical activity or experiment. Different institutions may use similar apparatus; they may have similar student numbers and engage students in a set of activities that follow the same steps. However, there is arguably little likelihood of finding two institutions that have implemented the same activity and allocated to it the same amount of time, resources and learning outcomes.

The model also suggests why a formal pedagogy for practical work in Higher Education does not appear viable – because the inclusion of such activity on a course is increasingly a pragmatic decision driven primarily by institutional/departmental factors rather than pedagogic considerations. Such factors often include: available teaching expertise, student numbers, educational level of students, degree structure, course structure, timetabling and laboratory facilities.

Remote experiments

Scanlon *et al.* (2002) report on the innovative way in which information and communications technology (ICT) has been incorporated into practical work. In their review, they report that ICT has been used effectively for providing collaboration and simulating experimental conditions. They argue that the use of simulation, or virtual science, in place of practical work has increased significantly over the past two decades. This can be accounted for by rapid development in the use of computer-generated graphics and the increasing use of ICT in tertiary education.

However, Cooper (2000), in comparing simulation and traditional approaches to experimental work, comments on the importance of spending time in a traditional laboratory, with the experience of manipulating and handling apparatus which is often compromised in the use of virtual science.

An alternative to virtual science is remote experimentation – the manipulation or control of traditional apparatus at a distance (as opposed to a graphic rendering of the apparatus). Scanlon *et al.* (2002) identified two main trends in the provision of remote experimentation when their review took place in 1999:

- experiments providing public access to scientific apparatus or findings
- consortiums where a number of universities with particular expertise or facilities share resources.

Undoubtedly, virtual science could play a role within the science curriculum of most universities, but the increasing number of remote experiments appears to indicate that this role may be limited. From informal monitoring of the research on remote experiments over a period of approximately three years, from 1999 to 2003, we estimate that the number of remote experiments in development or being used across the globe has tripled.

Cartwright and Valentine (2002) claim that the advantages of remote experiments include: enhancement of distance education courses; access to dangerous environments; access to rare or expensive equipment; and financial advantage opportunities for collaborative projects. They propose that there are three key requirements for a distance laboratory to compare favourably with a traditional laboratory:

- Students must have enough control of the laboratory equipment to start and stop an experiment and make appropriate adjustments.
- The experiment should be no more difficult to conduct than with the equipment physically present.
- Students need appropriate feedback.

(Cartwright and Valentine 2002: 40)

Arguably, the view taken by Cartwright and Valentine understates or simplifies the features which are necessary for favourable comparison.

The PEARL project

The European Union-funded PEARL project has researched and developed a system to enable students to conduct traditional experiments using computers. The aim of the project was to explore whether high quality learning experiences could be produced by bringing the teaching laboratory to the students, therefore increasing their access to science. There are other potential benefits too. For example, those working on the project have argued that there are a number of benefits that could arise from remote experimentation (Cooper *et al.* 2002). These include: overcoming constraints of time and space; meeting the challenge of increasing student numbers; and exposure to complex and expensive commercial equipment. Another benefit, and in fact one of the original motivations for the PEARL project, is linked to increasing accessibility to science for students.

The project extended the idea of Internet course delivery to accommodate collaborative working while conducting science and engineering experiments. This has been achieved by developing and integrating a collaborative working environment with accessible user interfaces, a modular system for flexibly creating remotely controlled experiments, and investigating an educational software framework based on templates and tutor guidelines that could enable some development of experimental programmes using this system. The project also researched the pedagogic impact of this approach by conducting validations of its developments in different educational contexts and subject areas in science.

The educational model adopted by PEARL

We developed the idea of practical work based on a model of collaborative working focused on experimental work in a remote laboratory, with feedback to students on their experiences being provided by tutor comments and peer interaction. The first step in the project was to establish a technical infrastructure that would enable the necessary interactions between students, equipment and their tutors. An analysis of the pedagogical requirements of the system was conducted in two stages: first, a literature review on practical work and, second, interviews and questionnaires with teachers in higher education about the needs of such systems. We found the work of the European Labwork in Science Education project (for example, see Leach and Paulsen 1999; Psillos and Niedderer 2003) offered a critique of how practical work in higher education in science is currently organized and recommended that the purpose and the learning objectives of the practical work be clarified.

We found the conversational model developed by Diana Laurillard useful in thinking about what interactions were necessary between learners and their environment, and with other learners and tutors. Laurillard (2001) considers the learning process as a sort of conversation. She produced a classification of media that is based on a conversational framework that identifies the activities necessary to fulfil the learning process. The learning process, she argues, must be viewed as dialogue between 'teacher' and student. The classification system she developed is based on the type of interaction between instructor and student that is made possible by the use of a particular medium. She argues that the best approach to teaching is likely to require an integrated combination of several media.

The technology involved in PEARL

Colwell *et al.* (2002: 67) describe the PEARL system as follows:

> The PEARL system involves a complex structure of network server and interface technologies, equipment control technology, video cameras, microphones

and streaming media technology, and collaboration tools. These technologies work together to allow students to issue commands from their PC to the remote laboratory, which in turn carries out the command and sends the feedback to the student. The student can then see the laboratory equipment being controlled via a video-stream and can communicate in real-time with a number of other students about the experiment.

There is, however, still the need for a technician/tutor to be on hand should the equipment fail in the laboratory. Human intervention is also required at the beginning of the experiment, for example, to light Bunsen flames or ensure chemical stocks are sufficient for the experiment to proceed.

This technical infrastructure supports four separate teaching experiments which have been developed at four universities involved in the PEARL project: The Open University (OU), the University of Dundee, Trinity College Dublin and the University of Porto.

The PEARL experiments

Each of the four universities that took part in the project developed their own experiment. Collectively, these covered a range of activities for students at different levels in different disciplines. The experiment implemented at the University of Dundee involves Year 3 undergraduates in cellular biology. It allows them to examine samples with an electron microscope to investigate the content and behaviour of biological cells. In the traditional laboratory, the students do not use the microscope themselves but are shown samples by the lecturer, who demonstrates the use of the equipment. The microscope is a large piece of expensive equipment housed in a small room. On many occasions the number of students to be accommodated prevents them using the microscope individually.

The experiment implemented at Trinity College Dublin involves the inspection of printed circuit boards. Students use a range of equipment, including cameras, lighting heads, lenses and computer vision systems. At the University of Porto, the experiment implemented for undergraduate students involves a digital electronic bench to design and test digital circuits, using programmable integrated circuits. This experiment is integrated with a web-based course via the PEARL system. The rationale for implementing remote experiments at both Trinity College Dublin and the University of Porto was similar in that both institutions reported that there was limited equipment which few students had access to, and providing access to that equipment for students enrolled on a particular course was difficult in view of timetable design and staffing issues. Therefore, the remote implementations at each university could provide access to equipment and an important hands-on experience for the students.

The OU's experiment was originally part of an introductory science course for residential school. The PEARL system implemented enables students to carry out flame tests and to use optical spectrometers and colorimeters in the analyses of substances. In the case of the OU, we were particularly interested in the feasibility of remote experimentation as a way of providing for those students who, for whatever reason, cannot attend a residential school to gain some experience of practical work.

Before we consider these issues in detail, it is important to note that, at the outset, the leader of the PEARL project, Martyn Cooper, set realistic aims for the project by stating that the PEARL system would not be able to reproduce the gestalt of working on traditional experiments in the laboratory (for example, the smells of a chemistry lab, see Cooper 2000).

Spectrometers, flames and spectra

For the rest of this chapter, we concentrate on a detailed discussion of our experiences in implementing and validating the OU experiment. We focus on this experience as the OU was the only partner that attempted to implement a remote 'copy' of an activity carried out by students in the traditional laboratory.

Background to the remote experiment

The experiment implemented at the OU was a remote-access version of an experimental activity that currently forms part of a residential school for one of the OU's foundation level science courses, SXR103: *Practising Science*. This course, unlike most other courses offered by the OU, is studied by students at a residential school. This is a week-long event where students are exposed to the laboratory environment and apparatus at a traditional UK university. Students then also study at a distance in preparing for the course and in completing part of the assessment.

Historically, the residential school was a mandatory component of the main foundation course S103: *Discovering Science*. S103 continues to recruit more than 3000 students every year and almost one-third of those students opt to study SXR103 too. In the past, many S103 students had problems attending the residential school because of work or home commitments and, in some cases, because of disabilities. This highlighted an issue that remote access to experiments could potentially solve: rather than the student having to attend the residential school, the residential school could come to the student.

We focused on remote implementation of two activities which were taken directly from the curriculum of the residential school. One activity involved chemical analysis techniques, the other concentrated on physics. Both activities were set within a scenario of environmental monitoring. These activities were designed to provide experience in using experimental apparatus, making and recording observations, analysing and interpreting data and working collaboratively with other students. The experiments include:

- a series of 'wet chemistry' tests – adding reagents to sample solutions and observing the results;
- a series of physics tests – examining the spectral wavelengths of different light sources and the analysis of those wavelengths. The aims of this set of activities

included: gaining experience of carrying out a flame test; gaining experience of using a hand-held spectroscope; experiencing the setting up and calibration of a spectrometer; measuring angles of diffraction using a Vernier scale; and identifying elements based on their spectral signatures.

In this chapter, we focus on the activity linked to the physics of light spectra. There are five tasks that students carry out at the residential school in relation to this activity:

1   There is a series of flame tests where students place a particular metal chemical compound into a Bunsen flame. The students are asked to observe with the naked eye what colour the flame changes to.
2   Students repeat the flame tests, observing the resulting colour change of the flame through a hand-held spectroscope.
3   The students set up and calibrate an optical grating spectrometer.
4   Students use the optical grating spectrometer to determine the spectral signature of a sodium lamp.
5   Students use the optical grating spectrometer to determine the spectral signature of unknown metal ions in a solution being blown through a Bunsen.

At the residential school, these tasks have been designed to take approximately half a day (three hours) to complete. In the next section, we outline our attempts to implement these stages as a remote experiment.

The development process

Producing these remote implementations seemed relatively straightforward at the onset of the project. The plan was to take existing apparatus, exactly like that handled by the students at the residential school, and implement a way of using it remotely with robotic manipulation. For example, an optical grating spectrometer has two main parts: a telescope and a collimator (see Figure 3.2.2). The collimator is pointed at a light source. At the end of the collimator is a slit, like two elevator doors, which can be adjusted to let in more or less light. The collimator slit width can be adjusted with a round dial which can be turned clockwise or anticlockwise. In the remote laboratory, the idea was that the turning of this dial for the adjustment of the slit width would be carried out by a motor shaft.

However, as the development and planning work progressed (more slowly than planned, which is often the case in technological projects) we found ourselves faced with a problem of sourcing affordable technology that would let us provide a comparable learning experience to that which students encountered at the residential school. We found ourselves having to compromise on what the students could achieve. For example, one of the first things the students learn to do with a spectrometer is to focus the telescope. This is done by pointing the telescope at a distant object (at the residential school this was usually a tree outside the laboratory). Reproducing

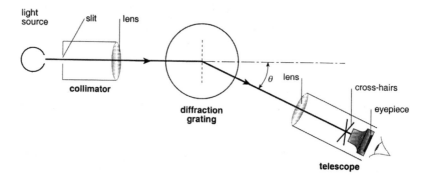

Figure 3.2.2 The main components of a grating spectrometer, including collimator, diffraction grating and telescope.

this experience would be untenable in the remote laboratory so we decided to focus the telescope for the students.

Originally, the tasks involving the flame test were intended to be implemented as remote control tasks but, following a detailed specification of the activity, it became apparent that such an approach was not feasible within the lifetime and resources of the project. Again, the main difficulty was finding a cost-effective robotic solution to what is a relatively simple procedure carried out by the students in the traditional laboratory.

As an alternative, this part of the activity was implemented using pre-recorded video of the activity broadcast over the Web. A series of video clips was produced and embedded in a web-based text which outlined the purpose of this part of the activity and also provided the student with details about the procedures they would carry out in the traditional laboratory.

The clips demonstrated the response of a Bunsen flame to the insertion of a chemical substance along with the procedures for cleaning the wire with which the chemicals are inserted into the flame and the consequences of the wire not being cleaned properly. These are all aspects of the learning experience that are high-lighted in the traditional version of the activity.

In the remainder of the activity, students worked with a spectrometer (see Figure 3.2.2) which was implemented remotely, but with compromises made to some of the initial setting-up steps students would carry out in the traditional laboratory.

As mentioned previously, we carried out the initial focusing of the telescope for the students. Further to this, students in the traditional laboratory setting are expected to insert a diffraction grating between the telescope and collimator. Again this was a step we had to carry out for them. Deciding to perform these steps for students was based on an examination of whether or not they were linked to the main learning objectives of the task. Arguably, the focusing of the telescope and the insertion of the diffraction grating do impact on one of the main outcomes of the task, as they allow students to become familiar with the workings and setting up of the spectrometer. However, given that the key outcome of the task was appreciating that there are quantitative differences between light spectra, we argued that performing these steps for students did not detract from this overarching goal of the task.

The challenges of real-time action

Along with developing the robotic technologies to perform these tasks, a considerable amount of time was spent developing and testing a user interface for the students to carry out the task. One of the major issues we were faced with was: how to provide real-time movement of the spectrometer's components?

If a student uses the spectrometer in the traditional laboratory setting, he or she can move the telescope freely within approximately a 180-degree radius. This free movement means that 'sweeping' large movements of the telescope can be made to initially find a set of spectral lines, or very small movements made when the lines need to be centred in the telescope. Unfortunately, we could not provide free real-time movement and real-time video; this was due both to technological factors and design issues associated with developing an interface that would also be accessible for visually impaired students. Instead, we opted for a system where movement was limited to coarse–medium–fine (see Figure 3.2.3), where 'coarse' was the largest of the available movements and 'fine' was the smallest.

Another issue was the quality of video. We provided students with three video feeds (see Figure 3.2.3):

- to illustrate what was happening in the remote laboratory (so the students could see the equipment moving);
- to show the measurement scale of the spectrometer (so the students could take a reading of the diffraction angle);
- to provide students with a view down the telescope (so that students could see the light spectra as they would in the traditional laboratory). In the traditional laboratory setting, if students look through the telescope they see a pair of spectral lines (doublet) close together at the zero order, first order and second order positions. We could not source affordable camera technology with sufficient resolution that would let students see the doublet. Instead, students saw a block of light.

In addition, the interface also integrated accessibility features for students with disabilities (predominantly students with either hearing or visual impairments). Each of the 'buttons' or actions on the interface could be executed using the computer keyboard. There were also visual cues in the form of status bars that indicated when an action or button was completed. For instance, if a student wanted to move the telescope one coarse movement to the left, they could press 'L' (to select a left movement) then 'C' (to select a coarse movement). The status bar under the left-coarse button would then change and finally beep when the action had been completed.

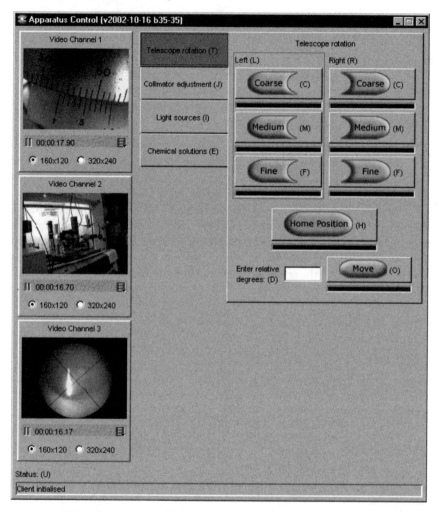

Figure 3.2.3   The interface designed for rotating the telescope, also showing the three video feeds.

What did students make of the activity?

Having built the remote laboratory equipment and, through previous testing, refined a control interface for the system, we carried out an educational evaluation of the system.

We were interested in answering a number of questions:

- Did it provide a successful and productive learning experience?
- How did it compare with the experience of students carrying out the same activity in the laboratory?
- What was its future potential?

The testing of the system was carried out by six students: three had studied S103 and SXR103 and attended the residential school for the course. The other three students had studied S103 but had not studied SXR103 or attended its associated residential school. Furthermore, as three out of the six students were registered with the OU as disabled we were also able to examine the accessibility of the system. We hoped this mix of student experiences would provide a rich insight into the experience of carrying out a remote experiment.

The students worked in pairs to complete the experiment, as they would at the residential school. We asked each pair of students to come along to the OU in Milton Keynes and take part in the testing for half a day where our recording facilities are based. In each session, we located one of the students in one room and the other student in another room (to recreate the notion of working on this experiment from their home). During the session, they communicated with one another and a tutor located elsewhere on the university campus using a collaboration tool called NetMeeting. This allowed the students to communicate with one another using both audio and text chat. We also set up web-cams in each of the rooms so that the students could see each other. They could both communicate with the tutor using the same program, but only through text chat.

The students were observed and video recorded using the system and, following the session, they were interviewed about their experience of carrying out the remote experiment.

The interview was divided into four sections in order to:

- investigate their past experience of practical work;
- determine their affective response (or general feeling towards the activity);
- provide a forum where they could reflect on what they felt they learnt during the session;
- consider how they had managed the different aspects of the task.

A few months earlier, we had used the same interview format to collect data from twelve students at the residential school about their experience of undertaking the same activity.

In the following sections, we outline what we found from each part of the interview and we compare the findings from the students who carried out the remote experiment with those that undertook the activity at the residential school.

Past experience of practical work

We asked students about their past experience to get a sense of what they generally thought about practical work and whether their views were dependent on the amount of practical work they had previously conducted.

Bliss (1990) reports on a project carried out in the 1970s which explored the experiences of physics students at ten universities in the UK. The project found that students reported more bad experiences of practical work in the early part of their undergraduate degree. Generally, they reported that bad experiences of practical work were characterized by them feeling insecure and doubting their own ability or feeling annoyed at the teaching or the fact that equipment had failed. Experiences of good practical work were characterized by experiments that worked, the achievement of a result and learning about something, being given autonomy in what they could do and feeling that the experimental process was not just a repetition of a 'recipe book' experiment.

The students from the residential school and the students from the evaluation of the remote experiment session both gave similar accounts. Most of the students had done varying amounts of practical work at school, but not much since and, for a lot of students, it was over a decade since they had studied any science.

They reported that experiences of good practical work enabled them to understand the course content more and, most importantly, many quoted that it gave them an opportunity to 'see it for real'. With limited experience of practical work, students who attended the residential school and those that used the PEARL system reported that bad practical work was marked by boring subject matter and procedures, along with failing equipment.

The students generally agreed that getting hands-on experience was the most enjoyable aspect of practical work while writing-up was the least enjoyable. They also agreed on the benefits of practical work: getting hands-on experience and increasing their understanding of science by making sense of the theory they had been taught.

General responses to the activity

In this part of the interview, we wanted to determine what students generally thought about doing the experiment, for instance what they enjoyed, what parts they found interesting and what parts of the task they found frustrating.

Students in both groups (residential school and PEARL users) reported that they enjoyed the activity, in particular, the flame tests and using the spectrometer. However, both groups also reported similar levels of frustration in using the spectrometer, particularly in finding the spectral lines.

One significant way in which the groups differed was that the remote experiment students felt they could have benefited from more help from the tutor and clearer instructions. We tried as much as possible to use the same instructions in the residential school labscript as for the remote experiment. However, the role of the tutor during the remote experiment was quite different from that of the tutor at the residential school.

At the residential school, a number of tutors walk around the room, visiting each pair of students to monitor their progress. They can also be called upon to assist students in difficulty. From observations carried out at the summer school, when a tutor visits a pair of students, the students often run through what they have done so far and outline any concerns or problems they have. We can think of this as being an active role taken by the tutor. In the remote experiment, however, the tutor could see what the students were seeing on their computer screens, but the only conversation they were privy to was that carried using the text chat facility. As most of the collaboration between the students took place using audio, with the students talking to one another, the tutor reported that a lot of the time he was unsure about what the students were planning or arranging. Therefore, the tutor only communicated with the students when they approached him using the text chat, when he felt a significant amount of time had lapsed without them performing an action or when he could see they needed some further instructions on completing the task. We can think of this role, then, as being significantly more passive than that of the residential school tutor.

Achieving the objectives of the activity

In the European Labwork in Science Education project, Millar *et al.* (1999) surveyed university science educators on the nature of the learning objectives commonly associated with university-level practical work. They identified a number of common objectives and these could be separated into two basic categories. The first category of objectives is associated with the process of doing experimental work; the second is linked to the conceptual content of practical work.

We took these objectives and asked an experienced tutor/course team member to outline how they related to the activity students would complete with the flame tests and spectrometer. We then asked students in both the residential and remote experiment groups to tell us how the activity linked to these objectives. In comparing the responses of the students with those of the tutor, we can examine the extent to which the activity met its intended teaching objectives (see Tables 3.2.1 and 3.2.2).

As indicated in Table 3.2.1, students in both groups felt they were able to 'learn how to use or set up a standard laboratory instrument' (i.e. the spectrometer). Understandably, the PEARL students felt less confident than their residential school counterparts, since only a few managed to complete the task and the students acknowledged that some of the things they would be asked to do in a traditional laboratory were done for them.

The reports of students in both groups indicated that only a few individuals believed that they had achieved the other objectives in the table. This is what one student from residential school said in relation to setting up the equipment, stressing the importance of this activity:

> You are using [equipment] you can't just pick up around your own house and start using ... and things you can't find on the High Street generally ... so being able to use real laboratory equipment: the microscopes help you understand how, as scientists, we interact with the equipment and what you have to do with the equipment to keep it at its optimum performance ... the safety aspects as well ... it's first hand experience. That is invaluable.

In the excerpt above, the student is highlighting not only the importance of being exposed to the equipment but also the experience of using the equipment as a 'scientist'. In contrast, the excerpt below is from another interview where the student was

Table 3.2.1 Process objectives for practical work taken from Millar *et al.* (1999) applied to the OU light spectra activity

Process objectives	SXR103 tutor response	PEARL students	Residential school students
To help students learn how to use or set up a standard laboratory instrument	Set up and use optical grating spectrometer	The students reported that they believed the session had helped them learn how to set up and use the optical grating spectrometer and they generally felt confident about being able to use to the equipment in a traditional laboratory	This was the same as for PEARL students
To help students carry out a standard procedure	Calibration of spectrometer using light of known wavelengths	Most students got further than half-way through the calibration and setting up of the spectrometer before time ran out. A number of students felt they needed time before the session to look at the labscript to overcome the time issues	This task was completed in its entirety by the students at the residential school. These students were also able to recount the steps they took in setting up and calibrating the spectrometer in greater detail
To help students learn how to process data	Processing of calibration data. Use of calibration data to calculate unknown wavelengths from diffraction angles	Generally, the students reported that the calibration data needed to be processed in some way, but generally they failed to mention that processing the calibration data led to the extrapolation of elements	This was the same as for PEARL students
To help students learn how to use data to support a conclusion	Measured wavelengths allow students to deduce which metal ion is present in the solution	This was mentioned by a few students	This was the same as for PEARL students

asked what the conclusion of the experiment was. The response was initially interspersed with a number of pauses, evidence that this was an uncomfortable question for the student and one they found difficult to answer. This was the case for students in both groups and this excerpt hints at why this might be the case:

Table 3.2.2   Content objectives for practical work taken from Millar *et al.* (1999) applied to the OU light spectra activity

Content objectives	SXR103 tutor response	PEARL students	Residential school students
To help students identify objects and phenomena and become familiar with them	Identify and become familiar with light spectra	This was achieved to a certain extent, but the students often made little mention of light spectra characteristics	This was achieved to the extent where students mentioned characteristics of different spectra
To help students learn a concept	Each element emits light with a characteristic light spectrum	This was achieved by seeing it	This was achieved by seeing it
To help students learn a relationship	Demonstrated using the grating relationship: $d \sin \theta = n\lambda$	This was mentioned by one student. The main relationship students reported was one between elements and light spectra	This was not mentioned. Again, most of the reports centred on elements and light spectra

We were discovering ... as a whole group ... which solutions ... we were identifying the main events ... from there the spectral wavelengths. In most cases it related well ... I don't know, by the time you get in [the laboratory] there is so much going on that you ... you are fascinated by the equipment. The aim tends to go out of the window because you're more interested [in getting] your hands on the equipment. But the overall aim was that you can find out different elements have different spectra.

Table 3.2.2 shows that students in both groups reported that they had learnt the core objectives of the activity – that elements have differing spectral signatures and also the need to quantify spectral signatures. However, it appeared students in both groups were not able to report an understanding of the grating relationship as a core objective of the experiment they had achieved. This report, from one of the residential school students, could give some insight into why this happened. Many of the students in both of the groups reported feeling pressured to achieve too much in a short space of time and the statement below seems to indicate that students felt directed towards doing things rather than understanding why something is done:

You don't get enough time for reflection ... you've got a limited time in the laboratory. You're in there doing the experiment and you're working at their pace not your own. That was one of the key things here. You are working a pace set by the OU not your own comfortable pace … I think that was a problem.

This quote, and similar reports from other students, seem to point to a problem with the amount of time students were given to complete the experiment. In fact, the students interviewed at the residential school often reported that most of the other experiments they conducted were done in a rushed manner. This could point to a potential advantage for the PEARL experiment in that students could have more time for reflection by spreading their experiment over a longer period.

Carrying out the activity

In this part of the interview, we asked students about how they managed the various components of the activity, i.e. completing the tasks in the allocated time, working with another student and working in the laboratory. Students at the residential school felt they had enough time to carry out the task while the students using the remote system felt they needed more time because they needed to communicate with their partner about what to do. Taken with the findings reported in the previous section this suggests that students at the residential school believed that, although they had enough time to carry out the experiment, they did not have enough time to engage with all aspects of it, including time for reflection.

In terms of working in a pair, both groups reported that a clear advantage to this arrangement was the ability to have someone on hand to advise and check what had to be done – we found students in both groups often began the response to the questioning with 'two heads are better than one'. An interesting finding, however, came from the students at the residential school who reported that being with a large group of students throughout the week of the school developed their enthusiasm for the subject and provided a large support network outside the laboratory. However, one student who had done the remote experiment expressed a particular preference from the more relaxed situation of working just with one other person:

I think when there's a whole group of people doing the same thing you feel more pressurized to go at their speed and what have you. It's just you and the person you're working with here, isn't it.

A small number of students in both groups, however, reflected that one disadvantage to working as a pair was disparity in skill and rate of reading/comprehension.

In relation to the tutor, again both groups of students were positive about the role and presence of the tutor, although the students at the residential school repeatedly mentioned the benefits of the tutor wandering around the laboratory motivating them with their infectious enthusiasm for the subject. Students using the remote system commented that the tutor responded to their enquiries but one, in particular, valued the perceived greater anonymity:

I suppose if he was here in the room with you it'd be easier to talk to him. But having said that he's not looking over your shoulder and you don't feel so conspicuous so that is an advantage.

Considering the experience, overall, students were quite enthusiastic about the remote experiment. They tended to have reservations about whether the system would fully replace the traditional laboratory experience but were convinced that remote experimentation was more effective than working with a simulation. For example, one student asked if the same effect could have been achieved with a simulation said:

I think this is better to be honest with you … Because it's actually happening. I know it's hard to explain, but I know what I mean. When you're doing it on CD, it's doing what it's supposed to be doing isn't it?

The student continued by adding that one advantage of the remote experiment in comparison with a simulation is the ability to make mistakes.

Conclusions

Few would contest the importance of practical work in science and engineering courses, yet it is increasingly held hostage by demands to reduce costs and cater to a greater number of students. In view of these demands, institutions are investigating the potential of using ICT and the Internet as an alternative that is considered both cost-effective and appealing to a broad range of students. As a result, there appears to be a current boom in the use of the Internet for remote experimentation.

In this chapter, we have focused on a project that has attempted to harness the power of the Internet to offer students remote access to traditional experimental equipment. The process of achieving this has by no means been an easy one, but this is often the case in developments involving technology and education.

In testing the system we developed for the OU, we focused on a foundation level physics activity of exploring light spectra. We compared the reports of students who used this system with a similar cohort of students who attended a residential school and undertook the same experiment in a traditional laboratory setting. Our findings from a small sample of students suggest a real potential and opportunity for remote experimentation to provide an alternative to practical work in the traditional laboratory setting. This has also been reported by academics to whom we have demonstrated the system. The system has the appeal of being flexible and of providing exposure to equipment that some students would ordinarily never get the chance to use. However, a significant barrier is the cost involved in implementing and developing remote experiments.

But what of the future? The aim of the PEARL project was to extend access to science to those who are unable to attend residential schools. Currently, students with disabilities are considered and given appropriate support at residential schools. These students were enthusiastic about their PEARL experience:

I definitely see a place for it for people that cannot do their residential schools and can't do the hands on. It's a good substitute ... at least you're doing something. You'll never replace the hands on but as I said it's a good substitute.

The response to our development of a remote experiment has been very positive, from students and academics alike. Our experience indicates that there is real potential in this approach but the finished product is the result of a time-consuming and, at times, challenging process. Many of these challenges have been in producing the technology to support remote access experiments.

In this chapter we have detailed the design process because we believe this is central to the success of any such endeavour. We have also documented key issues raised in our evaluation study. It remains to be seen what role remote experiments will play in the curriculum studied by the next generation of scientists and engineers, but it is likely that the traditional laboratory will be brought closer to the homes of students in a way that has never been seen before.

References

Bliss, J. (1990) 'Students' reactions to undergrad science: laboratory and project work', in E. Hegarty-Hazel (ed.) *The Student Laboratory and the Science Curriculum*, London: Routledge.

Cartwright, H. M. and Valentine, K. (2002) 'A spectrometer in the bedroom – development and potential of Internet-based experiments', *Computer and Education* 38(1–3): 52–64.

Colwell, C. Scanlon, E., Cooper, M. and di Paulo, T. (2002) *Computers and Education*, 38(1–3), pp. 65–76.

Cooper, M. (2000) 'The challenge of practical work in an e-University – real, virtual and remote experiments', in *Proceedings of the Information Society Technologies Conference: The Information Society for All*, Nice, France.

——, Donnelly A. and Martins Ferreira, J. M. (2002) 'Remote controlled experiments for teaching over the Internet: a comparison of approaches developed in the PEARL project', in *Proceedings of the 19th Annual Conference of the Australasian Society for Computers in Learning in Tertiary Education*, Auckland, New Zealand: UNITEC Institution of Technology.

Hegarty-Hazel, E. (1990) 'The student laboratory and the science curriculum: a model', in E. Hegarty-Hazel (ed.) *The Student Laboratory and the Science Curriculum*, London: Routledge.

Jervis, L. (1999) *Laboratory Work in Science Education: An Evaluation with Case Studies*, Plymouth: Science Education Enhancement and Development (SEED) Publications, Faculty of Science, University of Plymouth.

Laurillard, D. (2001) *Rethinking University Teaching* (2nd edn), London: RoutledgeFalmer.

Leach, J. and Paulsen, A. C. (eds) (1999) *Practical Work in Science Education: Recent Research*, Roskilde, Denmark: University of Roskilde Press.

Millar, R., Le Maréchal, J.-F. and Tiberghien, A. (1999) '"Mapping" the domain: varieties of practical work', In J. Leach and A. Paulsen (eds) *Practical Work in Science Education: Recent Research Studies*, Roskilde, Denmark: University of Roskilde Press.

Psillos, D. and Niedderer, H. (2003) (eds) *Teaching and Learning in the Science Laboratory. A Book based on the European Project 'Labwork in Science Education'*, Dordrecht, The Netherlands: Kluwer Academic Publishers.

Scanlon, E., Morris, E., Di Paolo, T. and Cooper, M. (2002) 'Contemporary approaches to learning science: technologically-mediated practical work', *Studies in Science Education* 38: 73–114.

3.3 ICT for science education

Current prospects and trends in research

Eileen Scanlon

Contemporary approaches to teaching science make use of information and communications technology (ICT). Current work on enhancing learning in science is influenced by the role that ICT plays in the working lives of scientists and engineers. This chapter acknowledges the opportunities for learning and working in science with ICT. A number of uses of ICT in science education are also described and a variety of current research projects used to illustrate ways that science learners may use computers in the future. A final section considers the emerging issues for research which arise as a consequence.

Computers have been used in science teaching for the past forty years in a variety of ways, so there is a long history of projects, initiatives and experience to draw on in consideration of what will work for science learners. In recent years, the increased access to computers for users has resulted in a proliferation of these initiatives which have been studied in a variety of ways.

It is important to remember that the uses to which computers are put are influenced by their inherent properties. Initial uses of computers in education were influenced by their computational capacities. There was a significant period in which learners were expected to develop knowledge of programming languages, sometimes special-purpose languages such as Logo (for example, see Papert 1980). Considerable hope was also placed on tutorial programs, as Wulf notes:

> In the early 1960s ... it was thought that every student could have at its disposal a tutor who was non judgmental, patient and continually reinforcing. The potential seemed limitless.
>
> (Wulf 2003: 19)

In recent years the convergence between the computational and communication properties of computers has led to many new possibilities for learning. DISessa, who has done pioneering work in this area, is clear that:

The emergence of computational media can't work by falling into an existing niche.

(DISessa 2000: 235)

However, there are times when the arguments for using computers in science education are more complex than simply examining the properties of the technology. For example, the introduction of computers into learning situations has sometimes been encouraged as a result of research findings that suggest increased motivation for groups of learners using ICT. There may be a need for caution with this approach. Boohan expresses this as follows:

> Computer technology is powerful. Whether ICT is a powerful learning tool, however, depends on how it is used. ICT should not be used, for example as a reward or because it is motivating. Motivation is a complex issue and ICT is not a magic button that can be pressed to make pupils more interested. In any case, many pupils may have far more entertaining things they can do on their computers at home. ICT should not be used in science lessons simply as a way of teaching ICT skills. It may indeed help to develop skills, and science teachers need to be aware of how their subject contributes to and builds on pupils' ICT capability in the context of the whole school. Additionally, to enable pupils to use specialist hardware and software, some skills will certainly need to be taught explicitly in science lessons. But the central justification for using ICT in science lessons has to be that it can make a positive contribution to pupils' learning in science.

(Boohan 2001: 212)

Using computers in education

The properties of computers which have been used are: the interactive possibilities which allow for adaptive interaction with individual students; the simulation and modelling capacity which allows events to be inspected by students; the storage capacity which allows students to have access to information; the input and output devices which can be used by students with disabilities; and, increasingly, the communication capacity which allows student access to information resources and to working with others. Each of these features has particular applications in the teaching and learning of science.

These properties of computers have been explored in a range of experimental settings (for example, in classrooms and universities). The educational potential of simulations was quickly recognized for science. For example, their potential for giving students access to dangerous situations like chemical reactions was noted. Further uses included situations where time needs to pass to see the effect, such as studying the development of populations over time. Simulations also became popular because they can help to simplify complex situations and they can incorporate models that can be run to enable students to investigate the behaviour of the simulation. Sometimes even the model underlying a simulation can be inspected (for example, see Hennessy *et al.* 1995; Smith *et al.* 1991). Further to this, there have been some useful examples of projects in which students themselves are engaged in modelling (for example, see Jackson *et al.* 1994; Mellar *et al.* 1994).

Microworlds were a further innovation. These are a particular class of simulations, popularized by Papert, where students can write simple programs and run them (for example, see Papert 1980). Tutorial programs presented the possibility of offering individualized instruction to learners, with appropriate feedback based on their responses (for example, see Cox 1992). The potential of different input and output devices was exploited, particularly for students with disabilities (for example, see Eisenstadt and Vincent 1997), and in the mid-1980s, technological developments made vast improvements in the graphics and sound capacities of computers, which were used for multimedia programs (for example, see Taylor *et al.* 1996). Finally, the development of the Internet and the World Wide Web in the early 1990s opened up a new range of possibilities (see Scanlon 1997, for a review). The communication capacities of computers on which these developments depend have allowed new forms of collaborative working (Mason and Kaye 1989). The context for both teaching and learning in science has been profoundly influenced by this convergence of communication and computational tools.

Scientists as computer users

Over the past fifteen years, the working practices of scientists have also changed as a result of this convergence and the incorporation of new tools (for example, see Rzepa 1999). Advances in information technology have enhanced the measurement, data handling and communication capacities of computers. These tools provide opportunities for collaboration, such as the pooling of resources and the sharing of information, the possibility of being involved in experimental investigations even though physically distant from the hardware, and the development of databases, virtual libraries and the multimedia capacities of web publishing.

At the same time, communication possibilities have involved students in discussion or collaboration with others on projects. Wulf has written extensively about these trends (for example, see Wulf 1998) and most recently writes:

> The information technology obviates the need for the university to be a place. With powerful ubiquitous computing and networking each of the University's functions can be distributed in space and possibly in time. ... Academics tend to identify more closely with their disciplinary and intellectual colleagues than with their university. Freed from the need to be physically present in the classroom, laboratory or library they are likely to find grouping by intellectual infinity more appealing.
>
> Some disciplines that do need shared physical facilities – say a telescope – suggest the need of a place. But large scientific instruments such as telescopes and accelerators are already run by consortia and are shared by faculty from

many universities, and many of these facilities do not require the physical presence of investigators. They could be online and accessible via the network.

(Wulf 2003: 20)

Current uses of computers in science education are influenced by developments in technology (as we have seen) but are also influenced by a developing view of the learner.

Somekh (1998) discusses the value of supporting learning through ICT in relation to a number of theoretical perspectives including behaviourism, constructivism, authentic learning and metacognition. There are examples of computer use in educational settings which are influenced by each of these different views of the learner. Much of the practice of science education is influenced by a view that what scientists do should be reflected for the students, so this shift in science practice should be reflected in science education practice. Contemporary approaches to science learning have moved away from an acquisition or construction metaphor towards a culture or participation metaphor (Sfard 2001). The notion of students, like scientists, participating in a community where communication is enabled by ICT is therefore quite powerful. The participation metaphor is arguably the strongest contemporary metaphor for teaching and learning.

Researching learning with ICT

The preceding part of this chapter offers a description of the possibilities offered by the properties of computers but, as Laurillard points out:

The properties of a medium do not determine the learning that takes place.

(Laurillard 2003: 15)

Research projects have been conducted to establish exactly what happens when computers are used in science teaching situations, for each of the possible uses of computers described above.

Research in this area is conducted by many different groups. These include science educators, computer scientists, educational technologists, psychologists and cognitive scientists. Often, these projects are conducted in multidisciplinary teams. This means that there are many journals in which relevant research is published, and many examples of projects conducted for a specific purpose which provide us with helpful indications for future uses of computers.

A number of studies have shown that observing learners working with technology can be a very productive way of exposing ideas and learning processes (for example, see Scanlon 1990). Barnard and Sandberg (1992) conducted interviews with ten scientists asking about the link between their theory of learning and how technology would support the kind of education they envisaged. Their responses highlighted their opinion of the importance of the computer as a way of testing learning hypotheses. In effect, these studies argue that detailed observation of students using technology can reveal something about the learning process as well as providing information about how to reshape the design of instruction using technology. This approach underlies much of the work at The Open University (for example, see Taylor *et al.* 1996).

Promises, promises

Reviews or meta-analyses of studies of the effectiveness of computer-assisted instruction have been conducted periodically. So far, these do not show striking evidence of the benefits of incorporating ICT in science education (for example, see Bangert-Drowns *et al.* 1985; Plomb and Voogt 1995; Niemiec and Walberg 1987). However, these studies are rather old and pre-date some significant work on, for example, the use of computer-based laboratories. The section on 'computers as tools' (see p. 193) outlines this more recent work.

Recent studies have used different approaches to establishing effectiveness. For example, work on the use of ICT in Britain, such as the ImpacT2 study evaluating current uses of ICT in the school curriculum, have taken the approach of documenting case studies of successful uses (Somekh *et al.* 2002) while lamenting the relative shortage of these. There have also been concerns that the huge levels of investment necessary for ICT have not had a noticeably large impact on learning outcomes (for example, see Cuban 2001; 1986). Other critiques have focused on the need to integrate ICT-based approaches properly with curricular approaches and teacher influences.

While reviews of research give only limited evidence of effectiveness, the potential of ICT in education has been sufficiently recognised to produce significant investments of time and money, as the following quotation describes:

> In 1998 new government programmes were announced which will provide funding of over £1.2 billion towards the National Grid for Learning, ICT for all initial teacher trainees and an ICT training allowance for all initial teacher trainees and an ICT allocation of £460 [...] for every practising teacher. Yet, despite these initiatives and inducements there is still only a limited uptake of ICT in science education (DfE 1995; Stevenson 1997) and only a minority of science teachers use ICT regularly in their teaching. Clearly the majority of science teachers are unconvinced about the value and useful role of ICT.
>
> (Cox 2000: 190)

Cox summarizes the difficulties associated with using ICT and attributes these, in part, to teachers losing faith in their own teaching expertise. For example, she points out that:

> ... in the case of using a science simulation, this should be related to previous topics and concepts; it should be introduced with clear aims and objectives; and pupils can be given planning tasks and writing up tasks, as with a laboratory experiment, to help them relate the ICT activity to their work.
>
> (Cox 2000: 194)

The next section describes some recent evaluation research projects, which examined simulations and modelling programs.

Simulation and modelling

There are many examples of research projects investigating the use of simulations in science education. For example, the Conceptual Change in Science project studied the influence of science simulations on students' development of scientific ideas (Hennessy *et al.* 1995). A study of a class of 12–13-year-olds working with mechanics simulations on a computer-based curriculum lasting for six weeks detected a significant amount of conceptual change, by comparing pre- and post-tests and performance on worksheets and interviews. The project combined real laboratory experiments and computer simulations successfully. More recently, Laurillard *et al.* (2000) investigated the impact of using multimedia packages to learn as part of the *Multimedia Enabling Narrative Organisation* project. They explored topics in science and history with a range of age groups focusing on the ways that certain features of multimedia design influence students' experience and learning outcomes. This project worked with a number of multimedia CD-ROMs, including an activity on the finches of the Galapagos, adapted for schoolchildren. The project compared different versions of the program with different narrative structures. Whitelock (1998) reported on the development of a suite of multimedia CD-ROMs provided as part of the introductory science course at The Open University, UK, and considered the different ways in which these have supported science learning. There are many other examples (see Ross and Scanlon 1995 for a review).

Niedderer *et al.* (1991) conducted a review of research evidence into the contributions of computer-based modelling to physics education. They found that, at the secondary level, such work:

> ... enlarged the set of phenomena studies in high school physics by the study of more complex realistic topics and shifted the focus of instruction towards conceptual understanding and the reconstruction of meaning.
>
> (Niedderer *et al.* 1991: 95)

Computers as tools

The computer has been used extensively in practical work in recent years, not least to facilitate data logging. For example:

> Data logging offers enormous potential. ... For example, a temperature probe can be used to measure the way in which the temperature of hot water changes as it cools with the graph plotted in real time. It means that we can shift our focus from the mechanics of taking readings and plotting them, towards the interpretation of the shape of a graph and the development of scientific understanding.
>
> (Boohan 2001: 212)

This is only one example of a line of work which uses the computer to collect data by means of sensors. Frost (1998a, 1998b) summarizes other examples. Barton and Rogers (1991) have illustrated the potential of using computers for measuring and for sensing data in a number of areas and projects. In particular, they found that using computer sensors to collect data directly freed pupils to concentrate on interpretation (Barton and Rogers 1991).

Newton (1997) observed and recorded the conversations of pupils in the first two years of secondary school who were using temperature sensors connected to data loggers and computers and reported the importance of the teacher in emphasizing and becoming involved in making sense of the data as it appeared. Barton (1997) conducted a comparison of approaches to data collection and graphing, including computer-based practical work involving data-logging. He used a conventional practical and a non-practical approach with 12–15-year-olds involved in measurement of electrical characteristics of circuit components. While many pupils were clear that they often preferred non-practical approaches, data-logging offered advantages including significant time savings and a different focus of attention (to trends in the data rather than data points) to the groups using it. Studies have also been conducted with primary school pupils (Mc Farlane *et al.* 1995). Harlen reviews the prospects for such work, and she says:

> Opportunities to extend primary pupils' experience are particularly rich, given that the use of conventional measuring instruments with sufficient accuracy to be useful in some contexts is not feasible.
>
> (Harlen 1999: 21)

Communication

In recent years, uses of the communication capacities of networked computers have included work on collaboration, virtual experiments, access to resources and access to others. For example, the *Kids as Global Scientists* project (Songer 1996) studied the impact of a six-week weather curriculum in middle school classrooms where groups of students exchanged information with children at a distance using an 'Internet infused environment'. Children worked in local groups carrying out experiments where they looked for patterns in images. They also discussed particular areas, such as wind or cloud patterns, with an expert, online. Then, in the following three weeks, the exchange period, children sent questions to other students who were studying the same areas. The learning through collaborative visualization (Co-Vis) project is in the same area (Gordin and Pea 1995).

Access to virtual experiments is being explored in a number of projects, based in schools and universities. The trend towards sharing sophisticated instruments over the Internet is growing and examples include the Hands on Universe project, giving high school teachers and students access to the same tools and images as research astronomers (Asbell-Clarke and Barclay 1996). *The Practical Experimentation by Access to Remote Learning* (PEARL) project, based at The Open University (Di Paolo *et al.* 2003), has explored the feasibility of students participating in laboratory work from home using spectrometers and electron microscopes remotely and collaboratively and it has reported some encouraging findings.

One of the new possibilities provided by the Internet is remote access to resources. For example, websites provided by science museums provide a resource for planning real visits and allow virtual visits. In addition, science museums have also experimented with communications tools to host online discussions. Part of this is a mission 'allowing the general public and schools directly into places of interest such as space centres and research laboratories' (Jackson *et al.* 1994).

Using the Internet for access to other people for learning is a contemporary trend. In distance-learning universities, the advent of computer-mediated communication over the past fifteen years, in such applications as conferencing systems, have provided new learning opportunities for students, allowing the possibility of contact with other students free from constraints of time or place. At The Open University, UK, a research programme into such uses of computers has been investigated their impact (for example, see Mason and Kaye 1989). These conferences are used in science and science education courses (Scanlon 1997). Oliver and Shaw (2003) report on the use of such communication in medical education. Issues about how teaching proceeds by this means are also addressed, for example, noting how moderators of these communications were a key factor in their success.

Such systems are also being investigated in school settings. For example, *Speakeasy*, an electronic discussion tool (Bell *et al.* 1995), enables students, teachers and scientists to collaborate in the construction of explanations of a science event. They argue that such systems help to make thinking visible by modelling how experts discuss their ideas. In addition, they highlight how such systems encourage autonomy by supporting students as they learn discussion practices, gain useful knowledge from each other and consider how their ideas differ from those of others.

Integrated approaches

The Knowledge Integration Environment (Linn 1995), which, in turn, was part of the large *Computer as Learning Partner* (CLP) project (Linn and Hsi 2000), is an example of an integrated approach. Over a period of fifteen years this ongoing programme of work based at the University of California, Berkeley, has made an extensive study of the use of computers, both face-to-face and online, in middle and secondary school science classrooms. The work involved developing 'pragmatic pedagogical principles', engaging students in practical inquiry, encouraging students to build on their ideas, investigating personally relevant problems and developing a generalizable inquiry process suitable for diverse science projects.

The computers were used for real-time data collection, using probes and graphing, which simulated investigations. The research was conducted as a partnership between scientists, classroom teachers, cognitive researchers and technology experts. As Linn and Hsi note:

> Real-time graphing and simulations of personally relevant problems made science ideas more accessible to students ... the expert tool of real-time data

collection made graph concepts more accessible. The dynamic character of a graph makes more sense when it occurs in real time. Real-time graphing led us to consider additional ways to make thinking visible.

(Linn and Hsi 2000: 72)

The strategy proposed by Linn and her colleagues involves a range of approaches to scaffolding student inquiry. One overriding conclusion from this work, which also emerges from other studies taking a constructivist approach to instruction (for example, see Hennessy *et al.* 1995), is the importance of selecting fewer topics, but making sure those topics are explored more thoroughly.

Over a number of years, White and Frederiksen have built up an approach to the development of inquiry-based science:

In creating this curriculum we were particularly interested in counteracting the view that science is an abstract and difficult discipline that is accessible to only an elite subset of the population – namely, to high-achieving students over the age of 13 who it is argued are the only ones capable of the abstract, complex reasoning processes needed to learn or do science. ... Based on research revealing the importance of metacognition, our hypothesis is that the reason students have difficulty with science, particularly physics, is not that they are too young or lack intelligence, but rather that they simply do not know how to construct conceptual models of scientific phenomena and how to monitor and reflect on their progress. ... Thus, if you teach students about the processes of scientific inquiry and modelling and if you also teach them to how to monitor and reflect on their inquiry processes, then they can engage in inquiry and learn physics as well as older or higher achieving students can.

(White and Frederiksen 1998: 5, 6)

A further, related, project supports the scaffolding of collaborative investigations within an inquiry support environment – a metacognitive tool that enables young students to embody and test theories of the cognitive and social processes needed for inquiry and how to support them (White et al. 2002).

Future trends

There are a number of recent issues being explored in research which may result in outcomes influencing future science education using ICT. Three of these are explored below: portability, reuse and virtual reality.

The advent of portable devices

Some current researchers are exploring the potential of portable tools for learners and workers. Building on previous work with graphical calculators and palmtop (or handheld) computers in supporting secondary school- and university-level mathematics, and in secondary schools more generally, researchers are beginning to explore a range of situations in which these portable devices are used for learning and working. These explore, for example, the use of handheld computers as flexible tools that can be adapted to suit the needs of a variety of teaching and learning styles (Curtis *et al.* 2002). Further work, such as the Handler project, has focused on the technical features required in such devices (see Sharples 2000). There have been a number of school-based studies, some of which involve pupils taking this equipment into the field for scientific data gathering (Rieger and Gay 1997; Staudt and Hsi 1999; Soloway *et al.* 1999) and other approaches (Roschelle and Pea 2002; Bannasch 1999; Tinker and Krajcik, 2001).

The Electronic Guidebook project at the Exploratorium science museum in San Francisco (Bannasch 1999) aims to understand how the introduction of wireless technologies might change the experience of visitors to a museum. The access to mobile web resources was received positively but users felt that the devices did interfere with their interaction with the exhibits.

In studies involving portable computers, some science classrooms have become virtually paperless. It is difficult to argue, however, that handheld computers will replace paper in the classroom.

The unique affordances of handheld computers include permanence, accessibility and immediacy as well as portability. They can get access to documents, data animations and software tools. This means that:

> ... whether students are at home, in the classroom or beside a river, they can get what they need right when they need it. They have access to work from earlier weeks. The ease of aiming your handheld at a partner during a collaborative task to 'beam' information has turned some typically individual activites into learning opportunities involving substantial discussion and peer-to-peer learning ...
>
> (Curtis *et al.* 2002: 23)

and:

> The unobtrusive nature of portables encourages students to spontaneously communicate face to face with each other more than desktop computers do.
>
> (Hennessy *et al.* 2001: 274)

Reusability of resources

There are many practical issues related to the production of ICT resources which are not covered here. One contemporary theme is ways in which existing resources can be produced and catalogued so that they can be used or reused. An attempt to do this was the *Source* project which took resources produced in a variety of different universities and investigated how they could be reused in others (Blake *et al.* 2001). Recently, there has been a large amount of work in the area of the definition of metadata in order to attempt to catalogue such resources as 'learning objects' for easier description and reuse (for example, see Greenberg 2001 and Boyle 2003, this volume).

Virtual reality

Several researchers have begun to explore the potential of virtual reality for teaching science drawing on its unique attributes. Crozier *et al.* (2000) describe these as:

> ... the ability to visualize and manipulate objects that cannot be ordinarily seen in the real world, the capability of taking on different perspectives and providing a medium for presenting complex three dimensional concepts.
>
> (Crozier *et al.* 2000: 329)

Crozier *et al.* (2000) describe these features in a report on a study looking at the application of virtual reality in secondary school science. They describe the development of an approach to teaching radioactivity. Although some good results were obtained, there were difficulties of integration into the curriculum and meeting the practical needs of teachers. Jelfs and Whitelock (2000) have considered possibilities of such systems for higher education.

Issues for research

When I reviewed the prospects for learning science online in 1997 (Scanlon 1997), I used five key features to review those using new communication technology. These were reliability (of access to information and technology), scaleability (how issues of scale would influence uptake and resourcing), integration (whether the activity is embedded into a curriculum), pedagogy (expertise in effective appropriate use of the technology) and evaluation (evidence of effectiveness). Today I would add a further feature, portability.

Looking at evaluation, it is interesting that so few studies of the use of ICT do more that describe uses of the technology. There is a need for more critical accounts. I would argue that such accounts should consider evidence of learning outcomes, detailed accounts of the process of learning and both students' and teachers' perception of the learning experience.

There is a tradition of comparative studies of the effectiveness of approaches using different media (for example, see Clark 1983) but these are not unproblematic for a number of reasons. In Kirkwood's view, the core problem of this comparative study approach is that:

> It is based on questionable methods and (very often) unacknowledged assumptions about the process of learning. The method and procedure is derived from medical-biological research in which the effects of different 'treatments' on matched samples of 'subjects' are compared for their efficacy of outcomes. Because the research design aims to hold all variables constant or matched with the exception of the 'treatment' all other aspects have to be as identical as possible.
>
> (Kirkwood 2003: 130)

There are several reservations about this methodology in education. These include the passive view of learning underlying the notion of delivery of a 'treatment'.

Some reports are focused on the technological developments which underlie new uses of a learning technology such as simulation or access to digital resources. Sometimes, the purpose of studies is to provide information to improve the design of a particular example. An instructional designer could use information collected during a formative evaluation, such as details of learners' use of the system, to help improve the design.

Producing formative evaluation to influence design is one of the purposes of research in this area. However, studies of the ways that students learn science using information and communication technology are still needed. Further research, run over significant time periods, would help to inform these issues.

What is not available from many studies (formative or summative) is good quality longitudinal data on the effects of long-term use of such systems. We also need to look at studies conducted over significant time periods to detect the effects of use.

I have described here ways in which I can see the potential of information and communication technology coming to fruition. The following quotation is a useful reminder that we should not assume that technology will solve all of science education's current problems.

> If computers are to serve as valuable tools for advancing and enhancing high school students' science learning then a broader view of their potential use in terms of what has already been proposed as necessary for improving science education is required. [...]
>
> There are no easy answers involving computers to the current problems besieging science education. The challenge is to make best use of the affordances provided by the technology while being mindful of, and minimizing, the effect of any possible associated disadvantages.
>
> (Thomas 2001: 38, 39)

References

Asbell-Clarke, J. and Barclay, T. (1996) 'Discovering the scientist within: hands on universe', *Hands On!* 19(2): 4–5.

Bannasch, S. (1999) 'The electronic curator: using a handheld computer at the Exploratorium', *Concord Consortium Newsletter* fall, 4–5, available on the Web at <http://www.concord.org/newsletter/1999fall/> (last accessed 24 July 2003).

Bangert-Drowns, R., Kulik, J. and Kulik, C. (1985)'Effectiveness of computer based instruction in secondary schools', *Journal of Computer Based Instruction* 12: 59–68.

Barnard, P. and Sandberg, S. (1992) 'Interviews' *AI Communications* 3, 4 and 6: 148–51.

Barton, R. (1997) 'How do computers affect graphical interpretation', *School Science Review* 79(287): 55–60.

—— and Rogers, L. (1991) 'The computer as an aid to practical science – studying motion', *Journal of Computer Assisted Learning* 7(2): 104–13.

Bell, P., Davis, E. A. and Linn, M. (1995) 'The knowledge integration environment: theory and design', in *Proceedings of the Computer Supported Collaborative Learning Conference*, CSCL 95, Bloomington, IN: Lawrence Erlbaum Associates.

Blake, C., Beetham, H. and Twining, P. (2001) 'Adopt, adapt, assimilate, frameworks for software re-use in higher education', paper presented at *The Association for Learning Technology Conference*, ALTC–2001, September, Edinburgh.

Boohan, R. (2001) 'ICT and communication', in S. Amos and R. Boohan (eds) *Aspects of Teaching Secondary Science*, London: Routledge.

Boyle, T. (2003) 'Designing multimedia e-learning for science education', in R Holliman and E. Scanlon (eds) *Mediating Science Learning through Information and Communications Technolgy*, London: RoutledgeFalmer.

Clark, R. (1983) 'Reconsidering research on learning from media', *Review of Educational Research* 53(4): 445–9.

Cox, M. (1992) 'The computer in the science curriculum', *International Journal of Educational Research* 17: 19–35.

—— (2000) 'Information and communications technologies: their role and value for science education', in M. Monk and J. Osborne (eds) *Good Practice in Science Education: What Research has to Say*, Buckingham: Open University Press.

Crozier, J., Cobb, S. and Wilson, J. (2000) 'Experimental comparison of virtual reality with traditional teaching methods for teaching radioactivity', *Education and Information Technologies* 5(4): 329–43.

Cuban, L. (1986) *Teachers and Machines: The Classroom use of Technology since 1920*, New York: Teachers' College Press.

—— (2001) *Oversold and Underused: Computers in the Classroom*, London: Harvard University Press.

Curtis, M., Luchini, K., Bobrowsky, B., Quintana, C. and Soloway, E. (2002) 'Handheld use in K–12: a descriptive account', in *Proceedings of the IEEE International Workshop on Wireless and Mobile Technologies in Education*, Vaxjo, Sweden.

Department for Education (DfE) (1995) Survey of Information Technology in Schools: Statistical bulletin issue no 3/95, London: The Stationery Office.

Di Paolo, T. *et al.* (2003) 'Redesigning practical work', in R Holliman and E. Scanlon (eds) *Mediating Science Learning through Information and Communications Technolgy*, London: RoutledgeFalmer.

DISessa, A. (2000) *Changing Minds: Computers Learning and Literacy*, Massachusetts: MIT Press.

Eisenstadt, M. and Vincent, T. (eds) (1997) *The Knowledge Web: Learning and Collaborating on the Net*, London: Kogan Page.

Frost, R. (1998a) *Datalogging in Practice*, London: IT in Science.

—— (1998b) *Software for Teaching Science*, London: IT in Science.

Gordin, D. and Pea, R. (1995) 'Prospects for scientific visualisation as an educational technology', *Journal of the Learning Sciences* 4(3): 249–79.

Greenberg, J. (2001) 'Metadata applications for the Plant Information Center (PIC): a web-based scientific learning center', *Interactive Learning Environments* 9(3): 291–313.

Harlen, W. (1999) *Effective Teaching of Science: A Review of Research*, Edinburgh: Scottish Council for Research in Education.

Hennessy, S., Fung, P. and Scanlon, E. (2001) 'The role of the graphic calculator in mediating graphing activity', *International Journal of Mathematics for Education in Science and Technology* 32(2): 267–90.

——, Twigger, D., Byard, M., Driver, R., Draper, S., Hartley, J. R., Mohamed, R., O'Malley, C., O'Shea, T. and Scanlon, E. (1995) 'A classroom intervention using a computer-augmented curriculum for mechanics', *International Journal of Science Education* 17(2): 189–206.

Jackson, S., Stratford, S., Krajcik, J. and Soloway, E. (1994) 'Making dynamic modelling accessible to pre-college science students', *Interactive Learning Environments* 4(3): 233–57.

Jelfs, A. and Whitelock, D. (2000) 'The notion of presence in virtual learning environments: what makes the environment real', *British Journal of Educational Technology* 31(2): 145–52.

Kirkwood, A. (2003) 'Classic review: Richard E. Clark (ed.), Learning from Media', *Education, Communication and Information* 3(1): 130–6.

Laurillard, D. (2003) 'Rethinking the teaching of science', in R Holliman and E. Scanlon (eds) *Mediating Science Learning through Information and Communications Technolgy*, London: RoutledgeFalmer.

——, Stratfold, M., Luckin R., Plowman L. and Taylor, J. (2000) Affordances for learning in a non-linear narrative medium', *Journal of Interactive Media in Education*, 2.

Linn, M. (1995) 'Designing computer learning environments for science and engineering: the scaffolded knowledge integration framework', *Journal of Science Education and Technology* 4: 103–26.

—— and Hsi, S. (2000) *Computers, Teachers, Peers: Computers as Lab Partners*, London: Erlbaum.

Mc Farlane, A, Friedler, V., Warwick, P. and Chaplain, R. (1995) 'Developing an understanding of the meaning of line graphs in primary science investigations using portable computers and data logging software', *Journal of Computers in Mathematics Science and Education* 14(4): 461–80.

Mason, R. and Kaye, A. (1989) *Mindweave Communication: Computers and Distance Education*, Oxford: Pergamon.

Mellar, H., Boohan, R., Bliss, J., Ogborn, J. and Tompsett, C. (eds) (1994) *Learning with Artificial Worlds: Computer Based Modelling in the Curriculum*, London: Falmer Press.

Newton, L. (1997) 'Graph talk: Some observations and reflections on students' data logging', *School Science Review* 79(287): 49–54.

Niedderer, H., Schecker, H. and Becge, T. (1991) 'The role of modelling in learning physics', *Journal of Computer Assisted Learning* 7: 84–95.

Niemiec, R. and Walberg, H. J. (1987) 'Comparative effects of computer assisted instruction: a synthesis of reviews', *Journal of Educational Computing Research* 3(1): 19–37.

Oliver, M. and Shaw, G. (2003) 'Asynchronous discussion in support of medical education', *Journal of Asynchronous Learning Networks* 7(1): 56–67.

Papert, S. (1980) *Mindstorms*, Sussex: Harvester Press.

Plomp, T. and Voogt, J. (1995) 'Use of computers', in B. Fraser and H.-J. Walberg (eds) *Improving Science Education*, Illinois: University of Chicago Press.

Rieger, B. and Gay, C. (1997) 'Using mobile computing to enhance field study', *Proceedings of the Computer-supported Collaborative Learning Conference* (pp. 215–23), Toronto, Canada.

Ross, S. and Scanlon, E. (1995) *Open Science: Distance Teaching and Open Learning of Science Subjects*, London: Paul Chapman Press.

Roschelle, J. and Pea, R. (2002) 'A walk on the wildside: how wireless handhelds may change CSCL', *Proceedings of Computer Supported Collaborative Learning Conference*, Colorado, 51–60.

Rzepa, H. (1999) 'The Internet as a medium for science communication', in E. Scanlon, R. Hill and K. Junker (eds) *Communicating Science: Professional Contexts*, London: Routledge.

Scanlon, E. (1990) *Modelling Physics Problem Solving*, unpublished PhD thesis, Milton Keynes: Open University.

—— (1997) 'Learning science on-line', *Studies in Science Education* 30: 57–92.

Sfard, A. (2001) 'On two metaphors for learning and the dangers of choosing only one', *Educational Researcher* 27(2): 4–13.

Sharples, M. (2000) 'The design of personal mobile technologies for lifelong learning', *Computers and Education* 34: 177–93.

Smith, R., O'Shea, T., O'Malley, C., Scanlon, E. and Taylor, J. (1991) 'Preliminary experiments with a distributed, multi-media problem solving environment', in J. M. Bowers and S. D. Benford (eds) *Studies in Computer Supported Cooperative Work: Theory, Practice and Design,* Amsterdam: Elsevier.

Soloway, E., Grant, W., Tinker, R., Roschelle, J., Mills, M., Resnick, M., Berg, R. and Eisenberg, M. (1999) 'Science in the palms of their hands', *Communications of the ACM* 42(8): 21–6.

Somekh, B. (1998) *Designing Learning Tasks with ICT*, available on the Web at <http://www.nie.ac.sg: 8000/~wwwera'conf98keynote/somekh.htm>.

——, Lewin, C., Mavers, D., Fisher, T., Harrison, C., Haw, K., Lunzer, E., Mc Farlane, A. and Scrimshaw, P. (2002) *ImpacT2: Pupils' and Teachers' Perceptions of ICT in the Home, School and Community. A Report to the DfES, BECTA*, ICT in Schools Research and Evaluation Series, No. 9.

Songer, N. (1996) 'Exploring learning opportunities in networked enhanced classrooms: a case for kids as global scientists', *Journal of the Learning Sciences* 5(4): 297–328.

Staudt, C. and Hsi, S. (1999) 'Synergy projects and pocket computers', *Consortium Newsletter*, Spring, 3, available on the Web at <http://www.concord.org/library/1999spring/synergyproj.html> (last accessed 24 July 2003).

Stevenson, D. (1997) *Information and Communications Technology in UK Schools: An Independent Inquiry*, London: The Independent ICT in Schools Commission.

Taylor, J., Scanlon, E. and Hodgson, B. (1996) 'Multimedia and science education', *Education Research and Perspectives* 23(2): 48–58.

Tinker, R. and Krajcik, J. (eds) (2001) *Portable Technologies: Science Learning in Context*, New York: Kluwer Academic/Plenum Publishing.

Thomas, G. (2001) 'Towards effective computer use in high school science education: where to from here?' *Education and Information Technologies* 6(1): 29–41.

White, B. and Frederiksen, J. (1998) 'Inquiry, modeling, and metacognition: making science accessible to all students', *Cognition and Instruction* 16(1): 3–188.

——, ——, Frederiksen, T., Eslinger, E. and Loper, S. (2002) 'Collins Inquiry island: affordances of a multi-agent environment', in P. Bell, T. Stevens and S. Satwitcz (eds) *Proceedings of the Fifth International Conference of the Learning Sciences* (ICLS), Mahwah, NJ: Erlbaum.

Whitelock, D. (1998) 'Formative testing of S103 multimedia CD ROMs', *Program on Learner Use of Media* (Reports Nos 104, 110, 127,130), Milton Keynes: Open University Internal Reports.

Wulf, W. (1998) 'Science and the Internet', in E. Scanlon, R. Hill and K. Junker (eds) *Communicating Science: Professional Contexts*, London: Routledge.

—— (2003) 'Higher education alert – the information railroad is coming', *Educause Review* 38(1): 12–21.

Endpiece

Eileen Scanlon and Richard Holliman

Computers have a role to play in science education. In this volume we have presented accounts of the different ways that science learning can be supported by computers, the ways in which the experiences for science learners using information and communications technology (ICT) can be designed and constructed, and the role that evaluation can play in this design process. We also have considered the different ways that the computer can extend access to science knowledge and considered some future prospects of this work.

It is striking that the various authors contributing to this volume use a very wide range of terms to refer to the use of computers in science education. These include: technology, educational technology, learning technology, information technology, information and communications technology, computer-mediated instruction, computer-related teaching, assistive technology and e-learning, among others. This is an indication that this area of interest is developing and the terminology is also shifting.

One chapter is particularly interesting, where terminology is used in a specific way. Linn provides a perspective on technology for science education based on a very broad interpretation of the term 'technology'. She defines ICT as including automated data collection, genetic engineering, data modelling and integrated circuit design. Taking this broad interpretation, she is concerned with the challenges that advances in science present to educators wishing to prepare students for the demands to be made of them, both as future scientists and as citizens interested in lifelong learning.

Central to all chapters is the role that the computer plays in learning. Researchers both celebrate and worry about the extent to which the experience for the learner is altered by the use of the computer – that is, when it becomes a mediated experience. As Crook argues:

> Mediation is one way to capture the multifaceted nature of this technology. The computer mediates our action – it exists between us and the world and it transforms our activity upon the world. For one thing, it encourages us to act upon that more elusive quantity: information.
>
> (Crook 1994: 21)

If the impact of using computers on science education led to a decrease in 'real' experience for learners, science commentators would rightly be sceptical about its value. However, if we look at some of the examples presented in this reader, we see ways in which this mediated experience offers new possibilities for learners. For example, Scanlon has noted how practical working can be enhanced by the use of data logging and di Paolo *et al.* have documented ways that opportunities for remote access to practical work and working with others are made possible. In addition, Cooper has outlined the ways in which computers are tools that enable people with disabilities to participate in education, noting how they are being used increasingly in the delivery of the curriculum at all educational levels.

The chapters in this volume have either explicitly or implicitly communicated their particular perspectives on science learning. For example, Wellington raises general concerns about authenticity. Linn, in particular, organizes her work around a scaffolded knowledge integration framework for understanding and designing her learning environments, drawing on educational technology. She shares with other science educators such as Gunstone (1988), a belief in the importance of making predictions before carrying out experiments. However, despite her convincing illustrations of the potential of technology for science learners, she is also concerned by the ways in which technology can thwart learning.

Some of the chapters foreground the construction and analysis of designs of instruction and analysis. For example, Laurillard seeks to examine what new media can offer science teaching, and uses her conversational framework to analyse academic learning situations, using this to guide her classification of educational media. The potential of this approach for analysis of learning situations is very apparent, although designs based on the analysis made using the conversational framework are still rare. Boyle notes the main challenges for multimedia designers, abstraction and complexity in science education, and then discusses how designers use visualization and scaffolding to address these.

Leach and Scott provide an examination of the design and evaluation of teaching sequences and, in particular, try to determine the links between their design and the teachers' role in staging them and they introduce the notion of social constructivist perspectives. These are given as 'staging' the scientific story, supporting student internalization of new concepts, and handing over responsibility to the student. They also introduce the term 'learning demand' and use it in the context of calculating the difference between the scientific story and the commonly understood views of a topic.

There are challenges to this perspective, however. For example, Millar has expressed doubts about whether constructivist principles have implications for instruction, arguing:

> … most of us who think we understand some science concepts did not arrive at this understanding by experiencing teaching programmes structured on constructivist principles.
>
> (Millar 1989: 589)

The key role that evaluation can play is highlighted in both chapters by Oliver and that by Scanlon. Like Crook, these chapters recognize that:

> Computers are unlikely to function as magic bullets – effortlessly releasing their therapeutic effects at points identified by teachers. The unfamiliarity and wizardry that surrounds them may cultivate such notions, but the real impact of learning through this technology may need to be measured with attention to how it is assimilated in the surrounding frame of activity.
>
> (Crook 1994: 9)

It is significant how many of the uses of the computer in science education reported here focus on enabling collaborations with other learners or teachers. Wellington discussed the challenges of using ICT from the teacher's perspective. Many of the knowledge-integration activities described by Linn depend on collaborations. Laurillard's work considers the role of communicative media, students and teachers collaborating with each other. Di Paolo *et al.* report on the way that collaborations are part of the remote laboratory experience, and both Boyle and Scanlon note the moves towards the development of re-usable materials, based on standardized design principles. This trend is a significant shift from early uses of computers in science education which were aimed more at the individual learner. ICT now has the potential to facilitate collaborations between learners, between teachers and between those designing and evaluating technology.

References

Crook, C. (1994) *Computers and the Collaborative Experience of Learning*, London and New York: Routledge.

Gunstone, R. (1988) 'Teachers and learners', In P. Fensham (ed.) *Developments and Dilemmas in Science Education*, London: Falmer.

Millar, R. (1989) 'Constructive criticisms', *International Journal of Science Education* 11: 587–96.

Index